AS A RESULT OF THE HELIOGRAPHICA SUSTAINABILITY PROGRAM, 10 CENTS FROM THE PROCEEDS OF THIS BOOK WILL BE DONATED TO ENVIRONMENTAL CAUSES THAT SUPPORT FOREST PRESERVATION AND ENVIRONMENTAL EDUCATION FOR CHILDREN.

ON THE EDGE OF GRACE

Mystical Stories of True Transformation

Written and compiled by

Christine Watkins

On the Edge of Grace

For information:
Heliographica
2261 Market St., #504
San Francisco, CA 94114
www.heliographica.com

Library of Congress Control Number: 2004111598
ISBN: 0-9753233-1-8

Printed in the United States of America

Cover design by Scott Segerblom

TABLE OF CONTENTS

FOREWORD

This book is a multiple encounter with the love of God and the Blessed Mother interested in our spiritual welfare.

In the following events, the Lord, the Mother and the angels gently talk to the people who have shared their stories and create for them opportunities for spiritual change and growth.

The One who has made the first move has always been the Lord, and His love has been the prompter for the final "yes" to his invitation; then everything starts making sense, and the joy of walking in the light slowly becomes one's new reality.

Father William Lauriola O.F.M.
April 6, 2004

Some names have been changed to protect the privacy of individuals mentioned in this book. All Scripture references are taken from the New American Bible unless otherwise specified.

Each story is compiled from the person's own words—usually spoken, sometimes written, and thus retains the individual's unique voice and character.

INTRODUCTION

Sometimes, as human beings, we find ourselves on the edge of grace. At that edge, an abyss falls away before us, and we are helpless not to tumble into it unless grace reaches out and saves us. We do not always know how we arrived at such a precarious point; but once there, we know we need healing, meaning, love, peace, hope and happiness. We know that we are seeking something to fulfill us and take away our angst and our sadness. What we do not know, is that we are seeking God.

Each true life story in this book reveals a person who has teetered on the edge of grace, in seemingly hopeless situations, and discovered hope and healing in a loving God. The people—an atheist, a stripper, a car thief, a woman who had two abortions, a sex addict, a lonely youth, a woman who told God to go to hell, a woman who hears the voice of God, a priest, a man with the hidden stigmata, and a homosexual man abandoned by his mother—all possess, as diverse as they are, vital elements in common: they have truly found God, and they have received help in their journeys of faith through the Blessed Virgin Mary's presence and messages in Medjugorje.[1] Each story, therefore, ends with a message that Mary has given to the world, a message which speaks to that person's life, and perhaps to our own.

The book begins with my own story. I am the atheist.

CHRISTINE

Rescued from the precipice of death

One night, as I lay in bed at age nine, an agonizing thought shot through my mind: "I am going to die one day." As much as I tried to think otherwise, I could not see a way out of it. "If I'm going to die and be nothing, then why am I here?" I wondered. "What is the point of life?" "Mom! Mom! Come here!" I shouted. My mother came into my room, and I asked her, "What will happen when I die?"

She knelt down next to me and said, "It's nothing to worry about."

"It's nothing to worry about?"

"No. What will happen to you is what will happen to everyone. When we die, we become like the earth."

"Like the earth? Will I know that I'm dead?"

"Probably not, because you won't be around."

"I won't be around?"

"Well, not completely. You'll be like soil in the ground. You'll either be cremated—that's when your body is burned and then you'll become like dirt that can help nourish other plants, like trees, or you'll be buried underground."

"Oh," I said, "It's nothing to worry about?" finding her answer horribly worrisome.

"No. It's nothing to worry about. Try not to think about it." Then she got up and said, "Goodnight."

"Try not to think about it," I reminded myself. "It's nothing to worry about . . ."

As she left my room and shut the door, dread filtered quickly through my mind into my body and left me shivering. "It's nothing to worry about?! . . . But I will be nothing," my thoughts chanted. "There will be no more me to even remember that I once was!" After that, I thought of death often, usually at night in my bed, staring into the darkness of my room, paralyzed with fear.

I did not like Christians

I was raised in a non-religious home, and I did not like Christians. I found them hopelessly misguided by a fairytale, and at best, annoying.

My derogatory view began one Christmas when my parents took me to see a manger scene in the spacious backyard of a home near ours in Berkeley, California. Covering the side of a hill were electrically-lit Wise Men and camels and cows and angels and sheep and shepherds and a mom and a dad and a baby. When I looked at the display, I thought it was the most beautiful sight that ever could be. My five-year old heart felt like it had been transported to heaven, and I thought, "How wonderful it is that my parents have taken me here!" Normally bothered by the cold, my body felt light and expansive inside my winter jacket, and the crisp winter air around me twinkled with joy. I could not take my eyes off the manger scene, and I did not want to leave. When my parents said it was time to go, I asked if I could stay longer. I gazed at the lit figures on the hill which seemed to wink back at me. Not knowing what the scene meant, I asked my dad, "What is this? Who are the people?" "They're part of a fairy tale about a special baby that was born in a manger and people came to see him because they thought he was the Son of God," he said. "It's not real?" I asked. "No," said my dad. "Are you sure?" I asked again. "Yes, I'm sure, honey. Now, let's go home." Reluctantly, I took my dad's hand and immediately wondered when I would see it again. I did not get a chance to return until years later. And when I did, the scene was gone, and so was my wonder.

So I learned, very young, that the Christian story was not real. I was never going to be a Christian—of that much I was sure. In my youth, I also perfected the fine art of worrying and suffered from very low self-esteem and mild depression. I walked with my shoulders hunched, head forward, eyes lowered, and my heart raced wildly at the thought of speaking up in school or talking to a boy. I did find joy, though, in ballet, and practiced it diligently for years with such commitment and passion that I ended up dancing professionally with the San Francisco Ballet Company. At age seven, I decided that I was going to become a professional ballet dancer, and I became one. I was going to dance until approximately age forty, so I planned. Ballet was my destiny. Nothing else even remotely satisfied me.

Not having been raised in any religion, I did not know there was a God, so, for me, ballet quickly became my personal God. At age nineteen, at the height of my dancing abilities and fully in love with my profession, I suffered from foot injuries and had three foot operations. This ended my career and took away the only God I ever knew. Devastated, I grew depressed, lost my identity, and lost my hope.

In my sadness, I looked to the New Age movement for answers, and for four years wound through a dizzying maze of practices and therapies. None of them brought me any lasting relief, and I ended up worse off than when I began. My search for "enlightenment" began when I read a book called "Many Lives, Many Masters" by Brian Weiss who claimed that his hypnotized client was telling him of her past lives. "I will live again!" I cheered as my latent fear of becoming dirt when I died disappeared for the very first time. Having opened a door into the New Age, I stepped through it and tried rebirthing, holotropic breathing, the I-Ching, runes, aura-readings, visualization, transpersonal psychology, shamanic meditations, numerology, astrology, chakra balancing, energy "healing" through touch, heart-opening rituals, yoga, colon hydrotherapy, yeast-free diets, past-life regression, crystal healing, and psychic readings.

I chanted and sang before Indian gurus, or pictures of them. I sat in a large theater listening to a female Indian Guru from New York who I later found out was involved in covering up her torture of her brother, the sexual abuse acts of her predecessor, and her organization's questionable financial practices. I sat on the floor in a lotus position, in front of an Indian Guru named Mata Amritanandamayi as she rocked rhythmically to "bhajans" (devotional songs), occasionally reaching her left arm into the sky with an odd laugh that was anything but contagious. I gathered in a home with people who sat and sang, chanted and meditated in front of a large picture of Sai Baba, a guru from India with a very large afro.

I read books by Shakti Gawain, Chris Griscom, Shirley MacLaine, W. Brugh Joy, Ram Dass, Brian Weiss, Louise Hays, Deepak Chopra, etc., etc., etc. I walked into musty, dimly-lit, smoke-filled rooms for tarot-card readings; and I stayed up late pouring over New Age books to learn about my past life as an Egyptian princess.

For a full year, from 1993 to 1994, I followed the advice of a psychic named Rita after receiving an "attunement" session from her during which I fell into a trance-like, peaceful and pleasurable state. She told me she saw a dove which meant I was saved, that a man would come into my life and pay for everything, and that the words "Matthew Fox" were written over my head. Convinced something supernaturally important had happened to me, I followed her advice to take a semester of graduate classes at Matthew Fox's New Age "Sophia Center" and moved into the dorms there and into deeper debt and confusion. I kept thinking I would find the secrets to higher consciousness, that they were right around the corner, but turn after turn led me to dead ends with more questions.

Rita acted like she knew the answers, so I called her after a semester and asked what to do next. She said I should move from the west coast to the east coast, so I did, and moved in with my aunt and uncle. Once there and still confused, I called her again. "I'm here. What do I do now?" This time she said I was to take Harvard summer school class. I got a catalogue, called her back and said, "Which one?" since none of them appealed to me. She told me to read her the catalogue of classes and with partial conviction stated, "You are to take the anthropology class."

Now, very much in debt from student loans, I took the anthropology course, and in each class, as I sat with a group of undergraduate students who looked like smart twelve-year-olds, I waited for the vital, life-changing, at least relevant information that this class would bring me. It never came.

One day, a couple weeks later, numb from running around between scattered promises of spiritual healing, I sat still in a lotus position and badgered my "higher self" for answers. Rita! I thought. She is the reason I am here in the first place. I should go see her and get some help. I phoned up her office and made an appointment, and my aunt gladly loaned me their car when she found I was using it to get counseling.

The day to see Rita finally came. Full of hope, I drove an hour to the next town, parked the car and lay down on the grass in front of Rita's office waiting for the time of my appointment to arrive. Without warning or provocation, a burdensome fatigue came over me in an odd and disconcerting way. A fearful question blew through my mind. "Is there something seriously wrong with me?"

When the time for my appointment came, I slowly peeled off the grass and was told by Rita's assistant to wait in the counseling room. I walked into a cold, damp room and sunk into a hardwood chair, like a rag doll with half its stuffing. Twenty minutes passed. Finally Rita entered and sat down across from me. The woman I saw scarcely resembled the woman I remembered. Her eyes darted about through rapidly blinking eyelids, as though focusing on one visual area for too long gave her sharp eye pain, and on top of her slightly plump, seemingly swollen body, her head jerked and wobbled nervously and apparently involuntarily. She seemed unable to sit still without twitching, as though a small animal were scurrying within her. As nicely as I could muster, I said, "I wondered if you were coming. I've been here for quite a while." "Well, you should have come and gotten me," she said. "You should take more responsibility for yourself." The injustice of her telling me to wait, leaving me alone to freeze, and then reprimanding me for it, irked me.

Thus the session began with a wrong turn and then began to spin out-of-control with 360-degree turns. I asked her for another psychic reading, but she said that counseling was what I most needed. Dissatisfied with her decision, I began to tell her how I wasn't sure what I was supposed to be doing on the east coast, that I was running out of money, that I didn't learn anything that interested me in the anthropology class, and that I felt ill and depressed much of the time. Rita responded by telling me that I needed to do something to boost my self-esteem—something to make me feel good about myself. She mentioned that she had just seen one of her clients who had always wanted a nice, new car and so she suggested to her that she go ahead and buy one, put it on her credit card, and worry about paying it off later. This suggestion, she said, transformed her client and gave her a new lease on life. "You should do the same," she said.

"I don't want to buy a car," I responded. "I don't need one. My aunt and uncle are lending me theirs." Upon hearing this Rita insisted that I look into getting a new car. "I've never driven a new car, and have no desire to," I said. "Besides that, I'm already in debt and don't need to rack up a needless credit card debt as well." Shaking with irritation and twitching, she countered, "You just don't appreciate yourself enough to do something nice for yourself." Silently, I thought, "You're nuts, and I never want to speak with you again."

Pulling quickly out of the parking lot, I drove away watching Rita's office shrink inside my rearview mirror. I had stepped out of our session as though stepping off of a spinning teacup ride and could barely hold my head up or peer through my tears to see the road home.

I made it home with patient effort, and as I opened the front screen door, I overheard my aunt speaking on the phone in a tone of hushed concern. She smiled sheepishly at me, held out the receiver and said, "Rita's on the line, she wants to talk with you. I think it's extremely wonderful that you're seeing someone." "Yes, wonderful," I thought facetiously. "Hello, Rita," I said.

"Christine, you owe me one hundred dollars for the two phone calls you made to me over the last month."

"I don't understand," I said. "Those weren't counseling sessions. I just asked a couple quick questions, and you never told me about any charge."

"You should know better than that and should know that I'm a professional."

"I disagree with your charge."

Raising her voice an octave, she said, "Look. You owe me money, and you're going to have to pay."

Not one to love controversy or pick a fight, I screamed, "I don't owe you anything!" "Yes, you do!" she yelled back, "and I'll keep calling until I get it." Scared by the weirdness of it all, I retorted, "Goodbye, Rita, and please don't call here again." Hanging up the receiver with a shaky hand, I thought, "I've been following the advice of a cantankerous loony-toon."

My aunt walked back into the room and said, "Rita and I had a very nice chat. She's concerned about you. We both are, really. I'm so glad that you have someone like her to talk to." Too tired to disagree, I responded with a polite "Thank you."

Stunned into giving up on Rita, but continuing my desperate search for answers, I began to frequent a Hindu/New Age/Holistic healing center where I would sit down in a circle of silent anonymity among an average of five strangers. One day, the group leader, a short, blond man who looked like John Denver, sat down on his meditation pillow, taking more time than usual to quiet himself, twice restructuring his lotus position with trembling hands. Normally, he began our group with chanting, but this time he spoke, struggling to find words which sounded uncharacteristically fragile: "I have unfortunate news to tell you." He paused and took a deep breath. "I have discovered that the gurus I have been following, gurus who claim to be Avatars, incarnations of the divine, have engaged in behaviors which"—he paused, focusing on a spot on the floor in front of him—"which don't honor human dignity." I recalled that the hallway leading to the meditation room had looked bare, but I hadn't noticed why. Now I realized that his string of pictures of gurus had been taken down.

Becoming hesitantly assertive, he continued, "We must only go to the Source of all Oneness and not use mediators. We can always trust the Source, the One who is Universal Consciousness, who is us, who is All." "This is deep," I thought to myself.

Needing to explore those depths, I sat, knelt, bowed, and then knelt, stood and bowed and sat, and so on in a humorless center for Buddhism and dutifully arose when it was my turn to visit the Buddhist "master" who sat regally on the floor in a side room with his serious female assistant. "You may kneel before the master and ask him a question," said the assistant. I recoiled at having to kneel before a stranger, especially one with a look of great self-importance, but purposefully stashing away my first impressions, I said, "I came here to the east coast because a psychic told me to, and now that I'm here I'm not sure what to do with myself or my life. What is the meaning of life, anyway?" The master, a tall, white, all American with the look of a quarterback, said in a booming voice, "I cannot answer that. What do you think?" "I don't know," I said, "What do you think?" He paused allowing enough time for an awkward silence then said, "I don't know. What do you think?"

I felt sick inside my soul

The false New Age promises of healing and enlightenment were not my only destructive hopes. From an early age, and especially after I lost my dance career, I looked for comfort and happiness in intimate relationships and sunk ever deeper into a mire of sin. I had felt so unclean just after I became sexually active, but as I continued with my behavior, that insidious feeling went away. Sex never attracted me much, though, I simply wanted to be loved and held. I felt temporarily filled with life when I was in a relationship, but when things failed, as they inevitably did, I was left with an even larger empty, dark and lonely hole within me. When I did not have a boyfriend, my mind would scramble for comfort and fixate on who might be next. If I could not think of someone, I found fleeting satisfaction in pulling out a list of men I had slept with as though it were a trophy. Life without a boyfriend meant desperate misery, so I would scan rooms, streets, and clubs with a lonely hunger, like an emaciated cub in search of its mother's milk, hoping to find "him." That summer on the east coast, I signed up for New Age workshops, hoping to find Mr. Right, if not nirvana, or the answer to life's mysteries, but inevitably walked away with nothing and no one.

Despite the inevitable pain, I was always searching outside myself for something or someone to make me happy, and I never felt a sense of inner peace. Life centered around my own desperate need for meaning, for healing and for love.

I can vividly recall one particularly hot day of that summer in 1994 when I awoke under the pall of a lingering nightmare and with sense of dread over life's insistence of a new day. I got up and stared at a frightening morning face in the bathroom mirror. Who was this person staring back at me? She had the same straight brown hair and brown eyes, but her complexion, normally an olive color, looked red and lumpy, and her features, normally youthful, drooped downward forming a heavy depressive frown. Her eyes looked muddy and her years looked advanced. When I tried to raise my eyebrows and facial muscles to feign happiness, she stared back at me forlorn and unconvinced. I wished I had never laid eyes on her.

I was twenty-seven, and my health was declining precipitously along with my sense of purpose and mental well-being. I began vomiting without cause, my hair was falling out more than usual, I was bleeding internally, I could not tolerate most foods, I ached, and without warning, energy would escape my deadened body, as though life had dropped me. Worst of all, I felt sick inside my soul. At times, I would call out in guttural despair; at times, I would rage at life's inconveniences; and at times, I could not stop crying once I started.

In a last attempt at healing, I attended a Reiki hands-on "healing" workshop the following day, and as I lay down on a massage table and the participants placed their hands on me, an energy poured into me that filled me with despair. I climbed off the table before they were finished and curled up in a hidden corner to cry. When the workshop ended, and people began to leave, I wanted to run up to someone, anyone nice, and shake him and scream, "Can you help me? Can anyone help me?" But I caught myself in my own madness and thought, "No human being can help you." Still sobbing, I got in my car and drove off chanting the words, "Hold me. Hold me. Hold me!" and wondered if anyone on earth or beyond could hear me.

The only friend I had left that summer, the only person who could handle my extreme distress and cathartic crying spells, was a man named Joseph who lived near my home on the west coast. Time and again, Joseph patiently listened to me pour my sadness into the telephone receiver. I knew Joseph possessed something special, something that gave him deep contentment. While life tossed me about like a ship in raging seas, his rudder remained plunged deep into still waters. I could not hurt him with my pain. Talking to him, I felt safe. I knew he was different.

The morning after the Reiki workshop, as I lay in bed, overcome by fatigue, I received a phone call that would change my life. It was Joseph. He told me that for the past six weeks he had been woken up in the middle of the night by a vision of me calling out to him saying, "Help *me*. Show *me* who you really are." At first confused, he ignored my image, and taking the message metaphorically, began to help various women in his neighborhood by assisting young women with homework and walking elderly women across the street. But the more he disregarded it, the louder I cried out. "Help *me!* Show *me* who you really are." I had known Joseph for five years, and he had never talked to me about his faith, but that day on the phone, in his distinctive, soft, articulate voice, he began to speak to me about my soul and about God's love. His words pierced the inner recesses of my heart, and I started to feel light and expansive, as though my body was filling the entire room. I told him what was happening to me, and he said, "Christine. You are being saved."

We soon realized that God wanted me to see Joseph urgently. With the little energy I had left, I drummed up the courage to take a battery of medical tests and flew to the west coast for what was to be the most miraculous week of my life.

You were a way station

I looked forward to spending time in Joseph's room. I needed solace and rest, I felt so ill. I had so little strength of my own, and Joseph's room had always nurtured me. Joseph rented a room in a house in Kensington, California that felt grand enough as to be uninviting, but his room felt like an oasis of peace—cozy, feminine and elegant. Pictures of angels and Notre Dame Cathedral in France hung over wallpaper of Victorian ladies, their suitors, and distant sailboats. Beauty towered over function. Postcards and ribbons and trinkets were placed so delicately on display that whenever I bumped into one thing, about fifteen other things fell down at the same time. Two windows opened to an expanse of San Francisco Bay—to trees, sky, city lights, a Bay Bridge, morning light, sunsets and a backyard of short sculpted hedges reminiscent of an ancient king's private garden. That week, I would stare out those windows often.

The evening I arrived, I entered his home, placed my bag in a room adjacent to Joseph's that he had reserved for me, placed myself on the bed without the energy to change clothes or lift up the covers, and went to sleep immediately.

In the morning, Joseph woke up wondering how he might help me. "I'll need to pray today," he said," and ask God why you're here. It would be good if you could spend the day in prayer as well."

"I don't know how to pray," I told him. "I've never prayed before."

Joseph looked at me incredulously as though he'd encountered an extraterrestrial, "*You mean to tell me you've never prayed?*"

"Joseph! I wasn't raised with any religion! Just assume I have no clue."

Joseph grew introspective, looked at the ground, and began to shake his head. "I just can't imagine life without prayer," he said.

I slept most of the rest of the day and when I woke up, Joseph had left a note saying that he had gone to the beach. Unsure of what to do with myself, I decided to take a twilight walk around the block. As soon as I walked out the door, I felt a happiness and tranquility that seemed otherwordly. My normal feelings of physical pain and emotional torment left me. As I walked along the neighborhood sidewalks, my feet felt like they hovered slightly above ground, my legs lifted and lowered weightlessly, and my eyes could see a supernatural beauty in nature that I had never seen before and have never seen since. Flowers, shrubs and trees seemed illumined from within. As I looked around me, I blinked several times to test if what I was seeing was real. It was, and I began to cry in wonder.

After an hour had passed, I walked to Joseph's home and waited for him to return. As I waited, the gift of expansive peace slowly subsided from me, and I again felt restricted to my aching body, yet not the same. Although I felt my physical symptoms creep back, my spirit remained joyful. When Joseph finally arrived, I told him about my heavenly walk. His pensive reaction puzzled me. Normally, he openly delighted in the good fortune of others, but as I spoke, he listened to me quietly and was slow to respond. "How was your time at the beach?" I asked. Joseph sat down in a chair next to me, sighed deeply, and told me that as he was sitting on the sand, he suddenly felt spiritually attacked. A weight of evil pressed down upon him from above, and he felt like his bones were literally being crushed. Fearing that he might not survive under the weight, he called out to God and to Mary for help, and finally the assault grew weaker and eventually stopped. He then looked up to see the outline of a dark demonic figure, glaring at him and screeching a hideous cry of angry defeat as it skimmed the ocean, moving further and further away until it fell away from view.

He looked down at the sand around him and couldn't believe his eyes. It was covered with his blood, and then he noticed, so were areas of his skin. He had sweated blood from the stress of battling Satan. What he had experienced in the spiritual realm had affected him physically. Joseph then peered behind himself to see a couple strolling by on the beach who, when they noticed him, looked fearful and began to walk faster. "I'd better wash myself in the sea," he thought. "Lord knows what I look like."

"I didn't know until now," Joseph said to me in a serious tone, "that the devil doesn't just live inside human beings, but is actually a being—conscious, fully alive and deadly."

Not knowing what to say, I stammered in a whisper, "It's incredible that as I was experiencing a moment of freedom from all my torment for the first time, you were being tormented like never before."

"It's not a coincidence, Christine."

"What do you mean?"

"All the demons that were in you came after me."

"Oh, my God. Why?"

"They knew I was going to lead you to God, and they were furious."

"How many were in me?"

"You were a way station."

I recoiled at the thought of what had lived inside of me and started to feel sick, horrified that I was part of what happened to Joseph.

"Christine," he said. "What have you been involved in that caused all this?"

I honestly did not know. At Joseph's request, I began to tell him things about my life that I had kept secret: my depression after having to quit ballet, my dislike of life, my intimate relationships with boyfriends, my brief affairs, two of which were with married men I had worked with at a restaurant, my New Age retreats and practices. Joseph grew pale and looked increasingly dismayed as I continued. He told me that premarital sex was wrong, that God never wanted me to be thrown around from heartbreak to heartbreak, that sexual behavior put me at risk for getting deadly viruses, and that if I was going to unite with a man and become one with him, God would want that man to commit to me with a vow and love me for life. Then sex could be safe for my soul. "The Church doesn't just make this stuff up, you know," he said. "You lost God's protection when you lost your virginity, and you opened yourself up to the demonic realm. With every person you slept with, more demons entered your soul. And you also hurt the souls of those you were with."

I defended myself saying that no one ever told me that premarital sex was wrong. How was I to know? Then I remembered how at a deep level inside myself, I did know something felt wrong, but I had ignored the feeling. I could not bring myself to defend my participation in adultery, though. I had rationalized away any feelings of conscience at the time, saying to myself, "Well, he must not have a very good marriage, anyway. If it's already bad, I'm not causing any more harm." But I never forgot the evening when I served my lover's wife at a restaurant table. She looked up to thank me with sweet eyes and innocent smile that pierced my conscience like a fiery lance. My whole body flushed with a warm rush of shame.

Struggling to find something redemptive about my life, I said to Joseph, "Well, at least I was growing in my spirituality by going to New Age workshops and working towards a higher consciousness."

"Christine. None of that helped you. The New Age movement does not honor the true God. Time and time again, God reached out to you to help you change your path, but you walked right up to the edge of a precipice and were about to fall off. Only grace has saved you."

I sat in stunned silence and put my head in my hands, barely able to breathe, devastated by the news that my search for love and meaning was not only a waste of my life, but the destruction of it.

That night, I lowered myself to my knees. Exhausted by the truth and by sickness, I dropped my head to the floor and, one by one, remembered each man I had been with and told God I was sorry for what I had done. Then I lifted up to God my whole history of spiritual confusion and said, "I'm sorry that I offended you. I'm sorry that I hurt you so much. Please forgive me."

You are as blessed as you are loved

I slept that night as though in a tomb. My health had declined to a perilous degree. I was bleeding internally, my abdomen was distended, I was vomiting often and in a lot of pain. My food would not digest, my muscles ached, odd pains surged through my body, and with no energy, I often collapsed with fatigue. I wanted help. I wanted God. But I wanted nothing to do with Jesus or Mary. For years I had wanted nothing to do with them. Once when I had seen a picture of the Madonna and Child, it made me so angry that I wanted it taken down. Another time, I had read a self-help book that I had enjoyed except for its fleeting references to Jesus. I knew that Jesus and Mary were fanciful figures for the hopeless and misguided. For me, their names and images had provoked ire. I had always disliked them intensely.

But Jesus decided to save me, a sinner. I will never know why he chose me, and I do not have the words to express my gratitude. I would not be alive were it not for divine grace, unmerited and unasked for. Three days after my arrival on the west coast, as I lay down in Joseph's room with my eyes closed and half-asleep, I felt the presence of God within and around me. Then suddenly I saw a gray, pulsating mass and then heard a loud "pop" sound within me. The mass disappeared. I opened my eyes and saw Joseph sitting next to me. "Did you hear that?" I asked him.

"No. What did you hear?" he asked.

I explained what had just happened to me. He paused pensively and said, "It was important that you came here as soon as you did."

"Why?"

"Christine. Jesus just cured you of cancer."

"What!?" I exclaimed, catching my breath. "What are you saying?"

"You had cancer, and you had six weeks to live."

"What!? How do you know that?"

"I was deep in prayer just now, and Mary and Jesus came to me and spoke to me. At the same time you were sensing the presence of God with you, Mary told me that she saw you flailing in life, like a fish that couldn't find water, even though an ocean was just next to you all along. She took pity on you and asked her Son to save you."

I sat upright, speechless. I tried to say a word, but could not. Somehow, I knew he had spoken the truth.

Over the next three days, all my physical symptoms vanished. I called the east coast to find out that a papsmear I had received was abnormal, but feeling completely assured and at peace, I did not worry and did not follow up on it. I have had healthy check ups ever since, and I have learned that promiscuity can lead to cervical cancer through exposure to the human papyloma virus. My sexual sins had helped bring about not only the death of my soul, but the death of my body. Jesus, at Mary's request, had saved my soul and my life. Even though I had hated them, they had always loved me.

The next day, Mary again spoke to Joseph and told him that I should pray the rosary whenever I needed her help and she would come to me. And Jesus told him that I should sin no more, join the Catholic Church, and help bring to it, "compassion, love, kindness, and generosity." I had never before set foot in a Catholic Church as anyone but a tourist, but I wanted to learn how I might "sign up."

"If you had died before Jesus saved you," Joseph told me, "you would have been in excruciating pain, not only in your body, because the cancer would have spread to your bones, but in your soul, because you would have wasted much of your life. Then after death, you would have entered into a dark, gray place of great pain and suffering for what would have seemed like thousands of years.

"Thousands of years?" I asked him in disbelief. "You got that in prayer, too?"

"Yes," he said. "Time is different in purgatory than here, but to you it would have seemed like an eternity."

I told him I thought I was going to be born again into a different body here on earth, but he assured me that that belief was not true, that it was a deception. We are born into this life only once, he explained, and where we end up—whether in heaven, purgatory, or hell, depends upon how we live our lives here.

"Heaven," he said, "is worth anything, any suffering on earth. The joy souls experience there is indescribable. They are completely fulfilled and live among beauty that does not exist here on earth."

"You've actually experienced heaven?" I asked him.

He blushed and looked away, then grew silent and contemplative, but did not answer. After a few moments, he turned his face towards me, caught my eyes with his and said, "Even if a person's sins are scarlet, heartfelt repentance can lead one into paradise."

That evening, after I was cured, I remember hearing a symphony. I was in Joseph's room and thought that perhaps the radio was on. I checked everywhere—in the hall, out the window, under the bed, even in his desk drawers, to see where the music might be playing; but I soon realize that the beautiful music was coming from within me. I realized then that heaven was rejoicing because one sinner had been saved, and the heavenly hosts were letting me join in the celebration.

That same night, Joseph had a dream. He saw me staring with amazement at my own hand to see it brilliant with radiant light. I gasped as my eyes traveled from my hand to the rest of my body to see divine light permeating and illuminating all of me. "See Christine," he said. "You walk in light. You worry about the pain in your feet and your body, yet this is who you are. You are as blessed as you are loved. You are a feather on the breath of God."

* * *

I am actually quite normal. My days with Joseph surpass my own understanding. Through him, Jesus and Mary showered me with more piercing love, genuine truth and immediate attention than I had been able to receive in all my years. Joseph entered into my life's desert wasteland, scorched and starved, and he prayed. Green sprouts of hope and small yellow flowers of joy peered out of my heart then budded through the cracks. In one week, God recreated me.

Before my conversion, whenever I gave myself to others, a pit of desperate need always pulled me back into selfishness; but after my conversion, God gave me his Holy Spirit, a spirit of loving sacrifice. Finally, I could look at the world and wonder what I could give, not what I could get. In the years that followed, I prepared for and received the Sacrament of Baptism, a gift from heaven of unmeasured grace, through which Christ gave me a share in his divine life. I worked for three years towards a Masters degree in Theological Studies at the Jesuit School of Theology at Berkeley and trained in spiritual direction there where all the great mysteries of life were at my fingertips, like ripe blackberries ready to be plucked. Then I studied for two years at the University of California at Berkeley to receive a Masters degree in Social Welfare, through which I learned the practicalities of living my faith on behalf of those in need. I ministered to women in prison, people with AIDS, and as resident minister in a college dorm. Then I began working with the dying and the grieving through hospice care, and, in addition, worked as a counselor, spiritual director, workshop conductor and parish mission preacher. In August of 2001, I entered into the Sacrament of Marriage with a loving man, and three months later, Jesus called me and my new husband, John, to go on a pilgrimage to Medjugorje. There, I received the grace to follow Mary's primary messages to the world—frequent reception of the Eucharist, Bible reading, prayer-especially the rosary, monthly Confession, and fasting on bread and water on Wednesdays and Fridays. It took me seven years, but I finally heeded Mary's call to pray the rosary.

My faith has nourished me, guided me, challenged me, held me aloft in peaceful joy and softened the blows of sadness, because now I know that no matter what life events might trip my steps or kick dust in my path, I have God, and he is all I need. I now know where mortal sin can lead, and I never want to go there again. My life is not mine any more. It is God's. It was God's all along. Being a Christian means everything to me. It means the difference between life and death.

* * *

Dear children, I have been with you nine years to tell you that God your Father is the only way, truth, and life—to show you the way that you can reach eternal life. Give good example to your children and to those who do not believe. You will not have happiness on this earth; neither will you come to heaven if you do not have a pure and humble heart and if you do not fulfill the laws of God. I am asking you for your help to join me in praying for those who do not believe. You are helping me very little. You have little charity or love for your neighbors, and God gave you the love and showed you how you should forgive and love others. For that reason, reconcile, and purify your souls by going to confession. Take your rosary and pray. Take all your suffering patiently. You should remember how patiently Jesus suffered for you. Do not impose your faith on the unbelievers. Show it to them with your example and pray for them, my children. Please pray for them.[2]

ALLAN

The hidden stigmata and unshakeable joy

My conversion began in August of 1974 when my sister invited me to a Catholic charismatic prayer meeting, and I was told by the leaders of the group that I needed to be baptized in the Holy Spirit. I was fourteen at the time, raised Roman Catholic and educated in Catholic schools, but I did not know what baptism in the Holy Spirit was about at all. In the early church, it was an important part of initiation into the body of Christ, which the Charismatic Renewal is restoring to the Church today. The baptism of the Holy Spirit is the release, or a deepening, of the graces of the Holy Spirit that one receives in baptism and confirmation. It is one's own Pentecost. It involves what Protestants call being born again and accepting the Lord Jesus as your Savior. John the Baptist speaks of it when he says in the gospel of Matthew (3:11) regarding Jesus, "He will baptize you with the Holy Spirit and fire." I was going away to a high school seminary at the end of the month to be a Franciscan friar, and the leaders of the prayer group knew that I would need spiritual power in order to survive the seminary ordeal, and boy were they right.

On August 23rd, 1974, the leaders of the prayer group laid their hands on me and prayed that I would receive baptism in the Holy Spirit. In that moment, I felt no emotion, only nervousness because my dad was waiting to pick me up, and I was late. When I finally got out to the car, my dad, annoyed and in a hurry, scolded me for making him miss part of the baseball playoff games. I could not stop from smiling because after they had finished praying over me I was filled with the joy of the Lord—much to the chagrin of my father. In his typical fashion, my dad dismissed what I was feeling as just my imagination. I went to bed as usual that night but awoke at about two o'clock in the morning speaking two words I did not know, "Mada Shunda." It sounds pretty funny, but I was horrified when I heard myself. I thought I had become psycho, like the people at the prayer meeting, or so I had judged. I thought of those people as a little weird and overboard in their love for Jesus. They were way too enthusiastic.

Strangely enough, after I said those words, I felt as if the Lord

Himself were standing right near me, at the foot of my bed. I didn't see him, but I felt the most intense love I have ever experienced in my life, and "being psychotic" didn't bother me anymore. Then I gradually fell back asleep, only to awake several more times uttering, "Mada Shunda." It cracks me up to think of it now.

When I woke up in the morning I told my seventeen year-old sister what had happened. She said, "Praise the Lord. You've received the gift of tongues." I, however, was not convinced. My sister advised me to go to my room and tell the Lord I wanted to speak fluently in the language, not just a couple words, if this was truly from him. Totally ignorant of spiritual etiquette, I demanded of Almighty God, "Give me this gift, and prove it to me, if this is for real!" All at once my tongue became thick in my mouth, and I began speaking words entirely foreign to me. I was amazed and again filled with that incredible love I had experienced the night before. The Mass and the Scriptures and everything else about my faith became alive for me, and I learned later that my parents feared my sister and I were getting involved in a cult.

Everyone stared at me blankly

Two weeks later, my parents drove me from our home in Wichita, Kansas to Cincinnati, Ohio to move me into a high school seminary there. Even though the seminary was filled with young men searching for God, it was a spiritual wasteland for me because no one shared my newfound joy in knowing Christ. I learned, rather quickly, to find my consolation in prayer before the Tabernacle. The Charismatic Renewal was new then, and nobody else at the seminary, except for one instructor, had had any exposure to it, so when I talked about my experience, everyone stared at me blankly.

Over the years I spent there, students began to confide in me that they, too, had experienced the baptism of the Holy Spirit in charismatic prayer groups in their own home parishes over summer vacation. Eventually we formed a student prayer group of about a dozen high school male seminarians.

The faculty at the seminary worried about our prayer group, so they sent a friar, a Scripture scholar with a doctorate in Biblical Studies, to observe our prayer meetings which were wildly enthusiastic. We clapped and sang and praised the Lord. All the while Father Hilarian . . . In Greek, his name means "joy," and he was the crabbiest priest I have ever encountered . . . Anyway, Father Hilarian sat with his arms crossed and his head down, as if asleep during our joyous praise and worship.

Finally, I asked him what he thought about our prayer meetings, and he answered, "I don't know how you dumb kids can be speaking ancient Biblical languages, but you are." "I'm convinced there might be something to this tongues thing."

We received many answers to prayer in that little group, including a miraculous recovery of a brother of one of the members of the group who was in a coma from a motorcycle accident. While we were praying for the young man in the coma, Jesus appeared to him in the hospital, took his hand, and told him to get up. He suffered no residual brain damage or any other disabilities as a result of the accident, leaving his doctors shaking their heads in disbelief.

Many unusual events occurred when I was in seminary. In my sophomore year, I was praying with my eyes closed one evening in the darkened seminary chapel, just a few feet away from the Tabernacle. All at once, a bright light startled me, so I opened my eyes thinking that someone had turned on the lights in the chapel, but they were still turned off. The bright, blinding white light I saw emanated from two approximately seven foot-tall and three foot-wide columns on either side of the Tabernacle. They looked as if two fluorescent light tubes had been placed on end. Inside of them stood two angelic figures in human form whose features I could not see clearly due to the brightness of the light. I could not see wings, nor halos, nor anything of that sort. I felt shocked and amazed to see the entire chapel filled with this light so brilliant I could barely stand to look towards it. I shook my head, rubbed my eyes, and blinked several times, but these columns remained. The angels did not speak to me or look at me, but focused all their attention to Jesus in the Tabernacle, bowing to him slowly and reverently, over and over.

I knew I had to find someone to see this, too. So after about five minutes of watching this spectacle, I leapt up from my chair, ran across the parking lot and through the gymnasium where a school basketball game was being played. I could not convince any of my friends to come with me to see these heavenly visitors. Nobody would peel himself away from watching the game because the score was tied. I couldn't believe it. So I ran back to the chapel and saw the light still there, shining through the windows onto the parking lot. When I got back inside, I returned to my place and prayed for about twenty minutes more, marveling at these angels who were still bowing to the Lord in the Blessed Sacrament.

Just as suddenly as they arrived, the angels left, without a word, leaving the chapel in darkness. They had been present at least a half an hour. I discussed this event with my spiritual director, a friar at the seminary, and he reminded me that angels are messengers from God, and that God allowed me to see them for a reason. And, "What would that be?" I questioned him.

"Well," he said, "What were the angels doing?"

"They were bowing over and over again before the Tabernacle," I replied.

"Well, maybe that's what the Lord is asking of you—to spend more time in reverent prayer before the Tabernacle." I did, and my prayer life deepened.

Angels have figured prominently in my spiritual life

After my initial experience of angels, they continued to visit in other ways. Once, during our charismatic prayer group, we heard angelic singing. It sounded as if a large choir of female and male voices were singing with us, thousands of them, complete with an orchestra. It was incredible. This happened once again when two of us were praying in the college seminary. Each time it lasted for at least ten minutes.

It is rare, now, that a month goes by when I do not see or hear an angelic presence. I do not usually see anything quite as dramatic as the two angels alongside the Tabernacle, but usually I see angels in the forms of flashes of light, or hazy figures around the altar at Mass, or at the side of the priest while he is preaching, or with my patients as they come into my chiropractic clinic. These angels I interpret to be guardian angels, since they seem associated with the person they are standing near. The only example I can recall of seeing an angel in actual human form took place when I was working in the inner city among the mentally ill homeless. As usual, I was running late and was on my way to lead a Bible study group for members of a parish I attended. As I hurried along the sidewalk to unlock the door of the parish, I noticed people already waiting outside to get in. After I unlocked the door and was about to close and lock it quickly behind me, a homeless man with the most incredible eyes approached me from the sidewalk. "Do you have a minute to talk with me?" he asked. "I'm sorry," I said. "I can't," and closed the door behind me. Instantly, I felt as if I had locked Jesus out, so I immediately unlocked and opened the door and looked all over for this man, but he had simply disappeared. This was not humanly possible since I had a good, wide view around me and did not see him walking or running away. I exhausted all possibilities by looking around the corner and behind any place he could have been hiding, and I never saw him again, whereas I saw the same homeless around there every day. I then knew he was an angel because he had disappeared completely.

That experience changed my perspective of how I look at the people I serve. I became more aware of what the incarnation was all about—Jesus enfleshed, even in the most humble and poor person, waiting to be discovered. The Scripture passage that says, "Do not neglect hospitality, for through it some have unknowingly entertained angels," became real to me. [Heb. 13.2]

Another interesting example of angels took place years later in 1994 while I was driving to a conference in a rental car with Tom, a fellow Catholic chiropractor like myself. We were singing religious songs a capella when I noticed a third soprano voice joining us from the rear seat. I kept turning back to look and see if anyone was there. Finally, I couldn't resist asking Tom if he heard the voice, too. He said, "Yeah, but I thought it was my imagination." We resumed singing, and we both heard the voice again. As long as we kept singing, the voice sang along with us. The reality of Emmanuel, God with us, became that much more alive to us as a result.

Angels have figured prominently in my spiritual life and development. Another angel experience I had involved my ministry in healing prayer which I have taught people for years now. As part of this ministry, Tom and Marita, my first intern in healing prayer, and I attended a conference on healing. Francis MacNutt, an expert in the field of healing ministry, was speaking. I had been acquainted with Dr. MacNutt and his wife, Judith, since 1985. He is a former Catholic priest who was officially laicized[3], and his marriage to Judith MacNutt was blessed by the Bishop of Jacksonville, Florida. He and his wife are wonderful and tremendously gifted by the Holy Spirit. At the conclusion of the conference, Francis and Judith stood at the speaker's podium leading the congregation in a final prayer. As we looked toward them, Marita and I both saw what looked like numerous basketball-sized globes of whirling white light around Francis and Judith. Suddenly, the globes stopped moving and formed an oval frame around their bodies. Then the globes burst into a brilliant flash of bright light. When our eyes could see through the brightness of that explosion, Marita and I both saw a huge, eight-foot electric blue angel standing behind them, with arching wings that towered over them. The angel then extended his arms around Francis and Judith from behind, encircling them with a tender embrace. At the conclusion of the prayer, the angel followed Francis and Judith down the stairs of the platform to their chairs in the front. Marita and I were astounded, and I prayed at that point, "Lord, if this is real, let me be able to talk with Francis and Judith afterwards." Marita, Tom, and I tried to approach them after the conference but were deterred by the crowds around them, and we finally had to leave in order to catch our plane. Marita then drove home, and Tom and I drove back one hundred and fifty miles to the airport in our angel-infested minivan.

I was more than a little disappointed that we could not speak with them. We had a connecting flight through Atlanta, and while Tom and I were waiting for our plane to Houston, guess who we saw walking down the concourse—Francis and Judith. We were able to have a few words with them before they rushed to catch their plane. I told Judith about the blue angel, and she replied, "Well, don't you know who the blue angel is?"

I said, "No."

She said in a factual manner, "It's the angel of healing."

As they proceeded on their way, I marveled at how, once again, the Lord was kind enough to give me a confirmation of his wonderful work in my life. I could go on and on with more angel stories. I have had so many angelic encounters they could fill a book. I will have to write one someday.

What I have learned in seminary, in my healing ministry, and in my experiences of angels is that they are pure spirit. They are not male and female as we are. That is why they are impressed with us so much. They are curious about us because we have corporeal, physical bodies, and Jesus does not live inside of them like he does in us. The incarnation exalted our nature to have the capacity to share his likeness. Physically we are created in God's image, and through the salvation of Jesus Christ, we can also share in his divinity. God sends angels to serve us, but they do not have the capacity to experience God as we can. We will never become angels and be handed a harp or a halo. Through the incarnation and death, Jesus has won for us a unique and special place in heaven as human beings.

Not all angels are good

Not all angels are good. Some are fallen angels, in other words, demons. I learned this the hard way when I was in college seminary and serving as a maintenance worker at a Franciscan school of evangelization in the Midwest. One day, the priest in charge received in his prayer that something unusual was going to happen that evening, so he made an excuse not to teach his evening basic evangelization class and left myself and Mike, another seminarian, in charge. Having learned the skill of delegation, I appointed Mike to teach the class of two hundred and fifty persons while I tended to my customary duties of setting up chairs, making coffee and greeting people as they arrived.

I was not, however, to get off the hook that easy. In my discussion group, which followed Mike's lecture, there was a medical doctor, his wife, two nurses, an accountant, a housewife, and a young legal secretary. The different groups totaling two hundred and fifty students were spread around the room, with ours in the middle, off to the side. We finished our session early and were standing around chatting in the classroom in the basement of the chapel when the legal secretary asked if we would pray for her because she had a stomachache. She didn't look disturbed and was professionally dressed, well-mannered and very polite. So we gathered around her to pray, and as soon as we touched her shoulder and grasped her hand to pray, she lifted up off the floor. Her head twisted ominously to one side, as if she were hanging from a noose. Only the whites of her eyes were visible. Everyone in our group saw this happening. The first comment was made by the medical doctor, a male gynecologist, who kept saying, "My God, something supernatural is happening."

As a ripple of horrified screams rose from the crowd along with pointing and shrieking, all but about thirty people ran out. I thought I was going to be fired because we hadn't yet taken the offering for the class. The thirty people who remained reminded me of rubber-neckers at a car accident anxious to see blood and guts, their fear quelled only by their curiosity. While all this was taking place, the priest in charge who elected not to teach the class, was watching from the next room to see how we would react. My first words were unpublishable. Okay, I'll tell you. I said, "Holy shit!"

The woman hovered motionless, about two to three feet off the ground, for about twenty minutes. Desperate, I begged the Lord to help me take care of the situation. While I was praying, someone tapped me on the shoulder. It was a middle-aged woman, nicely dressed, whom I had seen before in the class. She said, "Honey, would you like some help? I used to be a witch." I was dumbfounded. Here, I had a demonized person on one side of me and a witch on the other.

After about twenty-minutes, while I was talking to the ex-witch, the floating lady was suddenly turned horizontally and flung with tremendous force to the floor. We all thought every bone in her body must have broken. The medical doctor rushed to her side to examine her and was astonished to find normal vital signs. At that point, I sent someone upstairs to the chapel with a white Styrofoam coffee cup to collect holy water because I had seen "The Exorcist," and they loved using holy water in that movie. For the next several hours, I experimented. When I placed a drop of ordinary tap water on the poor woman—no response, while a drop of holy water placed on her skin evoked her loud protestations of, "Get it off me! Get it off me! It's burning! It's burning!" Her eyes remained rolled back in her head. She could not see if I was using the holy water or the tap water.

With the ex-witch encouraging me, I began to discern the names and kinds of evil spirits who were tormenting the young woman. This was an entirely new experience for me. It was as if I had been given a new pair of eyeglasses, and I could see clearly into the spiritual realm. I did not see anything through my physical eyes, but I knew what spirit was manifesting itself at each moment. For instance, I could sense a spirit of fear was in operation at one point. At another point, a spirit of anger was in her. I learned later that the gift I had received from the Holy Spirit to discern these things is called, "discernment of spirits." At one point the sound of a lion's roar came from her abdomen, interrupting our prayer and shaking us to our roots, because her mouth remained closed. Then, later, she assumed the posture of a snake and slithered effortlessly and rapidly across the floor. Something preternatural was propelling her because her movements were not humanly possible. I tried several times to replicate how she slithered and side-winded around the floor but was not able to get anywhere close to her fluid serpentine moves.

"What could be next?" we all thought, when tens of thousands of bird chirpings and squawkings came from her stomach. It sounded like a flock of birds of various kinds were housed inside of her. After she finally settled down a little, the ex-witch and I began to cast out the evil spirits, one by one. We first identified the spirit through our gifts of discernment of spirits. I either just knew what the spirit was or saw it with my soul and then bound it in the name of Jesus Christ and cast it directly to his feet, to dispose of as he willed. It never occurred to me to cease praying because I was so frightened. Most likely, this was a case of possession and needed the bishop's approval for an official exorcism. She exhibited classical signs of possession, like levitation and preternatural strength. During the time of casting out the spirits, it took four strong men to restrain her after she attempted to claw out her eyes and succeeded in deeply scratching her face.

While we were casting out the evil spirits, the priest who was watching came into the room to check on us. "Is everything okay?" he asked. I just looked at him like he was nuts to be so nonchalant, and before I could stop him, he left again.

After we finished, the young woman's eyes became normal, and she asked, "Why am I lying on the floor? And why is there blood on my face?"

I told her, "Someone will explain it to you later," and turned her over to the women in charge of the school's inner-healing ministry for further prayer. The whole thing had lasted several hours and was exhausting, and I didn't lose my job after all.

I later found out that the woman had been involved in the occult. She never remembered anything that happened during her deliverance. The school kept the details of her case confidential, as was their policy.

I was just twenty-one years old when it happened. That was twenty-one years ago. I should write a book about the over one hundred and fifty deliverances I have been in charge of since then, but I would rather not. I guess that will have to follow my angel book.

I asked Father why he didn't stay to help us, and he said, "Sometimes, the only way to learn is to grab the bull by the horns with things like this." He had performed many deliverances himself, and he told us that he was keeping an eye on us and praying the whole time. God had told him ahead of time that he would use Mike and me to do his work that evening, and that is why the priest left us alone. Mike had helped restrain her and had stirred the demons up in her because of his inspired teaching. Thanks be to God she was freed that evening despite our inexperience.

Christians do not need to be afraid of Satan

Prior to the floating woman, I did not have much experience with demons. They were not a part of my spiritual life, but that occurrence made a believer out of me. One word of caution I would like to add: Christians do not need to be afraid of Satan. Jesus Christ is Lord, and he has conquered Satan, sin, and death forever. But if there is anything I have learned from healing and deliverance ministry, it is that if we trespass into Satan's realm by delving into the occult, the New Age movement, or serious sin, we can open ourselves to the effect of demonic influence in our lives. Severe trauma inflicted on us can also be an entry point—like child-abuse, rape, or an accident.

The occult involves witchcraft, Satanism, Mind Control meditation, TM (transcendental meditation), tarot cards, astrology, consultations with mediums or psychics, wigi boards, Reiki, reincarnation, past-life regression, astral projection, spirit guides, aura-readings, psychics and psychic healers, attributing powers to crystals, attributing preternatural power to things, playing with chakras, séances, table-tipping, channeling, fortune-telling, all that stuff. It permeates New Age movement. All these things can infect a person with evil spirits, whether bidden or not. You do not have to invite them. They just come to you when you trespass into these expressions of the kingdom of darkness. Caution must be used in exploring eastern religions as well.

I know that this is true because I have seen these evil influences affect the people who come to me seeking freedom from their troubles. Most people are surprised that they have evil spirits inside of them. I have heard from professionals in the field that in any given crowd for an event, between ten and as much as thirty percent of those in attendance need deliverance, and this has born true in my ministerial work.

Demonic activity in one's life can range anywhere from simple temptation which affects everyone, to possession, which is rare and requires intervention, usually excorcism. People can be infested, which means that demons are inside of them, but they are not fully possessed. These thirty or so percent, as I mentioned, would need some form of deliverance to be healed. If a person is just tempted or oppressed, it means that demons are externally affecting him or her. In all cases, the remedy must include, if you are Catholic, regular Confession and reception of Holy Eucharist. For further reading on the subject, see "Deliverance of Evil Spirits" by Francis MacNutt, and "The Beautiful Side of Evil" by Johanna Michaelsen.

My family does not really believe me half the time when I tell them things that happen to me, but I have resigned myself to that. I told my mom that I was telling some of my spiritual stories for this book, and she said, "What stories?" "Mom," I said, "I'm one big story, basically. Where have you been for the last twenty-five years?" I have chiropractic patients who come to me, not to have chiropractic adjustments, but to hear my latest stories, or one of the many juicy ones pulled up from the archives.

People are going to think I am such a nut. I have had so many experiences, but I am nowhere near being a saint. Most people who know me well would laugh with great derision at the notion of me being a saint. So would I.

I have had experiences of being out of my body, what you would call in theological terms, mystical flight or "ecstasy." "Ecstasy," in that sense, is not a feeling, it is to leave one's body. "Ex statis", in Latin, is to stand outside of one's body, literally "beside yourself." (I feel like I'm bragging if I talk about these things.) My first experience of ecstasy happened when I was sixteen. Just prior to attending a high school seminary prayer group that prayed the rosary together, I had an argument with a fellow seminarian. I joined the group in prayer and when my turn came to lead the third Glorious Mystery, I felt like I was air leaking out of a balloon. I left my body. Looking down from above and off to the side, I could see myself down below, and I could hear everybody saying, "Allan, it's your turn."

All at once I saw the Lord standing before me, looking into my eyes. He was not happy. He scolded me and said, "Why are you coming to pray when you treated your brother so badly?" I felt very repentant and promised Jesus I would apologize to him. I cannot explain how beautiful Jesus was. He looked Arabic, with dark skin, brown eyes, brown hair and a white robe. His eyes were penetrating. They were angry eyes, but I still felt loved at the same time. He did not make me feel condemned or guilty, just repentant. Then all at once I was back in my body again and left with my own sin. I felt very disoriented and had to be helped back to my dormitory after the rosary ended. That was the same year I saw the angels in columns of light. I was sixteen. I have experienced things like that infrequently, about four times since then.

This all sounds very New Age, but it was not "astral projection" because I did not initiate it and did not want it to happen. It happened because of divine initiative. That is the difference between New Age experiences and true mystical experience. What happened to me is called mystical flight, and it is very rare. "Astral projection" is self-hypnotic and done by one's own initiative. It definitely can open you to demonic activity and is very dangerous. And you do leave your body. The New Age movement, which recommends the practice, is built on deception, and, as I mentioned, many good people have been deceived by Satan through it.

Another time I experienced mystical flight was when I was praying the Sorrowful Mysteries in front of the Blessed Sacrament. All of a sudden, through the Lord's initiative, I found myself at the foot of the cross as if I was a participant in what happened at Calvary. I saw Our Lord dying on the cross and Our Lady sobbing quietly, standing below him. When Jesus died, she crumpled to her knees and wept. I cannot begin to describe what Jesus looked like. Every inch of his skin was covered with bloody wounds. He was laboring to breathe. To gaze upon him was not a grotesque thing. His struggle was pure, unfathomable love.

The whole scene appeared in black and white. I felt shocked to be there. The only people I could see were Mary and John at the foot of the cross and the Lord Jesus. After Jesus died and was taken down from the cross, I stood behind Mary who sat with her dead Son in her arms. She was crumpled over and weeping with a piercing sadness. She was not the stoic Mary that we sometimes see in pictures; she was sobbing and sobbing. I knelt beside her and held her close to me and wept with her. I felt as if my heart was breaking for her. When I came back inside my body, I found myself sitting in the chapel pew crying, aware that I had been given an incredible glimpse into the death of Jesus and Our Lady's incomprehensible sorrow. Now whenever I pray the devotion of the Seven Sorrows of Mary I am struck with a poignant sadness.

I could not move a muscle

In many ways, I have experienced the adventure and mystery of suffering. I joined the Franciscan seminary because I knew I was to become a priest from my earliest boyhood. I still believe this will come to pass. I lack less than a year towards my theological training, but the Lord told me not to be a priest back when I was in religious formation, so I became a brother. As a Franciscan brother, I worked as the director of adult spirituality in a bilingual parish where I also led a healing ministry. When I was working there, a new pastor came in as an assistant to my good friend the pastor, and this new pastor kicked me out of the parish over a personality conflict.

In 1989, I came down with Guillain-Barre Syndrome, and because I was involved in healing ministry, I wondered why I had gotten ill myself. It got to the point where I almost died from Guillain-Barre Syndrome and was kept alive on a respirator for four months. I was hospitalized for a total of nine months, then in a wheel chair for two years. Thanks to my physical therapists and chiropractor, I slowly began to walk again.

When I was on the respirator, I could not move a muscle, and that was when the Lord told me I would be a chiropractor. I remember laughing inside and telling him, "Well, Lord, you have to be able to move to be a chiropractor." I never had considered it whatsoever. I had no background at all in the sciences or in healthcare.

While still in a wheelchair, I attended a weekend retreat for the Association of Christian Therapists. One of the members present, a charismatic Presbyterian Christian psychotherapist, was conducting a healing service during the weekend. I waited until the very end to approach him and his prayer partner because I didn't want to create a spectacle. Everyone else had left the room.

He prayed with me and asked, "Do you know you have a curse of death on you, Allan?" "No!" I exclaimed. "Get rid of it!"

He broke the curse with a verbal command in Jesus' name and

said, "Now, that's done. Get up and walk." Shocked by his command, I protested saying, "I'm in physical therapy, and I can't even bear my own weight without four people holding me up on the parallel bars!" I knew I would fall flat on my face, but he insisted. He lifted my paralyzed legs off of the footrest of my wheelchair, took my hand, folded the footrest out of the way, and said again, "Get up and walk." Instantly, my legs returned to normal, and for twenty minutes I walked with no difficulty around the empty ballroom where the conference had been held. I walked in a daze, not believing what was taking place. I thought it strange that the man who prayed for me and his female assistant did not seem happy for me, but I felt too stunned to even speak to them, and I left pushing my empty wheel chair back to my hotel room where I happily shoved it into a corner. I had been in a wheelchair for two years.

When I woke up the next morning, I expected to leap out of bed only to find that my paralysis was back. Dejectedly, I crawled over to my wheelchair and then found the man who prayed for me and asked him what the deal was. He said, "I didn't want to tell you last night . . . the Lord showed me that your healing would be only temporary, but that you should be patient because it will eventually be complete."

The curse of death was placed upon me when I was leaving my healing ministry in Detroit to spend the summer in Guadalajara to practice my Spanish. I had all my bags, books and boxes packed, when my spiritual director referred a young woman to me who was deeply involved in the occult. She was being used as a medium by a group of Santeria practitioners and was ambivalent about leaving. Santeria is an amalgamation of Christian and occult beliefs, similar to voodoo. It is what they call a syncretic religion that combines Catholic tradition with West African religious traditions, like animal sacrifice and possession trance for communicating with ancestors and deities. Since Santerians mix Catholicism with the black arts, they have saints on their altars as well as idols, or demon figures.

The young woman referred to me tried twice before to leave the Santeria group, but the first time she was struck paralyzed, and the second time her mother was struck paralyzed. I gave her an initial interview but did not do any prayers of deliverance, since we always employed a team for deliverance prayer. Then I got a second call from my spiritual director warning me not to see her again. Others in the ministry had been creeped out by her as well. I also received a message in prayer not to see her again, and guess what, I saw her again. We had made an appointment so I felt obligated. That was my rationalization for being disobedient. By being disobedient, I removed myself from

God's protection.

I saw her a second time, and she announced that she was afraid for my life because of threats the group had made against me. They put a curse of death on me, and two weeks later, while I was in Guadalajara in July of '89, I suddenly felt weakness in my legs. I woke up the next morning, and they would not move. The next day, my arms were also paralyzed. The Lord showed me that had he not intervened, I would have died. Although I had contracted the disease through contaminated shrimp, the fact that I almost died was the effect of that curse of death. After the sickness, I had deeper spiritual experiences. I also realized a great gem when I was back in the United States, paralyzed and on the respirator. I understood that my value before the Lord did not come from what I did for him, but from who I was in his sight.

Shake the dust off your feet and move on

A man from my order came into the hospital when I was on the respirator and told me that they weren't going to pay for my hospital bills. I had already made solemn vows, and I felt disowned over money. And while my Franciscan friend, the pastor of my church, visited me every day, bathed me, clothed me and carried me in his arms, the new assistant pastor who had kicked me out of the parish acted hateful and jealous towards me.

I was still a Franciscan at that time, but during my rehabilitation I took a two-year leave to decide whether I should leave the order or not. During that time, it took me ten minutes to get from my car to my apartment. After two years of praying about it, I got my answer when I read in Scripture, "If they do not accept you in one town, shake the dust off your feet and move on." These words shook me to my root, and I realized it would be the best thing for me to request a dispensation from my vows with the Franciscan order. The separation was painful, like a divorce. I felt lost without my family. They were brothers to me. I was also angry. Never in my life had I hated anyone, but I hated the assistant pastor who fired me. It took me years to forgive him. Now I can see him and talk to him and not have any ill will, but only after the hard work of forgiveness. I never had a face-to-face reconciliation with him, but I reconciled our past with God. You know you have forgiven someone when you can hear that person's name and not feel nausea in your stomach but even feel love for him or her. I do love him. I feel I have learned so much from moving through hatred along the long process of forgiveness.

I have been gone from the Franciscan order eight years now, and I still consider the friars my brothers. They treat me wonderfully now. When I left, I didn't tell the people in the parish why, and so the parishioners felt angry and resentful towards me, but I didn't want to disparage the assistant pastor's name. It got back to the provincial that I left without an explanation, and I received a black mark on my record. Then when I tried to become a priest in another religious community, I got a bad recommendation. This happened four or five times when I applied to other communities as well. The friars were telling lies, but I've forgiven them. I love them. They're human beings.

During my two-year leave from the Franciscans, I began to prepare to be a chiropractor and took a course in organic chemistry. It is amazing what resilience resides in the human spirit. That class was the most horrible thing I have ever been through in my life. A miracle occurred when I passed it. It didn't help that my teacher who was a Nobel Prize Winner spoke more Chinese than English in the classroom. Do you understand a word this guy is saying?" I asked one of the students next to me, and he said, "No. Nobody does."

Guillain-Barre Syndrome left me moderately disabled. My body is still partially paralyzed, and I walk with a limp and a cane. Many times, since 1991, I have asked for healing from the residual paralysis, and I have expected it because of prophecies given to me by others in the past. It hasn't come yet, but I'm not disappointed.

One of the prophecies happened in 1992 when I attend a non-denominational charismatic church. In the middle of the service the preacher asked me, "Are you here for healing?"

I said, "I guess."

"Come up here," he said. Using my walker, I came forward slowly. "This is a man of God," he said. "Is it true that Satan tried to steal your life? Is it true that Satan just tried to take away your ministry?" I nodded in amazement. "What the Lord tells you is this. The Lord will restore your full-time healing ministry to you, but this time it will be international in focus. You must be patient because your healing will come to you slowly."

At that point I was using braces on my legs and a walker. Then I went to using just a walker, and now I use a cane. Since that prophecy in 1992, I have visited four different countries to conduct healing services, Spain, Venezuela, Bosnia-Herzegovina and Portugal. It has all come to pass.

It is a privilege to suffer the pains of Jesus

In June of 1995, something quite remarkable happened to me. I was driving and praying the Sorrowful Mysteries of the rosary, just after returning from a pilgrimage to Betania, Venezuela. As I reached the third mystery, I could hardly hold on to the steering wheel of my truck because the palms of my hands were seized with sharp, stabbing pains. I considered pulling off to the side of the road to try to relieve the cramping in my hands, and I recall laughing to myself and saying, "Allan, don't get so much into these Sorrowful Mysteries while you're driving."

I attempted to forget about the whole thing, yet the pains in my hands continued. I felt too afraid to talk about it with anyone for several months. It disturbed me that even when I slept I could not find relief from this considerable pain. I would awaken at night, alarmed, when my hands would inadvertently hit the headboard of the bed, or when I would unconsciously roll over onto one of them. I could no longer shake hands with anyone. When I finally worked up the courage to mention this to my spiritual director, she raised her eyebrows and smiled and said, "I wondered when you were going to tell me about this." I just about fell off my chair when she said that the Lord had spoken to her months before and told her I would experience the wounds of Jesus.

I thought back to when I was sixteen years old and praying in front of the Tabernacle. As I was praying, the thought occurred to me to ask to receive the sacred stigmata, the five wounds of Christ, because I wanted to be like Saint Francis of Assisi. As soon as I expressed this desire to the Lord, I burst out laughing that I could be so bold as to ask for such a special gift. I shook my head in disbelief at myself and forgot all about it.

It was twenty years later, when I was thirty-five, that I received the pains in my hands. As that year unfolded, gradually I received pains in my feet, between my ribs moving into my heart, and finally on my head like a crown of thorns. When I began to analyze my experience with my spiritual director and wondered why some people had the wounds in their wrists, not their palms, and some on one side of the ribs or the other, she said, "You've been reading books about this, haven't you?" I was afraid to admit that I had read everything I could put my hands on. Then she told me, "I don't think that it's a good idea for you to read anything more about this. Just relax and let the Lord do his unique work in you."

After about six months, I had all five wounds and the sense of a crown of thorns around my head. It still feels like my head is in a vice with spikes driving themselves into my skull. It really is painful, and it is there all the time. I have experimented with every type of pain reliever and nothing abates the pain. I feel the pain more intensely when I am at Mass or in prayer. I live in constant discomfort. But, at the same time, it is a joy, a delight, and a privilege to suffer the pains of Jesus.

About six months after I started to experience pain in my hands and feet, side and head, I shared this experience with my parents. When I was on the phone with my dad, he said, “You’d better get an MRI. Maybe you have a brain tumor.” My only response was gales of laughter. My dad later told me that two years prior, a family friend confided to him that she received a message in prayer that I would soon be given the stigmata. She didn’t tell me that, but she told him.

When I was forty-one, one year passed during which I experienced particularly unrelenting, constant pain in my hands, feet, heart and head; and I started to fear that I could be imagining the whole thing, or, worse yet, could have fallen victim to demonic deception—despite my assurances from my spiritual director and confessor. They, along with my parents, were the only people who knew what was happening to me.

I asked permission of my spiritual director to begin a novena to Saint Therese of Liseux, “The Little Flower,” to once and for all settle this question for myself. I began a novena requesting of Saint Therese that I would receive, within nine days, three confirmations that my reception of the stigmata was genuine. So, after receiving three phone calls, all from people in different states in the U.S. who did not know one another, and who had essentially the same message for me—“Allan, are you okay? The Lord told me you have the stigmata”—I still doubted. I responded in disbelief and said, “Who told you? Why do you ask?” And when my friend, Marita, came to Galvaston, Texas from Michigan to visit me, I nearly drove off the causeway into the Gulf of Mexico when she said, “So, when are you going to tell me about your new gift?” “What!?” I responded, and she said, “You know. I don’t know what it’s called—that Padre Pio thing.”

If that were not enough, while I was praying that same novena at a local retreat center for a day of recollection, and in a foul mood from an argument with someone, I received a visit from heaven. I was not even praying. I was just sitting there mad. As I stewed over what was said, four feet away, a blank wall before me melted away (It sounds like I’m on LSD) to reveal billowing white clouds like one would see in the sky. I was astounded. Out of these clouds stepped Saint Therese herself, smiling radiantly and cradling a crucifix in her arms along with a bouquet of multicolored roses, some of which fell gently from her arms.

I thought to myself, "Oh my God, I must really be bad if she had to come to me and make a personal appearance." She didn't say a word, but after about ten minutes of standing there smiling and staring at me, the scene reversed itself, with her fading into the billowing clouds which then disappeared into the plain wall. I felt amazed, grateful and unworthy. I sensed that her smile was a divine smile of approval and favor. It was very humbling. One would think that would be enough confirmation. It would be for the average person, but not for me. I had traveled the world over, obsessively seeking confirmations until, while on retreat in Medjugorje, a friend put my mind at ease with her oh-so-witty comment, "Allan, aren't 'fifty-seven' confirmations enough?" Thus I was able to close that addictive confirmation chapter of my life. Onto another confirmation of something else . . .

The God of consolations

I think I have so many spiritual occurrences happen to me because my faith is so weak, and I constantly need reassurance. After all that has happened to me, I still have the audacity to sin and to doubt and to look for more confirmations that what is happening to me is real. It is part of my sinful nature to doubt that God is actually willing to waste time on me.

I have been blessed with good spiritual directors and confessors who have reminded me to stay balanced and prayerful and obedient to the Church through this whole experience. I am willing to submit all these experiences to the discernment of my bishop and will obey his wishes in every regard. I don't want to say anything that sounds like I'm bragging, and I would be willing to keep silent for the rest of my life if ever my bishop should ask me to do this. At this point my case has not been studied by the diocese, so I think it is okay to speak freely.

The wounds are visible at times. Lately they have been brighter. The pain is worse on Tuesdays and Fridays. In March, 1997, my feet were marked with dull red spots about the size of a pea. They have not bled yet, but are reminders to me that this is not all in my head, which is a good consolation for me. Often, my hands become marked at Mass or when I pray, but they have not bled and the marks go away after a few hours. I have noticed I have more pain Monday afternoons through Tuesday evenings and Thursday afternoons through Friday evenings and throughout Lent. Some who have had the stigmata have experienced the pain increase then, too. Good Fridays for me are excruciatingly painful. Excruciating is a great word to use because the Latin "ex crucis" means "from the cross."

Although I have received many graces from God, this is no indication of my holiness. Many saints and holy people, Saint Therese of Liseux and Saint Teresa of Avila, and Brother Lawrence of the Resurrection, for instance, suffered long periods of dryness and received very little confirmation from God. Brother Lawrence never saw one vision or heard one heavenly voice. Saint Therese, who was declared a Doctor of the Church, didn't either. I could not imagine myself ever approaching their intimacy with God.

I must rely on the God of consolations rather than on the consolations of God because consolations are so often emotional. This was revealed to me after an intense period of spiritual dryness myself.

I am the biggest sinner I know, and that's the truth. I have been ungrateful, and I have squandered so many of the graces God has given me over the years. I see myself as such a sinner in comparison to the unbelievable abundance of God's grace. When I act uncharitable or impatient towards people, or want to run them over on the highway for their stupid driving, I reflect on how far I am from gratitude and how far I am from being a kind, patient, and gentle person. That is why I am so encouraged when I see someone like Father Zlatko Sudac, a stigmatist priest from Croatia, who is so kind, gentle, patient, and truly loving.

I received the gift of healing

In 1997, during a prayer meeting, I noticed my hands were getting very warm. Somebody told me that it meant I was receiving the gift of healing, and I was dumb enough to believe him. I have been praying with people for their healing ever since. The way the gift of healing manifests in me most prominently is in the area of physical healing, although I have also prayed with people for inner healing and deliverance and continue to do so, as well.

Some peoples' hands tremble when they receive the gift of healing. Most people's hands get warm, which is an indication of the gift, but not a prerequisite. When I have laid hands on people and asked the Lord to heal them, I have seen the Lord heal everything from headaches to cancer, from congenital disease to broken bones, from blindness to deafness. He does all the healing, I just show up and call on him and pray.

Once, I was conducting a healing service and got a word of

knowledge about a particular woman there. I was able to point her out but didn't so as not to embarrass her. Instead, I said, "There is a woman here who is scheduled for heart surgery tomorrow. She should not worry, because the Lord is doing the surgery right now." When I gave that word of knowledge, she felt her heart moving and twisting within her. After the service I talked with her and found out she was a Lutheran who felt out of place in a Catholic setting. She described her experience to me, and I advised her to refuse the surgery and instead ask for more tests to be done on her heart, which she did, much to the disapproval of her surgeon. All the tests that were performed revealed that her heart had spontaneously performed a triple bypass, something unheard of in medical literature to that date. That same woman later came to me for inner healing prayer as a result of unresolved grief following three abortions. I think it was beautiful that the Lord healed both her physical and her spiritual heart. That is just one example of a healing.

When I was working full-time in healing ministry work in the Detroit area where our healing teams would pray over people, miracles like this commonly took place. During a typical week, our team saw 100-150 people for individual prayer appointments with two people who did healing prayer with them. We have seen healings over and over again. I have seen thousands of people healed.

These are healings verified with X-rays and MRI's. They are not surprising to me at all. I expect the Lord to heal people and he does, as long as we continue to have faith and pray. It has been humbling for me to pray for people in my disabled condition, and more than once people have challenged me and said, "What are you doing praying for other people, when you aren't healed yourself?" I say, "I'm just trying to be obedient to the Lord and share the gifts he's given me."

At this time, I feel God is calling me to found a new community for single Catholic laymen called "The Servants of Divine Mercy" that may in time become a diocesan religious community. I am looking for new recruits of single men sincerely seeking the Lord.[4] From my earliest boyhood, I knew that I was to become a priest. I still believe this will come to pass. Currently, I have a Masters degree in Theological Studies from Catholic Theological Union in Chicago, and I lack less than a year towards my theological training.

An outreach of "The Servants of Divine Mercy" is the "Holy Spirit Healing Ministry Internship," a 100-hour course that trains lay people in the basics of healing prayer.[5] Every believer, according to Mark, Chapter 16, is admonished to lay hands on the sick for healing. Some people receive a more pronounced charism of healing than others, but we are all called to pray for the sick.

Look for me in the sun

I have received so many gifts and graces from the Lord. One of them is the opportunity to go on pilgrimages—often. Most people dream all their lives to go on pilgrimage to go to a place like Medjugorje, Bosnia-Herzegovina or Lourdes, France, just once; and I have been almost gluttonous in my extensive travels to nearly every major Marian shrine in the world. I save up my money every year for the chance to go on a pilgrimage. It is the highlight of my year. If I start to feel pangs of guilt about my repeated pilgrimages, I remember what a holy friar once said, "It's okay to be a hog at the trough of the Lord. There's plenty of grace to go around for everyone."

I first heard about Mary's apparitions in Medjugorje when they started in 1981, and so I asked Our Lady, "If you're really appearing in Medjugorje, please get me there somehow." And she has—three times, in fact. My first pilgrimage to Medjugorje was in April, 1989. I was a Franciscan brother then, co-directing a group of fifty-five pilgrims, mostly from the Detroit area. Since we had also visited Rome and Assisi, only three days were allotted for us in Medjugorje, which was not nearly enough.

After drenching ourselves in the peace of that holy place, we boarded the bus to leave for Dubrovnik to begin our trip home. As I took my seat on the bus, I heard Our Lady say to me interiorly, "Look for me in the sun tonight." I thought her words might just be in my imagination, but I decided to look anyway when we arrived at our hotel in Dubrovnik. I had often heard Our Lord speak to me this way, but not the Blessed Mother, so I was anxious to see if it would come to pass.

The sun was much too bright to even glance at it at 6:30 p.m., but then precisely at 6:40 p.m., a white disc appeared over the sun, dulling its brightness, enabling us to look directly at it without injuring our eyes.

The disc began turning, both clockwise and counterclockwise, and moving vertically as well as horizontally over the sun, turning everything from scarlet to silver to copper to royal blue to purple to green. I definitely did not see any pastels, but I did see brilliant, breath-taking colors. Some British tourists, who were not members of our group, happened by and were astounded. In the midst of our joy and excitement, we told them about the events of Medjugorje while we watched the sun pulsate, strobe (appear to be flashing on and off), and exhibited every hue of the rainbow.

Meanwhile, my mom stood three floors above us on her balcony, as I stood down below on the veranda with about ten others. After we watched the sun "dance" for twenty minutes, all at once, my mom, a friend, and I saw Mother Mary in dazzling gold with folded hands, the sun just coming up to her knees, as if she were standing behind the sun. "The Woman clothed with the Sun!" [Rev. 12.1] Then she opened her hands and extended them downward just as she appears on the Miraculous Medal. Others simultaneously saw a cross or chalice. All we could do was stand there in awe and cry.

Surprisingly, the rest of the group was eating and opted not to come out to see the solar phenomenon when we ran inside to tell them about it. (I was reliving my high school seminary experience of failing to get people to see the angels alongside the Tabernacle.) But the others did not have to wait long, because the next day when we returned to Rome, the sun repeated its spectacular display at 6:40 p.m. but with far less intensity of color, and all of the fifty-five pilgrims on the bus witnessed it. None of us could attribute these occurrences to anything other than the power of God revealed to us through his Mother. No natural explanation for it could suffice.

Before I saw Mary in the sun, I prayed the rosary occasionally, but I didn't feel a personal connection with Mother Mary. After seeing her, I felt close to her for the first time in my life. Mary was suddenly real to me. When I saw her in Medjugorje, I just wanted to be with her. I had an unquenchable thirst to be where she was and where she has appeared on earth.

I was able to return to Medjugorje, which is a tremendous grace. I think people long to go back there because it is so much like heaven, our true home. Nothing in this world can satisfy us like the peace flowing like torrents of grace from Our Lady in Medjugorje.

The second time I went to Medjugorje, I lead a group there and to Lourdes, France. When one leads a pilgrimage, one forgoes many of its benefits because of the demanding nature of the job. I decided to go to Medjugorje for a third time when I prayed after communion and asked the Lord where I should go on retreat in 2002. Immediately, I heard his voice interiorly, and he said, "Medjugorje, of course." By that time, even though I had received many graces from there before, my favorite places to go were Lourdes, France where the Virgin Mary appeared in 1858 and Betania, Venezuela where the she appeared in 1976 and continues to appear to the mystic and stigmatist, Maria Esperanza. I waited for the Lord to change his mind and give me those locations instead, but he did not. And being one who is addicted to confirmation, I did not believe that it was the Lord who had spoken to me until I got home that evening, booted up my computer, opened up my email, and was startled to read an email titled in bold letters, "MEDJUGORJE WITH FATHER SUDAC RETREAT." I do not know where that email came from. I never asked for such an email. I took it as a sign that the Lord, indeed, wanted me to go to Medjugorje. As a result, I met the most wonderful people I had ever met on any pilgrimage I have ever gone on, and I have been on at least a dozen pilgrimages. I have never laughed so much in a two-week period in my life. I had such a great time.

Joy is the affirmation that God is in control

One of the events that stood out for me in this pilgrimage to Medjugorje was my struggle to climb Podbrdo, Apparition Hill. I wanted to be on the hill early for the visionary, Ivan's apparition of Our Lady which was to take place at 10 p.m. I wondered if Our Lady would help heal me during the apparition. By 5:30 p.m., I started climbing the hill using my cane along with four fellow pilgrims. My climb was slow and laborious. About halfway up the hill, two hours later, I decided I had had enough and would be content to sit there and pray on the side of the hill for the rest of the evening. It is not a difficult hill for able-bodied people, taking them only twenty minutes to climb, but I was only halfway up the hill and exhausted.

I didn't even get a chance to sit down and give up when a strong, young local tour guide named Miki Musa, (who is a dead-ringer for Donny Ozmond, and tall, but everybody is tall to me), enlisted the help of an American man climbing with him, and together they formed a chair with their arms and hoisted me onto it. I curled my arms around their necks, and five minutes later I was perched proudly near the top of Apparition Hill at the feet of Our Lady's statue where Mary has appeared and would appear that night. Miki and his helper were drenched in sweat, and I felt so grateful to them. Of course, I did not even think about how I would descend the hill in the dark.

The experience of praying with hundreds of other pilgrims and the hushed silence when Our Lady appeared, (except for the ceaseless murmuring of the boisterous Italians), was incredible. I felt just thrilled to be in Our Lady's presence on such holy ground, despite the fact that I was not healed and saw no signs or wonders except for the peace of God and Our Lady's consoling presence. Then getting back down the hill turned out not to be a problem because several people from my wonderful tour group walked down it with me, step by step.

Another event that stood out for me on the pilgrimage happened during our retreat with Father Sudac on the island of Mali Losinj. When Father Sudac anointed me with the Sacrament of the Sick and then prayed over me, I rested in the Spirit on the floor among a few others. During that time, I enjoyed a deep peace, but I became a little distressed because I felt intense joy rising within me up to the point that I could restrain it no longer. Laughter seemed to bubble up out of deep within my belly and into my throat! The more I tried to quell it, the more powerfully it surged up within me, so I simply yielded to it. Aware that people around me were weeping, I did not want to behave inappropriately, but as I surrendered to the Holy Spirit and released the joy within me, I finally became aware of where the joy in me was coming from. All at once, I felt I was "gone," that I had left my body and was watching a movie. I was taken to an unfamiliar place. I found myself lying on my back in the middle of a wide, rocky road in a vast valley. The horizon up to my feet was dim and dark, but behind me, past my head, it was sunny and bright.

I could not rise from my back, and at once became aware of at first a few, then a multitude of people making their way towards me on the road. They were all strangers to me who literally beamed with radiant joy! They did not acknowledge me, but kept passing by—people of every age and race. They seemed intent on reaching their destination which lay behind me, in the direction beyond my head. With each passing cluster of people, I was again and again overwhelmed with intense joy, and I felt I would burst if I tried to contain it, so I laughed and laughed. This went on for some time until I realized that these people were souls streaming toward heaven as they left purgatory! Oh the inexpressible joy that shone from their whole beings as they entered into paradise!

Gradually, I felt myself back on the floor at the retreat center. This experience left me with such joyful gratitude. The whole pilgrimage was one of joy for me. Of all the fruits of the Holy Spirit the Lord has produced in me, joy is the most prominent. I have found that the Lord's joy within me has increased over time and is always present despite the circumstances. When I am disturbed or distressed, even depressed about something, I am always aware of the Lord's joy under the surface. Joy is the affirmation that God is in control, and that I am a child of the Father who loves me. Joy is God's antidote to our self-importance.

Joy is not a gift of the Spirit, but a fruit. A gift, or a charism, is an unmerited grace given to us so we can use it for others. A fruit is the result of God's action working in us over time. For example, there is no such thing as the gift of patience, but as the Lord works in us, converting and changing us over time, we become more patient. It is the same with all the fruits of the Holy Spirit—joy, peace, love, gentleness, humility—they can grow in us over time. But everything we have is God's gift to us. Nothing we have is our own.

The joy I speak of is not an emotion or a feeling, or simple happiness. It is a deep contentment. Happiness is just a passing emotion, but the joy I feel is a deep, spiritual reality that transcends emotion. Just as love is not a feeling, but a decision, joy is not happiness, but a conviction of an enduring relationship with a loving Lord. I am a co-heir of Christ who is King of Kings and Lord of Lords. I have no business walking around being sad. Saint Francis of Assisi used to send his brothers to Confession if they were sad because joy is the normal disposition of a Christian, not the doom and gloom so often found on the faces of people sitting in the pews. If you want to see joy, just visit a contemplative community of nuns and you will see what I mean. These women shine with God's joy because they know him deeply and love him with all their hearts. A child is joyful when he or she is secure in his/her parents' love. So it is with God's children. When we are secure in our relationship with him, joy grows within us. This joy is an unshakable belief that God is in control, that Jesus is Lord, that he has risen from the dead, and that we have a part of his risen life and his joy even now.

Sinner as I am, may my life be a testament to his joy and his unfathomable love.

* * *

In difficulties, when you carry the cross, sing, be full of joy![7]

JUSTINE

Abortion, the New Age, and God's healing promise

Lost. If I had to use one word to describe my life before my conversion, "lost" best captures it. My lost state stemmed from a profound sadness that began young. My pediatrician told my mother I had clinical depression at age five, and from age three to ten, I went through periods of getting nauseated to the point of throwing up blood. After a week or two of this, my parents usually placed me in the hospital, but tests always showed nothing physically wrong with me. When I lay sick in the hospital, death seemed like the only escape, and I prayed that God would let me die and come home.

I prayed to God because my family was Catholic, and we went to church on occasional Sundays. I prayed because I had been baptized, confirmed and learned about the existence of God. But we didn't practice faith, and we didn't practice love. For much of my childhood, I tried to hide from my parents because my father was an angry alcoholic, and my mother's mood grew stormy when he drank. To escape the rage in our house, I often huddled under the stairway or in closets, or stayed outside in the woods admiring the sunrays darting between the trees, wondering what it would be like to live there and never have to come home.

When I was six, I decided to commit suicide. I climbed up to the window of my bedroom, sat on the windowsill and tried to muster enough courage to jump, but I felt too afraid, afraid that I would severely hurt myself and not die.

Misery also followed me into adolescence. From age eleven until I left home after high school, my father's best friend, Mr. Thompson, who worked as a Methodist youth minister, molested me when I baby-sat for his family. My parents often left me at his home overnight to baby-sit, and I slept on the couch in the den, which left me vulnerable. Each time I stayed over, Mr. Thompson got up in the middle of the night after his wife had fallen asleep and came to molest me in the family room. This happened often for a good six years, and he and made it clear to me that I should keep everything secret.

When this first happened, I went to my mother for help. I wanted so much for her to rescue me. "I don't want to baby-sit there anymore," I said, terrified, desperately hoping she would ask me, "Why not?" and pull out of me the dark and awful secret I wasn't allowed to tell. But in a tone of condemnation, she responded, "You are being very selfish. Your father and I want to be able to go out with our friends, and why can't you help me?" Standing rigidly still, like a deer blinded by headlights, I stared at her blankly, too scared to find my voice. Finished with the conversation, she turned her back to me and walked away as I reeled from the sting of the first of many betrayals.

When I was eighteen, God gave me the grace to never let the youth minister touch me again. Perhaps because God's truth and love was not being communicated to me through the people in my life, God came to me himself, and, to my amazement, spoke to me in an interior locution. One day, when I was walking towards their house, I heard God say inside my soul, "You're having an affair with a married man." His words shocked me. I don't believe God was holding me culpable for an affair, but he was trying to tell me that it was wrong. After that moment, I never let this man touch me again. If he came near me, I screamed at him through my eyes.

At eighteen, I also heard through the neighborhood grapevine that Mr. Thompson was molesting an eleven year-old in our neighborhood. At the same time, I realized I needed help. I had been going to college for only a few weeks, when I began to notice I was damaged. I couldn't date. I felt so terrified of sexual tension that I pushed boys away. I was falling into a depression, sleeping a lot, unable to concentrate, flunking out of my classes, and emotionally distraught over the pressure of carrying a shameful secret. I didn't know what to do and felt I needed my mother to help me. Surely, I thought, telling her what happened would finally break open her motherly compassion, something I had never experienced before. Yet, at the same time, I feared she wouldn't care, and I would crumble. She had never cared for messes, and this was messy.

At home on a school break, I walked into her room and stood in front of her dresser as she watched a morning T.V. program and ironed. "I have to tell you something," I said. Without ceasing her chores or looking up from the T.V., she responded coldly, "What?" Trembling, I said, "Mr. Thompson has molested me since I was little, and it started when we lived on Drake Street, and I need you to help me." She looked up from her ironing and asked, "Is he still doing anything to you now?" "No," I answered. Then her look turned into a cold stare, "Well, if he's not doing anything anymore, then what are you telling me for? What do you want me to do about it?" I wanted to recite a litany of pleas:

"I need you to help me with school, with my depression, to protect me, to protect other neighborhood girls . . . ," but I didn't feel I could ask for or reveal anything. All I could say was, "I don't know." Then she started ironing, and I went to my room to cry. I knew from that moment I did not really have a mother. I didn't think I did, but now I knew I didn't. She died for me that day, and we never spoke of it again. My parents remained best friends with Mr. Thompson and his wife for the next twenty years.

In my distress, I thought, "If my mom won't help me, surely the pastor of Mr. Thompson's church will. Mr. Thompson works with children as a youth minister, and someone needs to stop him." Awkward and nervous, I walked into the Methodist pastor's office and sat down across from him. Skipping any formalities, I blurted out, "The youth minister in your church has molested me ever since I was a little girl, and I have to tell you that because I know he's in charge of children here, and I feel a moral responsibility to tell you, especially since I know he's done this to other friends of mine."

Then I waited in fear for his response. "Well," he said after an awkward pause, "that was in the past, and I really don't see it as a problem now. I don't understand the big deal. Thank you for coming in." And he showed me the door. I left his office in an ethical daze, feeling abandoned and trapped in a twisted parallel universe. "What the hell is the matter with the adults in my world?" I wondered.

A piece of me died

That same year, I started dating someone for the first time—my teacher. I had begun studying psychology, trying to piece together what had happened to me growing up. My instructor was a psychotherapist, an older man who I thought, at the time, was helping me since I was becoming more academically and socially capable at school. The relationship formed gradually, and I dated him sporadically from age nineteen to twenty-three. He was a broken man and couldn't handle any level of intimacy, whatsoever. Neither could I. The moment we became emotionally or sexually close to one another, we broke up. During one of these breakups, when he was with another woman, I discovered I was pregnant. Despairing, I did not see any way to keep the baby. I had no job, nowhere to turn, no church, no resources to help me. I had been getting checkups at Planned Parenthood where I met with a counselor, and once I talked through my situation with her, she made it seem like abortion was my only option. I walked out of the clinic believing that it did not make any sense to have the child.

The only problem was, it cost $350, and I didn't even have $50, so I called my ex-boyfriend who agreed to pay for the abortion. He picked me up and dropped me off in front of a clinic where people were picketing, carrying huge signs covered with images of fetuses. Some were praying, and some were yelling at me. The whole day progressed like a horror movie.

I remember lying on a gurney in a hallway for what seemed like an eternity—scared and alone, staring at the ceiling, waiting for the staff to take me into a room. To start preparing me for surgery, they had given me a preparatory drug without telling me it would paralyze my limbs and my body. Suddenly, I could not even open my mouth or speak. I wanted to run out of there, but my body would not move. I felt like screaming but couldn't. I lay there paralyzed for a half-hour, as people walked by me laughing and eating. Their actions seemed so impersonal and cold. Then they put a cup over my mouth and told me to take three deep breaths.

The next thing I can recall was waking up in the recovery room on a surgical table sobbing. Unconsciously, I must have known what I had done, even though consciously, I did not. After it was over, I sat out on the front curb of the clinic, bleeding, waiting for my ex-boyfriend to pick me up. A piece of me died that day, and it never quite came back.

Who are you, and where are you?

In my emptiness, I began looking for God. I wanted to come close to him, to experience him. "Who are you and where are you?" I asked him. I wanted God, but I didn't want Catholicism, the religion of my parents, since it felt very important for me to be *not like them.* At age twenty-four, I came across a bookstore carrying books on Eastern religions and New Age ideas. My friend, Sally, and I started going to talks the store gave on subjects such as meditation, psychic intuition, reincarnation, angels, chakras, and the Enneagram. People talked about experiencing God personally which intrigued me. Maybe I could experience him, too. Maybe he could heal me of a sadness I felt had no bottom.

Sally and I thought to use our vacation time to develop ourselves spiritually, so we decided to attend a week-long New Age seminar for spiritual growth in Arizona given by a man touted as a "high teacher" in New Age thought. For some reason, he latched onto my friend and me during the seminar and used us for instruction on "hands on healing." Honored to be chosen by this "high teacher" and eager to learn all we could from him, we willingly took turns lying on a table placed at the front of the room. He worked on each of us four or five times as he talked about healing, chakras, energy, light, vibrations, shamanic and crystal healing. In private, he was able to touch the back of Sally's neck and give her an orgasm. Energy shot down from her neck to her private parts. Somehow he had cultivated this strange metaphysical expertise.

Toward the end of the seminar, when talking about the structure of the universe, he said, "One of the things that Christianity says which is not true is that Lucifer is a bad angel. Lucifer is actually a good angel, and Christians misinform people about him." "What a strange comment," I thought, but at the same time, I wanted to believe him. He seemed to know so much.

After Sally and I went home, we did not feel right. We both started to have nightmares, and she began having visions of evil spirits, dark creatures which lurked in her house. Before the seminar, when I had closed my eyes and concentrated on God, I had seen a stunning white light, and if I placed my hands on Sally's head, her migraines had disappeared. When I returned home, I no longer saw the beautiful light, and I was unable to heal her. Instead, I started hearing cursing towards God in my head and around me, and something kept prompting me incessantly and against my will to take God's name in vain.

Frightened and bewildered, Sally and I met for dinner and tried to figure out what had happened to us. By recalling what the New Age teacher had said and what we experienced afterwards, we realized this man was promoting Lucifer worship, and through cultivating a relationship with evil, he had gained certain powers.

We decided to verbally renounce Satan. We said we did not want anything to do with the "high teacher" and wanted all his effects taken away. At that moment, we both sensed that a type of oppressive hood—a disgusting, horrible thing—had been placed over our heads. Then we felt God take it away. Fear seized us when it was lifted because we knew without a doubt that what this man had done to us was evil.

We let this man lay hands on us without knowing what he was up to and suffered the negative effects of evil without ever looking for it. It frightened us to think of what he had done without our permission. That is why I feel very resistant to allowing anyone to do body or energy work on me because I know that a person can channel "energy" into me that does not come from God, and not even know it is harmful.

Talking to me sweetly

I started going to the Catholic Church in a desperate search for safety. Even though I did not understand Catholicism and didn't believe in its moral teachings, I somehow grasped that God was there. It was part of my childhood—the only thing I knew. I walked back into the Catholic Church, and for the first time, God revealed himself to me personally—as love. As I sat in the pew, Jesus, himself, began talking to me sweetly in my soul. I didn't know, at the time, how unusual it was to actually hear his voice. When he spoke, I felt his great, yet gentle passion for me, which stirred in the center of my chest. Before then, I didn't know what it felt like to be loved. I didn't think such intimacy was possible from the Lord—his feelings for me were so warm and personal and traveled so deep into my soul, reaching places I didn't know lived inside of me. I had always thought of God as angry, far away, judging, keeping track of my wrongs and metering out just punishment. I never knew he was sweet!—possessing a sweetness so intense, it sometimes scared me.

Because Jesus' incarnation was male, when I felt his love piercing my heart, at times it sparked an irrational fear that the intimacy would turn into abuse. The words "I love you" from the man who molested me meant the precursor to something ugly, so when Jesus drew intimately close, I felt scared and asked his mother, Mary, to keep me safe. But with gentle kindness, Jesus always reassured me he would never, ever hurt me. Through his words, he guided me with great care, like an adoring father with his toddler girl.

One day, he told me he didn't want me to spend time with a co-worker who complained to me for hours each day about her life and left me emotionally drained. "She's not good for you," he said. When I wanted to go to different New Age workshops he said, "No. Don't go to that," and, instead, encouraged me to go to church. Some days he wanted me to go to a Catholic church and sit in silence, alone. I went without knowing that he, himself, was fully present there in the Tabernacle.

I attended church for a few months and felt solace, until one day the pastor gave a very fiery and condemning speech on abortion. Feeling unwanted and unwelcome, I didn't return.

Then the locutions stopped

Because of that one homily, Jesus saw me walk out the door of his

Church, and I think to console me, he continued to speak to me in full locutions. In retrospect, I can see how he was trying to keep me with him. But as much as he tried to keep me close, I pulled away. At age twenty-nine, I met a man through work named Jim whom I ended up seeing for the next eight years. Jim looked liked a young Jesus to me, with long brown hair and a beard. I found his appearance and gentle spirit extremely attractive. He was sensitive, but at the same time emotionally unavailable—able to reveal his own needs, but unable to take care of mine. This emotional side-stepping attracted me to him, as well, and made me feel uncomfortably at home. My parents had taught me the same dance. I fell for Jim right away, and at the same time heard Jesus say to me in an interior voice, "No. I don't want you to see him." It was clear. It was not ambivalent. No question entered my mind of who was speaking, or what was being said. But I wanted to be with this man, so I bargained with Jesus and convinced myself with thoughts such as, "Well, maybe it's okay for a little while." Pleased with my excuses, and unaware of the consequences of disobeying God, I decided to date Jim anyway. I didn't know that if I became sexual with Jim, then I would separate myself from the Lord. Jesus didn't go away at first. He kept asking me to stop seeing Jim intimately, and then I had a dream. In the dream Jim was married to someone else, and I was left devastated. Furious at God, I demanded, "Why would you bring this man into my life, let me care for him, give me a "No" and a hideous dream if you know I want to get married, and he seems like the right man?"

So, I continued to see Jim, and then the locutions stopped. Almost immediately after we started being intimate, I got pregnant. Jim implied that if I had the baby, he would leave me. He did not want to be a father, and I felt tortured with what to do. One overriding thought guided my mind—if I was going to be in any way a mother like my own, my child would be better off going to heaven than being with me. After painful deliberation, I asked Jim to drive me to a clinic, and I had another abortion. I don't remember being there at all. I only remember being home, lying in my bedroom, feeling completely hollow.

I didn't hear God speak to me in any more inner-locutions for another eleven years. In the long days that followed, I can say, in retrospect, that I know what it is to live in mortal sin. This manifested itself in me through things that culture acknowledges, like depression, isolation, despair, and feeling lonely, even in a group. I felt I could not find my reason for being. I could not find who I was. Looking back, I can see that if I was separated from my Creator, how could I find myself? That lost state of my soul went on for years.

You are out of grace with your Creator

Jim finally left me and within six months was engaged to someone else. That drove me into an even more desperate sense of soul-searching. Still feeling ostracized from the Catholic Church, I started looking for God elsewhere and dove into Eastern meditation, Buddhism and Hinduism more seriously than I had before.

For a short time, I followed two women gurus and sat at their ashrams, sometimes experiencing a peaceful, loving, very pleasurable, almost addictive sensation. But it never lasted. Enduring peace always seemed to evade my grasp. The gurus said they knew how to commune with God and felt it their divine role to teach and gather others to follow in their example. Enamored by their claims and exotic nature, I made these women my gods, yet no one who followed them, including myself, seemed to be healing from their emotional scars, many seemed worse, and one of the gurus, a beautiful woman from India who now lives in New York State, turned out to be very corrupt.

Disillusioned by retreats with Hindu ashrams, mantra chanting, and shaktipat (when a guru hits you on the head with a feather), I tried every kind of healing work I could find: healing of the inner child, hands-on energy work called "Reiki," acupuncture, EMDR, color therapy, aroma therapy, yoga, psychotherapy, tarot readings, psychic readings, crystal healing, chakra balancing, guided visualization, aura readings, massage therapy, craniosacral therapy, past-life regression, rebirthing, holotropic breathing, and even yeast-free and sugar-free diet that promised to heal my fragile emotional state.

Going to "spiritual healers" became very addictive for me. The elements involved paralleled any addiction. First, I experienced suffering and did not want to accept it. I sought to control it because the idea of endless suffering made me feel crazy. Second, I experienced temporary relief that helped me feel like I was doing something about the problem. Third, a carrot dangled in front of me offering a future fix. "If I keep going," I hoped, "I'll eventually get better." In my search for healing, somehow I didn't stop long enough to notice that no long-term changes ever took place.

So many well-intended "healers" manufactured a lot of easy answers to my emotional pain. A craniosacral therapist once told me, "Oh, your cranium is out of whack. Of course you're depressed." Another New Age therapist told me, "Your chakras are blocked. I'll open them up, and then you'll feel more free and alive." An acupuncturist told me, "Your meridian is weak. That's why you're out of balance. What's going on?

We'll need at least ten sessions to fix this." But all these therapies kept me from looking at what was really destroying me—my sin. I never heard anyone in the New Age movement or Eastern religions say, "You are out of grace with your Creator. That is the problem."

I have heard, "There are many paths to God, and they're all the same." An ongoing stream of New Agers have said that to me. I was to find out this just wasn't true.

This is your life without Me

My four years of fruitless searching ended when I walked into a Barnes & Noble bookstore. There on the front display shelf I noticed a book called "Looking for Mary" by Beverly Donofrio. The book had a picture of Our Lady of Guadalupe on the cover, and I liked the look of it, so I bought it. After turning the first few pages, I realized that the book concerned Medjugorje, a place I had heard of in college and thought of visiting one day.

I devoured the book in twenty-four hours, intrigued to read the story of a woman who had fallen away from the church and into a normal American life of sin. As a hesitant skeptic, she traveled to Medjugorje where the Virgin Mary is allegedly appearing to six visionaries, and there she experienced an enormous change of heart that altered her perception of life. That was what I had been looking for. I had been looking for God and for a way to have this awakening in me. Perhaps, I wondered, I might one day travel to Medjugorje, too.

Then, just two months later, I received a special phone call. My friend's brother, Gary, called to talk about spiritual matters. He had recently experienced a conversion to Jesus and took an evangelical Christian approach as he spoke with me. In the midst of our conversation, he invited me to kneel down and asked if I was willing to take Jesus into my heart as my Lord and Savior. Eager for any kind of healing, I said, "Yes," that I would, and immediately I felt the presence of Jesus just in front of me. It felt very hot, like an intense burning sun emanating heat towards my body and face. The sensation eventually faded, leaving me dumbstruck, feeling somehow changed.

That night I could hear evil spirits all around me, swearing angrily and taking the Lord's name in vain, furious at what I had just done. This torture went on all night long, and I feared the bad spirits would never leave.

The next morning, I had an interior experience of Jesus showing me a scorched landscape. I saw what looked like a city that had just been burned to the ground. What had once been full of life appeared charred and black with smoke rising from the debris. As he showed me this scene of ruin, I heard him say, "This is your life without me."

Mary's voice

The vision showed me that I had no hope without Jesus. Without understanding why I needed him, without comprehending that Jesus was the true God, the only name that could save me, the Savior to whom all of creation owes its existence, I vowed to find him again.

Still aware of evil swarming around me, I went to a Catholic store the next day and bought a rosary. I had heard it was a powerful prayer of the Catholic Church which meditated on the life of Jesus. I also vaguely remembered my grandmother on my mother's side saying the rosary, calling on Mary to intercede for us before God. Never having learned how to pray it, I said the Our Father prayer on every bead, and when I did, the evil spirits left me for a while.

Later, I realized I probably wasn't saying it correctly, so I returned to the store to ask the lady behind the counter for help. She showed me an instruction card, which I bought, took home and studied. Carrying the card with me wherever I went, I began to pray the rosary throughout the day, but then thought, "I'm not sure I believe in some of these rosary prayers," so I changed them. Just afterwards, I heard Mary's voice in my heart for the first time. "Don't change the words," she said. "Say them as they are written in the little card you have. And if you do this, I can help you." Her voice sounded so tender and motherly. Oddly, I heard her without surprise. It somehow seemed normal to me that she should speak to me, and I gratefully followed her lead, like a happy puppy at the heels of its master.

I prayed the rosary unceasingly and no longer felt under such spiritual attack. With this new sense of protection, I also started to feel called to go to Medjugorje as soon as possible. It was November of 2000, The Jubilee year, and I thought I might go in February of 2001 in order to spend Christmas with my family, but when I prayed, I sensed I should leave in a very short time, so I made reservations for a week-long tour that left December 22nd.

While at the airport on my way to Medjugorje, I suddenly felt terrified the plane would crash. My intuition, I thought, was telling me that I should not get on the plane, so I said a little prayer, "God, I'm really not ready to die yet. I'm not reconciled in my life, so please tell me if it's safe to go on this plane. Is this terror inside of me a message from you?" Then I walked into a little airport store to buy a luggage cart and heard the words, "You may go," in a clear, loud and reassuring male voice, a voice I had longed to hear for the last eleven years. With profound delight and relief, I thought "Oh, hello, Jesus! You're talking to me—after all this time!" I felt like an old friend whom I'd ignored had run up from behind and given me a big hug. I hadn't heard Jesus' voice in this way since I was twenty-nine, when I first felt his love. Smiling inside and pushing aside tears, I knew instantly that I would be fine and that I should go. His voice had all the authority and all the love there is. This time, I dared not disobey it.

Prepare the way

Our tour group arrived in Dubrovnik, in Bosnia-Herzegovina, the former Yugoslavia, at 11 p.m. Miki, our tour guide, met us at the airport, and we took a bus to the village of Medjugorje at midnight. Completely delirious, I stumbled into our pansion[8] at 3 a.m. where I checked into my sparsely decorated room and fell fast asleep. An hour or two later I woke up and couldn't quite remember where I was. Nothing hung on the walls except for one large crucifix. While lying in bed, I stared at the cross and asked God, "Okay, Lord, what am I doing here?" and to my surprise he answered me again. "Prepare the way," he said, with the same authoritative and compassionate tone I had heard in the airport. He was preparing the way in order to reside more fully in my soul, but I did not know this at the time. I had never read the Bible, and I didn't know of the passage from Luke, Chapter 3, verses 3 and 4, which says, in reference to the preaching of John the Baptist, "He went throughout the whole region of the Jordan, proclaiming a baptism of repentance for the forgiveness of sins, as it is written in the book of the words of the prophet Isaiah: 'A voice of one crying out in the desert: Prepare the way of the Lord, make straight his paths.'"

As I lay pondering what "prepare the way" meant, God impressed upon my soul that he was asking me to go to Confession. I didn't know that Confession, or Reconciliation, as it is now called, was a sacrament of the Catholic Church, or that it had any divine power, but I decided to go.

We ate dinner early, around 4 o'clock, and then went to stand in line at the confessional next to Saint James' Church. Outside was freezing cold and wet with rain—a dark Christmas Eve night. The long line for reconciliation moved slowly. Twenty or thirty people stood in front of me in the English-speaking line. Nervous and apprehensive, I stood wondering what kind of priest I would meet. I had always thought of Reconciliation as a priest's power trip and didn't know it offered the healing grace of God. I still did not know what I was doing, or why I was in a distant country among strangers.

While waiting in line, I heard a bell tower begin to chime. It was 5:40 p.m., and I had heard Mary was appearing to a visionary in the village at that very moment. Turning away from the confessional towards Saint James, I knelt down out of respect, thinking that perhaps Mary was inside the church. I prayed spontaneously to join my heart with hers, and after the bells ceased ringing, signifying that the apparition had ended, I asked God if he had a message for me and why I was in Medjugorje. Then I heard a crystal clear, strong male voice say to me, "My daughter, I will heal you." I knew it was God the Father! I was shocked. I never expected a response, and not from him! I had spent my whole adult life tying to heal my emotional wounds and for him to grant my deepest wish overwhelmed me. This was the one thing on earth I wanted more than anything else, and he knew this! I felt *completely seen* by him. He was answering a need so profound and so tender that perhaps even I did not realize its depths until it was addressed.

Just after that, I walked into the confessional, and my life changed forever. I opened the door and saw a very sweet, jovial Irish priest looking straight at me with a very tender gaze. His name was Father Michael. I burst into tears immediately, so he started patting me on the shoulder and reassuring me that everything would be fine. When I spoke, I told him that I hadn't been to Confession since I was thirteen years old—twenty-eight years earlier—and I proceeded to tell him about my life.

I realized in the telling what a serious state of sin I had been living in. Being in that holy setting of Reconciliation somehow helped me understand that my sin was my own doing. I already knew part of the healing I needed from God was because of mistreatment I received from others, but now I understood that part of it came from how much I had hurt myself and God by ignoring and disrespecting his laws and commandments. Although I hadn't fully understood his statutes, they still applied to my life, as they apply to all lives, and by breaking them I had created a division between my Creator and myself. That division, I realized, had led to the emptiness, depression, lack of direction, loneliness, and most all the other problems that had plagued me.

Meeting Father Michael moved me to tears because I knew God had chosen this priest for me. God knew I needed someone exactly like him—a living witness of Jesus. Up until that point in my life, I had never had an interaction with a man so selflessly compassionate and focused on my well-being. Father Michael wasn't trying to use me for anything, or get anything from me. He was extraordinarily kind, warm and friendly, not condemning at all—so different from any man I had ever met.

Father Michael gave me absolution, and I left to sit inside Saint James' Church. The sense of separation from God I had felt all my life was gone.

The day after my confession and my first Mass in Medjugorje, it was still raining, and I went with others to an apparition at 5:40 p.m. with the visionary, Marija, at a chapel called "Oasis of Peace." I arrived there about 5 p.m., and the chapel was already so full of people that we could not get inside and instead stood in the outer courtyard, praying the rosary. Is this truly about to happen? I wondered. Is Mary herself going to be with us? As my doubts faded, a buried pain surfaced in my heart, and I began to struggle terribly over my inability to think of Mary as my divine Mother. I had read Mary's past messages to the world that she had given through the visionaries, and she often spoke of her great love for her children. "What does that mean?" I cried out silently to Mary. I did not have any attachment or love relationship with my own earthly mother, and my inability to understand Mary's motherly love gave me so much angst that, while standing among the crown of pilgrims, I quietly asked her, "Please, Mary. Would you adopt me?"

At about 5:37 p.m., just before Mary was to come, I felt a peace descend upon the outer courtyard and upon the whole chapel. At the very time of the apparition, Mary's presence suddenly consumed me, and I fell to my knees sobbing. She embraced me and let me know I was her daughter. Her love for me felt more powerful and pure than any love expressed here on earth. It seemed to come straight from heaven it felt so otherworldly and celestial, while at the same time, very personal and intimate. She stayed with me for the duration of the apparition—about five minutes. People towered around me as I knelt on the courtyard floor, bent over and crying, watching my tears join with the rain.

Before that day, I had no idea what it felt like to have a mother, and after that day I have felt safe in her arms. I now feel what all children feel who have grown up with a mother who loves and protects them selflessly. If I am in trouble and call out to her, she is instantly there for me. She is the perfect embodiment of motherhood. For someone like me, who never sensed the safety of motherly arms, it was a miracle my heart could open to such a feeling. I can feel her right now as I speak. It feels like she is happy. She is so gentle and good it makes me cry.

She is saying, "Please say this so that other lost children know how to find me." Her tenderness fills a deep wound; it is like a salve I cannot get enough of.

I give myself to Jesus and not to you!

The next morning, evil showed its fury over my converting heart. I went to the English morning Mass at 10 o'clock and felt happy to see that Father Michael was presiding that day. Then just at the moment when he elevated the host, as I was kneeling at the pew, I sensed Satan on my right side. Overcome with fear, I felt him seize my soul in the center of my chest and say with viciousness, "You're mine." He was pulling at my will, and I sensed that he wanted autonomy over my soul. With the full force of every ounce of mental and spiritual strength I had in me, I said, "No! I give myself to Jesus and not to you!" But his power was keenly strong, and I started to lose. In terror, I felt my will slip away, as if after a critical moment of weakening in an arm wrestling match. I started praying madly for help, and the only thing that came to mind was something I had read in Teresa of Avila's "Interior Castle," that holy water was extremely powerful against the devil. So at the high point of Mass, I got up, went to the back of Saint James' Church and blessed myself with holy water while begging Jesus to help me in this fight. Finally, Satan went away, but I remained very afraid.

I could not understand why I had been so attacked until later when a fellow pilgrim explained to me that because of the way I had been living my life before Medjugorje, I had belonged to Satan, and he was making a last ditch effort to keep me for himself. It took every drop of strength I had in my being to reject him in a fierce battle of wills. I shudder to think what it might have been like at the moment of my death had I not converted.

I learned from Reconciliation and my terrifying experience at Mass that all the New Age and Eastern therapies I had tried and thought had something to do with God, did not. All the New Age "healings," such as the "Reiki," along with the abortions and the sexual sin, had allowed evil to enter me. I had unknowingly spent precious time, energy and thousands of dollars exposing myself to evil in numerous attempts to heal myself when my healing was going to be through Jesus all along.

I haven't forgiven myself

I returned home from Medjugorje committed to my faith. I belonged to Jesus again, and over the next few months, he continued to guide and heal me. Prompted by his Spirit, I cleaned out items from my home that felt spiritually unclean—old books incompatible with Christianity, Buddhist statues and Hindu art, immodest clothing and objectionable movies. After a week of purifying my surroundings, Jesus began to clean me on the inside as well, by healing me through frequent attendance at Mass, adoration, Bible study, the rosary, and Reconciliation.

Then, after being home for a few months, I went to Mass during the Respect Life month of October in the Catholic Church. The priest gave a very scathing homily on the subject of abortion, and I felt like I did years earlier when I had been attending Mass—unwelcome and condemned. I entered headlong into a crisis. This time I had embraced the Catholic faith far too deeply not to be a member of the Church, but I did not know how to stay there. I felt so emotionally torn that I didn't eat anything for about forty-eight hours.

In a frantic search for help, I found a weekend retreat called Rachel's Vineyard on the web by looking up, "Post-abortion healing." No retreat existed in my area, so just five days after that Sunday Mass, I found myself in another state, sitting in a room with strangers, terrified of the pain buried inside of me, wondering how I could possibly face it. But the weekend was very gentle, and I felt embraced by God's presence—almost with the same intensity I had experienced in Medjugorje.

The most significant thing that happened to me on the retreat occurred during an all night vigil in front of the Blessed Sacrament. Each participant had an hour to spend with Jesus during the night. When my turn came to sit with him, I told him I realized he had forgiven me, even though I had doubted it. "But," I said to him, "I haven't forgiven myself, and I'm really not able to." Then I felt him say, "I want you to hear something from your children." He was introducing me to my two children, a girl and a boy, who were already in heaven with him. I heard each one of them, one at a time, tell me that they forgave me. Their voices sounded so innocent and beautiful. I can't think of this without crying. I just could not believe that they could forgive me for taking away their lives.

The Rachel's Vineyard weekend[10] helped me to reconcile with myself, my children, my past and the Church. Because of the level of forgiveness I had just received, I felt I absolutely had no business holding grudges toward anyone. "If these babies can forgive *that*," I thought, "what business do I have being mad about anything?"

Upon returning home from Medjugorje Jesus had continued to reach out to me, especially through prayer, the Sacraments, and the retreat, yet I still sensed the need for further healing. Somewhere inside me remained a festering wound whose depths God's grace never seemed to touch.

I will never leave you

I came to find out that a retreat was being offered which included a week in Medjugorje followed by a week with Father Zlatko Sudac, a holy priest with the stigmata, on an island called Mali Losinj in Croatia.[11] Mary placed in my heart an incredible longing to see her again, so even with few resources I managed to go on another pilgrimage. After a week in Medjugorje where I felt like I received a long, loving embrace from my mother after not being with her for a long time, I went to the Bethany retreat house where Father Sudac gave talks, offered Mass, adoration and prayed over us. Being so close to him, I could see how filled he was with love and with the holiness of God. One day of the retreat, Father Sudac offered to anoint some of us with the Sacrament of the Sick, and to pray over us as we knelt before the Blessed Sacrament. Because of my childhood, I still carried a lot of emotional scars, especially from sexual abuse, so I stood up, walked forward, knelt before the altar and asked for healing. He prayed over me and anointed my forehead with oil, then I stood up and sat back down in my seat. Almost immediately, I became aware of a very deep grief rising up from the depths of my soul—a sorrow that felt bottomless. I started to cry and then began to sob, and I could not stop. My tears were uncontrollable. Then, all of a sudden, I started hearing Jesus' voice, and he said over and over again. "It's going to be okay, I'm here now." Then he said, "Go ahead. It's okay. Let it go." And I let out gut-wrenching sobs.

Every time I heard his voice, I cried more. When I was a little girl and needed him to tell me everything was going to be okay, I didn't sense him. He was giving me now what I needed all along. I sobbed for two hours. Then he said, "I will never ever leave you." I broke down even more when he said those words, and I wanted him to say them over and over again. I felt like he could not say them enough times to fully sooth my soul, so I pleaded with him, "Could you say it again?" And he said the phrase again, so lovingly, "I will never ever leave you." For the next two hours, I asked him to repeat it, and every time I asked, he responded with the same words and with indescribable patience.

I think Jesus was showing me how much sorrow I was holding inside. It truly seemed endless. I felt I could have cried from that day on into eternity and not have shed all the tears in my heart. But Jesus also had a plan in his heart to help me. Later that day, Father Sudac gave a healing Mass. At the moment of receiving communion, I heard the Lord say interiorly, "I will heal you today," and once I received the Eucharist, I felt his Spirit move into my soul. Then something beautiful happened which paralleled what Jesus says in the Bible, in John 7:38, "Let anyone who thirsts come to me and drink. Whoever believes in me, as Scripture says: 'Rivers of living water will flow from within him.'" I felt like places where pain had been locked up in my heart were breaking open and flowing with living water. The water was filled with love and for fifteen or twenty minutes it kept washing over and through my soul—washing away years of old pain.

When Mass ended, I felt truly at peace for the first time I could remember. Jesus had healed depths of sorrow within me which I had thought had no bottom. I tried to reflect upon which part of my past had been healed, and as I did, he said, "No." It was as though he was saying, "You've done a lot of work on memories and pain from your childhood, and I don't want you to worry about it anymore. It's done now."

* * *

Pray, pray! So many have followed other beliefs or sects and have abandoned Jesus Christ! They create their own gods, they adore idols. How that hurts me! If only they could be converted! There are so many unbelievers! But that can change only if you help me with your prayers.[12]

PHIL

God in a jail cell

I was an emotionally sensitive kid, and when I was in high school, I poured my powerful emotions into alcohol, drugs, sex and pranks. While I continued to go to church on Sundays, I worked at being "cool" in an all-boy's Catholic school in southern California. I caused all kinds of trouble for my teacher there. One time I threw a desk at my teacher when he gave me a grade I didn't deserve. Another time my friends and I turned up the heat because we wanted him to start sweating profusely. Later he had a huge heart attack. I don't doubt it was precipitated by the grief we caused him. I also remember putting noise-makers around the classroom that chirped, "F.U." everywhere and unabbreviated. Once I asked the teacher if I could go to the bathroom, and when he said, "No," I borrowed a fellow student's water bottle and poured the water in my lap. I grew quiet, and the teacher who was accustomed to my constant banter with other students asked why I hadn't spoken. "Is it because you still need to go to the bathroom?" he questioned. "I already did," I told him. Then I threatened to take him to the dean and get him fired. "Under California State Law," I said, "You can't deny a child his right to use the restroom." I stood up in front of the class with my pants down and underwear on, and had him wipe off the liquid with a washcloth. I did this to humiliate him, and I think he did it because he was fearful for his job. I was just selfish. I wanted everyone to laugh. The last straw for my teacher occurred when I wasn't in class. I think teaching at an all-boy's school for too long did him in. My fellow students told me that after they put ice down his shirt that slipped down into his underwear, he stood on his desk, grabbed some toilet paper, and pulled down his pants to wipe himself. Keep in mind this was an all-boy's school. I heard about what he had done and made sure that the dean heard about it, too. That got him fired.

Now I want to be a priest. I bet you're wondering how that happened.

In college, I began to wonder about the existence of God. If there was a God, I thought, then that God might be asking me to live a certain way. This idea really hit me when I found myself one day, in jail. Drunk and high, I had decided impulsively to steal a car by myself. I thought it would be something fun to do, a cool experience I could share with my friends. When I was driving it, I realized I was less likely to get caught if I returned the car to where I had found it; but after skidding around a curve and drawing attention to myself, I worried about driving any further, so I stopped the car on the side of the road. Meanwhile, someone had called the theft into the police station, and I got out of the car only to get into another one with sirens on top of it. Sitting there in the back of the police car, I prayed Hail Mary after Hail Mary. Then I decided to cut God a deal. I told God I would quit having sex with the girl I was dating at the time, and I would give up alcohol and drugs, if he got me out of trouble. I had just gotten into a good college on a glitch, and I was dead afraid of blowing the whole thing, and I didn't want to get charged with a D.U.I. on top of everything. All the time I was praying, it didn't seem to me that God was listening. Yet somehow I passed the drunk-driving test: I walked a straight line, I counted numbers backwards, correctly, and I was certainly more than drunk.

When I was thrown in a jail cell with about thirty other people, I grew scared and thought, "I'm going to find a Bible in this cell and show God how serious I am." I kept reminding him that I would quit my sins if he got me out. But I could not find a Bible, so I picked up a Steven King horror novel instead. For three days, I read, sat, thought, and prayed. On the third day, a large man, who looked hardened and drug-worn, and who hadn't eaten a bite or moved from his bunk the entire three days except to go to the bathroom, suddenly got up from his bunk, came over to me and asked me if he could read my book. I was the smallest and youngest guy in the cell, and I wasn't about to say, "No," but I thought it was a nasty thing to do because he took away my only form of entertainment. And not only that, he walked back over to his bed, put the book under his pillow, and returned to his comatose state.

I felt bummed. I looked over, forlornly, at my own cold and nasty bunk. But then, to my total amazement, right in the middle of my bed, I saw . . . a Bible. My heart began leaping all over the place, I felt so excited and grateful. I quickly picked it up and searched for a passage I could read that would express to God my plea of "Hook me up. Bail me out! I will change!" I'd had a fundamentalist Protestant friend, George, in high school, and I looked for a passage I knew he had liked. George, I thought, might know what passages really get through to God. But then I grew frustrated fingering through endless pages and came to the conclusion that the Bible was too big for me, so I gave up. Feeling dead tired, spent, and defeated, I stared down at my numbered wristband that categorized me as a prison detainee, and my eyes rested on the last three digits of my number, 683. I wondered if those numbers held any significance, so I picked up the Bible again and turned to page 683, which was the book of Jeremiah. I started to read. He spoke of how God was going to punish the Israelites because, in recompense for their sins, they were offering God animal sacrifices when God wanted their hearts and their good lives, not their sacrifices. At that moment, I realized that I was offering God the periphery of my life but not my own heart. God was asking me to choose him and to give my heart to him. If I did that, then my sins would fall away. A peace came over me, a peace that told me I would be okay—that everything would be okay.

My charges were dropped from a felony to a misdemeanor and the judge denied what the prosecution team desired—the first time he had ever done that. He said, "I can't do this ever again because I'll get a bad reputation, and no one will come to this court." I know it was because of that judge's radical and unusual move that I spent thirty hours doing community service rather than eighteen months to three years in jail. I will never forget his last words to me as I left the courtroom. He looked me in the eye and said, "Don't fail me."

My parents, on the advice of the judge, let me stay in jail a few more days rather than bail me out, in order to educate me further in the lesson of consequences. When they did pick me up after my release, they were terribly worried. I told them not to worry about a thing, that everything would be okay. But they were completely unconvinced, and my calm demeanor upset them even more. Not only was there son a criminal, but now he had gone crazy.

God chose me

At first I kept to all the sacrifices and promises I had made to God because I felt enthusiastic about my faith. For the first time, I knew unequivocally that I was chosen by God and cherished by God. And since I now understood how important I was in God's eyes, my initial burst of faith centered around an elevated idea of *me.* "God chose *me*," I thought to myself. I got such a kick out of that. My faith was easy for me my first six months as a believer, but when the initial thrill of it all went away, my *me*-centered faith left me very vulnerable to temptation, and I fell back into my old familiar sins. I failed walking my Catholicism. I had only felt what it was like to be carried. From then on, I knew that the way I approached faith was wrong. I also noticed that sinning was different for me. I had reverted to behaviors that in my initial conversion I had left behind, but I couldn't enjoy my sins like I had in the past because I now felt the pain of them. My sins also planted a seed of doubt in my heart, and I started to experience painful moments of unbelief that tormented me.

One day, I felt so upset over the destructiveness of my own sins that I just stopped. That started the best time I have ever had in my faith life. I read the book, "True Devotion to Mary" and came across the Medjugorje website[13] where I poured through Mary's messages. I knew about Medjugorje because my mother had gone there with my dad in 1987 when it was just an obscure, miniscule town in Yugoslavia. They saw the miracle of the sun, saw it change colors and dance in the sky, and my mother climbed up Apparition Hill with pictures of me, my brother and sister. She placed them near where Mary first appeared and consecrated our lives to her. When I was growing up, I knew that Mary was appearing there, believed it and didn't care.

Now that I was in college making a sincere attempt at giving my life over to God, when I read what Mary was saying in Medjugorje, I felt excited. Her messages felt very alive and spoke directly to me. They weren't something that happened in the past, like the lives of the saints. They were happening now, and because they were occurring simultaneous to my own conversion, they seemed more personal, more impactful and more credible to me. I sensed that her messages to the world were something I could participate in because they weren't over yet. I could have an active hand in promoting the messages, so I did. I started a daily email group and sent messages throughout the college dorms and beyond, every day. I also tried to do everything Mary was asking for in her messages. I relied on them. I was fasting on Wednesdays and Fridays; going to Confession/Reconciliation at least monthly; reading the Bible; praying the rosary—three mysteries each day; and attending Mass almost daily. There was no doubt in my mind that Mary, the Mother of God, was appearing in Medjugorje, and if that was the case, then there was no point in living for anything else.

My commitment not to sin and my interest in Medjugorje also began a time of great spiritual consolation as well as great personal loneliness. God started to teach me about faith and about the Church, the way a family trains a puppy. I knew so little, and I was alone, so he taught me himself. In prayer, I experienced moments of ecstasy, and I really longed to share my newfound knowledge and faith. I remember sitting outside the school cafeteria asking God to send me someone to talk to so I could share my new life in God. No one came. For three months, I spent approximately six hours a day in prayer.

I want to serve Him

My prayer for faith-filled companionship was finally answered when I participated in a campus ministry retreat and met my friend, Peter, and many others. Every person in my the group of friends that came out of that retreat came to be transformed by Medjugorje. But after a while, my old doubts about my faith being real began to plague me again, and Mary's Medjugorje messages supported me when nothing else did. I started clinging to them for dear life. As I began to question the existence of God and to wonder if faith was just a cultural phenomena, the messages kept me constant in my religious practice, if not my beliefs. I entered into terrible moments of darkness and doubt which left me feeling isolated, empty and emotionless. Over and over again, I asked myself, "Has everything I've believed in wholeheartedly over the last three years been a charade?" I was feeling trapped by a faith that might not be real, and was living it out of fear rather than out of love. Worse yet, for me, faith out of fear didn't seem worth living at all.

Even in that difficult time, I still received moments of brief rapture which were prompted by my Marian devotion, particularly my rosary prayers. And at a Marian conference in Northern California I received strength to continue believing. There, Father Svetozar Kraljevic, the Franciscan priest in charge of the English-speaking pilgrims in Medjugorje, said two things that impacted me. In his talk, he urged us to pray and said that, more than any other message, Mary repeats the words "Pray, pray, pray." "Why does she repeat them?" he asked. "Because we are not praying enough." And then he said later, "If you are not going to church on Sundays, then don't call yourself a Catholic because you are doing more harm than good." I believed that no one could be that sure of anything unless it were grounded in something real. And when the Medjugorje visionaries spoke, I also saw that they were convinced of what they were seeing and believing. When my faith failed, theirs sustained me. Medjugorje provided a reason for faith when I couldn't find any within myself.

The messages from Medjugorje nurtured my faith and helped me not to get lost in my temptations and doubt over whether Christianity was real. In my journey toward God, I continue to take two steps forward and one step backward in the moral life. I accept that my temptations may never leave me, but know that God won't either.

One day I knelt in a side chapel dedicated to the Virgin of Guadalupe and asked her what she wanted me to do and be. I felt that she was calling me to be her soldier for Christ. I had already decided that I wanted to be a priest, and this led me to believe that she wanted that, too.

* * *

My angel, pray for unbelievers. People will tear their hair, brother will plead with brother, they will curse their past lives lived without God. They will repent, but it will be too late. Now is the time for conversion. I have been calling you for the past four years. Pray for them. Invite everyone to pray the rosary.[14]

JOHN

husband

Mary won his heart in Medjugorje

My journal entry, May, 2000:

> What was going through my head when I shook hands with that homeless man? It was similar to what God said to Jesus after his baptism, "Thou art my beloved Son. With thee I am well pleased." (Mark 1:10) I felt that God was saying to me—"Johnny, I love you, and I am pleased with you. Out of your suffering you have found a great treasure. You share a kinship with the poor and broken hearted. God loves the broken hearted, the sinner. You don't have to be ashamed."

Growing up I felt neglected by my parents. My mom and dad were good people, but they were absent and not very affectionate. I felt lonely and thought my parents didn't care if I existed or not. I often hid in the closet for hours and listened to hear if anyone missed me. One time, I tried to hide in the basement but could not walk down the full length of the stairs because I grew terrified. The basement heater made noises which sounded like a monster lived down there, so I stayed near the door for hours watching people coming and going. As always, no one noticed I was gone.

From kindergarten through second grade, I walked home from school and lived with a fear that when I arrived home, everyone—my parents, sister and two brothers—would be gone, and I would have to take care of myself. I knew my parents were good people so they would leave me plenty of food and the house, but I figured they would one day just leave and forget to take me with them.

My feelings of abandonment began when I was very young and created a drive in me—a hunger and thirst to be seen and loved and held. In my pain, I began to look to God for comfort. At Saint Philip's Church, near where I grew up in Southern California, I would look up and stare at the sanctuary walls which are covered with a beautiful painting of God the Father in the clouds—a white bearded old man who looks like Santa Claus. Below him are saints, and below them are people celebrating the Mass. That image became my picture of God, so I thought God was in the clouds. Up until about second grade, when alone outside, I looked up at the clouds and talked to God. At those times, I felt his presence and his loving encouragement. I was very shy and alone, so God became my friend.

God, for me, was a lot like my dad. Every Sunday, dad took my siblings and me to church. At bedtime, he told us kids stories, rough housed with us, then prayed the Guardian Angel prayer, the Hail Mary, the Our Father and the Glory Be, and then topped of the night by tickling us. All my friends loved him, and he seemed to have everything I wanted—a lot of attention and a reputation for doing good works in the community, such as helping the poor, the elderly and juvenile delinquents.

When I was in second grade, my parents divorced and my mom remarried. By the time I was born, their marriage had already begun to fall apart. After the divorce, I did not talk to God anymore. I felt disconnected, with no control and no rudder, like a leaf floating down a river. To cope with life, I watched about five or six hours of T.V. a day from age five until twenty-five. A lot of my formative memories come from T.V. I also became intent on stacking up achievements and being popular in order to be like my dad and get some kind of attention; but what I truly thirsted for was to be loved.

I was drifting away

I took on the example of my dad as a working model of how to be in the world, and God disappeared. Years later, I understood that my dad was operating on a merit point system based on the self-focused idea that if you do a lot of good works, go to Mass, and get a lot of people to like you, then you will rack up points and be in good standing with God. I thought what faith really boiled down to was being popular and good.

Being good and popular at the same time proved too difficult, so I chose popular. By the time I entered middle school, I had developed a mean spirit. I did not care about other people, and to be cool, I openly made fun of anyone socially awkward. I knew God was not too happy with my behavior, so I hid from him by not being attentive at CCD[15] classes and by daydreaming, joking, and looking for distractions while at Mass.

By the end of middle school, I was very well-liked, good in sports, good in school and had lots of friends. I carried a false sense of being on the verge of satiation. By the time I approached my dad's age, I figured, I would be so popular that I would not have to work so hard at it, and everything would be in place.

Then I went from a small middle school to a big high school, the same high school my dad had attended, and there everyone told me I was just like him. I had his name; people said I had his looks; people said I had his everything. This brainwashing reinforced the thought that I would be like my dad and achieve my goal of being liked. What I found out, though, in a harsh way, was that I was not like my dad. High school academics were hard for me; I could barely manage them. I could have played sports, but at that point, I felt that unless I was going to be the best, then I should not even try. If I shared my gifts and did not prove good enough, then my weaknesses would be exposed, and I would know for sure that I was, in truth, useless.

Literally, I had no friends throughout high school. Not doing sports, I did not have any sports friends. Wanting to be good, I did not hang out with the troublemakers and the kids taking drugs—and in no way was I going to hang out with the nerds. I existed in a horribly lonely space, and during any break or recess I walked around as though I had a destination, but, in truth, I had nowhere to go and no one to be with. Compounding the loneliness was my fear and embarrassment over admitting my feelings to God or to my family, especially my dad. What if they thought I was a dork and did not like me? I learned to hide my weaknesses from others and from myself. I foolishly hoped that God, too, would overlook me, while at the same time, I worried he would do just that. So I created a trap for myself and shouldered everything alone. On top of it all, I felt a sense of hopelessness and despair because I realized that my dream, my hope of being well-liked was not going to be achieved. I began to self-destruct. I was not suicidal, but I did wish I were dead many times. I felt as though I was drifting away, and one day I would be gone.

That was my state of mind when around my sophomore year, at age sixteen, I went to Mass on a Sunday with my siblings and my dad. While they sat clustered in the middle of a pew, I sat at its end, physically and emotionally separated from them, feeling completely detached. I felt utter despair, almost to the point of wondering, why live? Just before the "kiss of peace," the moment of the Mass when people shake hands and say to one another, "Peace be with you," I yelled to God internally with all my heart, "Give me peace!" Then, in the next moment, I saw in the corner of my eye a homeless man in a pew behind me and by himself. The church was full, but no one had wanted to sit next to him. I had never touched, spoken to, or even seen a homeless person before, but I knew his state by the way he looked and smelled. His face was red and unshaven, his hands big and rough, and his clothes dirty and brown.

My family started shaking hands with the people around them, and I immediately felt drawn to the homeless man. I walked over to him, held out my hand, and simply offered him peace. Then an incredible wave of serenity passed through both of us at the same time. As we shook hands, I felt God hugging me and the homeless man together; I sensed God revealing to me that this man was my brother, that we shared a kinship in being broken and outcasts; and I realized that God really loved him—and loved me. Through this homeless man, God was giving me special attention, that full attention I craved. As God's love and physical presence rushed through me, I felt like I had come home from a very long and tiring trip, and my parents were there to give me a big hug and to let me know I was safe. Our hands parted, and the homeless man looked into my eyes and said, "There are a lot of good people here, but you're the only one who understands the message of the Gospel today."

I was afraid of many things

After the encounter with the homeless man, I began to pray again. The only way I knew how to pray came from my high school teacher, Father DeLancey, who told our class to simply talk to God: "You just need to say, 'Hello,' and wait for him to respond," he said. So that was what I did. I fully expected I would hear God, and I did, in subtle words and impressions on my heart. I entered into a year-long period of grace during which I felt God's presence and joined him in conversation. He literally spoke to me, telling me he loved me in many different ways, and I thought of this as completely normal at the time.

When I was seventeen, this time of grace ended. One day, as I lay on my bed at home and chatted with God nonchalantly, as I normally did, I asked him, "So God, what should I do? Should I be a fireman? A fighter pilot? Should I be a businessman like my dad?" I rattled off many different professions, and then I stopped and said, "Well, God, what do you want me to do?" And that was when God shocked me with a clear and challenging internal voice. He called me by name and said, "Johnny, I want you to forget about all these things. I want you to forget about what your parents want you to do and follow me." Up until then our dialogues were more casual, more encouraging, but this one challenged me. God called me to do something, and I felt terrified.

I was afraid of many things, afraid he was calling me to leave my parents' house, and I did not want to go, afraid he was calling me to the priesthood, or to be persecuted, or to die, or to go and speak in front of people, like a prophet, which was even worse. I felt that following God was an out of control choice, and I dared not say, "No." I feared if I said anything negative to God he would not like me anymore, so, I stopped talking to him. I pretended he did not say it, and I did not hear it.

Altogether, I stopped praying for ten years. I still went to church and said the Mass prayers aloud, but without my heart. I would not talk with God alone because I feared he was mad at me and would talk to me again in a louder voice. I went to church because I felt safe from him there.

Seeking to be liked

I attended college, regained a sense of popularity, and after graduating, spent five years in the business world, in sales, like my dad. During this period, I set off again on a path of hope that I could become likeable.

Those were very exciting times, and they were fun times. I had lots of friends, and we laughed a lot. But I also made a lot of mistakes. I lost my sensitivity towards others, towards the poor, towards the outcast. Desiring to be part of the crew, I walked a fine line between being good and being cool. I started drinking too much. I started getting involved in pre-marital sex, which ultimately led to disastrous consequences and served to add more pain to my wounds.

When I was twenty-one and in college, I started dating my first long-term girlfriend. She is the first person with whom I had intercourse. She is one who haunts me to this day, one of the monsters who remains in my dreams. At the tail end of our relationship, when she was also seeing other guys, I no longer had much of a moral backbone. I was still clinging to the fruitless hope that she would see my love for her and come back to me. Determined to get her back at all costs, I made my family and friends, even God, take a back seat. All I wanted was to be liked by her, while she used me as her safe standby guy. We were not having sex a lot, but one night when I went to her place, we saw a sexually charged movie—I cannot remember it, one with Sharon Stone—and we were both overtaken by lust and had sex afterwards.

I went home and had a dream that night—a very clear vision of conception happening. It looked like a scene from a Nova television program. I saw a light followed by a sperm connecting with an egg that then exploded into life with cells breaking up and multiplying everywhere. I sensed that the person created at that moment was a boy. I woke up and shared the dream with a friend who said, "Whoah, man.

Be careful not to get her pregnant."

A few weeks later, my girlfriend called me up to say only, "I need to talk to you," but in my heart I knew she was pregnant. Then she came over, told me of the pregnancy, said she was going to have an abortion, and added, "I know what your opinion is, and I don't want to hear it." I felt numb, powerless and neutral. At that point, her opinion of me seemed more important than what I thought was only the potential for the life of a child. I tried to be supportive of her. I helped pay for the abortion. I also drove my girlfriend to the clinic and waited for her there. The experience passed like a bad dream of which we never spoke. Then I blocked it out.

After the abortion and the end of that relationship, my heart became hardened. I kept a distance from people and tried to remain emotionally safe. I entered into other sexual relationships but did not care about them much; and I had a lot of friends, but never any close ones.

As the years passed, I grew very close to following in my dad's footsteps. I was making my way in the business world of sales, getting involved in different community volunteer activities, and becoming more and more miserable. I moved to San Francisco with a new job selling phone systems for Lucent Technologies and worked from my home in solitude, without friends again, in that same old place of loneliness.

I was reaping misery

I had always gone to Sunday Mass but decided to become more active in my church. As I started to get involved my faith again, the memory of God calling me to follow him started to gnaw at me, but I still felt afraid to sit down and truly listen to him. To appease the tugging in my heart, I started to get *very* involved in the church by volunteering, giving talks, and helping the poor, but I was still trying to do things my way—still trying to stay in control of my life.

I grew anxious and depressed and started to have panic attacks. In desperation I began to pray again and asked God, "What did you mean when you said, 'Follow me?'" I almost winced because I thought he would respond right away and perhaps be angry. But I did not hear anything back. After weeks of asking him and hearing nothing, I began to worry that maybe God had given me a one-shot deal and had forgotten about me.

In July of 1998, I wrote in my journal:

> I'm so anxious. I hate this feeling of fear. I can't see

> past it. I can't feel anything but its desperate grasping. My world is turned upside down. There is no meaning in my life. What's wrong with me? HELP!!!!! What did you mean when you asked me to follow you? The journey back is long, it's lonely and cold. I'm so tired. I can't make it home. GOD!!! JESUS!!! WHERE ARE YOU?!

I soon realized that no matter what I did, if I did not ultimately do what God had asked of me, my life was going to be fruitless. I knew I was holding myself back from God, that although I was willing to hear what he wanted to say, I was not willing, necessarily, to do what he wanted me to do. Thinking that, perhaps, he was calling me to become a priest, I decided, with the help and encouragement of an acquaintance who would later become my wife, to go to spiritual direction. I needed to discern his calling.

Through spiritual direction and Ignatian prayer,[16] I returned to that original experience of God calling me to follow him. I sat with it, journaled about it, and prayed over it for a few months. In one of my sessions with my spiritual director, she had me imagine myself as a priest and asked me what it felt like. I saw myself surrounded by children, working with the poor, being a voice for them, serving them and being in community with them; but I did not see myself administering the Sacraments. Over time, I realized my calling to be with the poor, but not to be a priest. In order to please God, I decided to cover all my bases and volunteered for almost every ministry at church, as well as at a homeless shelter for families where I worked with children. Fundamentally, though, I was still unhappy and struggling.

At age twenty-eight, I reached a point of frustration and realized that everything I was doing, or had ever done, ended up working against me. As I became more involved in church, I felt less peaceful. As I immersed myself in volunteer work, the results were fruitless. I did not grow more loving, and I do not know if I really helped anybody. The way I had thought to do everything was wrong. From my dad's example, I had learned that if you did a lot of things well, you would be rewarded, but I was reaping misery. I was a drone. I was successful at sales, but I had to be pushy and lie, and I acted meanly towards people. Rather than feeling free and loved, I felt trapped—even my good work in church enslaved me and did nothing to pull me out of my predicament. I had thought my good works would satiate my thirst to be loved, but my thirst was only growing. I was becoming physically tired with depression and anxiety. When my anxiety became unmanageable, I started taking Paxil and seeing a Christian therapist. I had reached my limits. I could not do any more than I was doing, and what I could do was not helping the least bit of my thirst.

One day, while I was praying in a fetal position on my bed, I finally flung up my hands to God and said in desperation, "God, everything that I've done has turned into shit. I can't do anything on my own. It all turns bad. Whatever you want me to do, I'll do. If you want me to be a homeless person, if you want me to be a priest, or a persecuted prophet, I'll be that—anything. Whatever you want me to be is infinitely better than the emptiness I feel now. And, God, whatever you want me to be or do, you make it happen. I can't do it on my own. Everything that I do turns to crap." Within two weeks, I quit my job at Lucent and got a job offer at a seventy-five percent pay cut, working with homeless families and children at the homeless shelter where I volunteered.

Finally, I did find a place where I felt at home. I was at home with the outcasts. That is where I wanted to be, and that is where God knew I needed to be. My weak and wounded character made me a chameleon who was going to do whatever social pressure called for. If I worked in an environment where it was important to lie, cheat and steal, then those were the traits I was going to adopt. God needed to put me in a place where my job would be to serve people, where the social character would be redemptive for me. But even when I got to the shelter, I continued to battle my old wound, my need to have attention.

God, I want you to know me

I began to have a recurring dream at this time when I began to question my motives, my drives. In the dream I am a man known by all to have superpowers. I am confronted with a monster, and just before engaging it in battle, I test my powers: I try to fly and cannot; I try to see if I can lift up a car and cannot; I try to bend metal and shoot lasers out of my hands, but I cannot. I stand before the monster who knows I have lost my supernatural abilities, surrounded by people who still expect me to have them. The monster enjoys seeing me posture, and so he does not destroy me, but continues to allow me to dance around pretending. I hit the monster. Nothing happens to him, and I wake up in the middle of trying to fight him, full of angst and powerless. The dream is ongoing. I still have it today.

The dream reflects the way I operated in the world, out of fear and pride, with inner tension, wanting to be liked, trying to use abilities which I was told I had, but somehow knew I did not. Satan was using my needs and weaknesses to control me and make me dance around in life so as to appear capable and wonderful. The set up suited him perfectly because I just went nowhere. I still live in the reflection of that dream, fighting lost battles, at times, so I can look good and maintain an image.

With the help of spiritual direction, I continued to reflect on the moment when I was seventeen and God called me to follow him. It scared me to think that out of billions of people on this earth, he had called me by name. But this being so, I knew he must care about me, and though I had let him down multiple times, he seemed to like me, even still. I discovered this when I put into practice something Saint Paul said in his letter to the Ephesians: "everything exposed by the light becomes visible, for everything that becomes visible is light." [5: 11b-14a] When I decided to try this and expose my sins to God, I expected him to come with judgment, but I found that he came with mercy. When road rage, for instance, consumed me completely because I stored a lot of anger inside, I began saying to God, "I want you to know this about me. I want you to know everything about who I am. You judge me, not me," and he gave me an infusion of peace instead of the merciless punishment and shame I normally gave myself. Or when a feeling of lust came over me, or when I harbored harsh judgments toward people, especially in church, I caught myself and said, "God, I want you to know me. Here I am. This is me." And each time I received a healing wave of peace.

I began to trust God again

In my journal on June 30, 2000 I wrote:

> God, you remember when my brother and I were little, and we poured all the milk on the kitchen floor—laughing and sliding back and forth. You are like my mother on that day. You are merciful and kind. The thing that I loved most on that day was seeing my mother's face when she walked in and saw us. My brother and I suddenly realized our predicament. "We're dead!" I thought. Then like a summer rain or a warm breeze, she looked at us and laughed. She saw our joy and pardoned our sins.

I began to trust God again. The process moved slowly, but I went from a faith of doing to a faith of relationship. When I stopped hiding from Jesus, he not only showed me mercy, but healed my deepest wounds of needing to be loved as I am. Most people who knew me thought, "Nice kid, nice boy," while my rage, bitterness, judgment and sins ate at me inside. Only Jesus knew who I really was. He became my only authentic friend, the only person with whom I trusted to share my burdens. Until then, I did not have much of a relationship with anyone. I was playing the roles of a good son, a good church person, and a good social worker, so I did not know who I was—my different personas limited my capacity to know myself, and I was not very interested in knowing other people. I was interested in them seeing my persona as likeable. My heart was disconnected, but as I began praying with God, sharing the dark sides of my life, lifting them up in the moment that they happened, his mercy changed me.

A couple years into that process, I had a dream which pointed to this conversion. In the dream I met a prophet, an old man standing on a platform preaching about Jesus, saying that the devil was real and that he was trying to destroy us. I joined the small crowd of people standing around him, and as I listened, I believed him and became his disciple. Then he said, "If you believe this message, then you need to start preaching it," so, in the dream, I started preaching to non-Christian friends in my life to whom I normally never preached for fear of persecution. As I began to tell people to repent because Satan was real, I became aware that Satan was now suddenly aware of me. Before then, he paid me no notice, but now that I was speaking the truth and speaking against him, he wanted to destroy me. As I was preaching to small groups of people, suddenly everyone disappeared, and I was left standing face to face with Satan. He looked like an ordinary man with curly black hair—no pitchforks, horns or red tail. Nothing distinguished him except for his qualities of evil and power. With a smug and disdainful look on his face he said to me, "God is not going to save you. I'm as powerful as God, and even if God cared about you, which he doesn't, because you're just one person among billions, he could not overpower me. I'm just as strong as he is."

I felt an urge inside of me to respond as I normally did, to posture, to pretend I possessed special powers and rail at him like a loud prophet, but instinctively, as I stood before him, I knew he could destroy me. Shaken, I thought, "I don't know how powerful Satan really is, but what he said made sense to me. There are billions of people, and is God really aware of me?" Then, in that moment, I remembered that Jesus had never left me. I knew he would protect me. I did not know how powerful Satan was, but I knew that Jesus defeated Satan because of the resurrection and because of my experiences of his healing mercy. My only thought of hope was the Lord, so I fell down on my knees and in a deep guttural prayer said, "Jesus, save me!" Then I collapsed into a fetal position, and with my whole body and my whole will, I held onto his legs in faith. "I'm going to hold onto you Jesus," I said, "even if Satan kills me. I'm going to hold onto you until I get to heaven."

Satan stood still in front of me. I had put myself in a weakened state before him, and I knew he could kill me, but I also knew that because I was clinging to Jesus, I was not going to hell if he did. Then a complete wave of peace overtook me. Jesus had responded to my call and saved me. I looked up and saw Satan. He smiled, shook his head, and walked away, but in his look I saw the words, "You're mine. I'll get you later." And then I woke up. I was sitting on the couch with a pillow in my arms and tears in my eyes. It was the middle of the night. I walked over to my bed and fell back to sleep, and when I woke up in the morning, I remembered everything, which was highly unusual for me. The dream was about my psyche, but it was also a dream in which Satan and Jesus were actually present. I am still able to recall what happened as if it were a real event.

With that dream, my model had broken. I came to find the peace of Christ in my utter defeat—a victory much greater than anything I could have measured. I had thought that if I did the right thing, I could save myself, and then God and people would like me; but I started to see that my faith was not so much about showing off my goodness, but more about recognizing my powerlessness and turning to God, the only source of good and the only one who could move me to goodness. So when I stood before Satan, I knew I could not save myself, and that was okay. I did not have to put up a powerful façade because the façade was not going to save me, Jesus was.

My hope was in Christ's blood

My relationship with God was deepening, but I still struggled through my relationships with people. I dated a gal for a couple years, and although I tried to make the relationship work, I did not emotionally invest in it at all. Shortly before we parted ways, she gave me a tape of a Protestant preacher who explained the beauty of the Sacrament of marriage using Paul's letter to the Ephesians, Chapter 5. Before that, I did not think I would ever show interest in marriage, but the tape explained its sacred nature by using Saint Paul's words in an appealing, non-sexist way. The preacher focused on the line, "Be subordinate to one another in reverence to Christ." From his words, I understood that marriage could be a journey towards Christ, and I saw, for the first time, that God was calling me to marriage as a vocation—but not with this young woman. The tape gave me clarity to end that relationship, and my next girlfriend, Christine, became my wife.

A month into dating her I had a dream in which I saw a bride and groom at a wedding Mass. A viciously demonic alligator, intent on bloody revenge, planned to tear them apart with his jaws, but I knew the woman was going to destroy it, and this gave me a sense of peace. The alligator, fuming with rage, began to charge at her and her husband to be. She stepped forward with a cup of Christ's blood that she had in her hand, threw the consecrated wine over the alligator, and it disappeared.

The dream was prophetic. I was the groom. My hope was in Christ's blood, and my hope was in the woman who represented my future wife. The alligator represented my fears, my shame, and my anger. The woman loved me and brought Christ's blood into my fears and cleansed me. And that is what Christine did for me in real life. I was able to put my trust in her. For the first time, I started to have a real, loving relationship with a person. The dream prophesied that my wife would be faith-filled and very instrumental in healing me by deepening my faith in Christ, and one of the ways she has done this is through her strong devotion to Jesus' mother, Mary.

Hello Mary, I've never written to you before

Just after our wedding, my wife sensed we were called to go on a pilgrimage to Medjugorje[17] where the Virgin Mary is appearing. I struggled with the idea of going quite a bit, because I did not have a relationship with Mary: I did not pray the rosary, had not grown up with any kind of Marian influence, and my entire faith life had centered around Jesus. I felt very fearful of having anyone, even Mary, stand between us.

After much prayer, I finally submitted to God's calling through my wife. Saint Paul's line from Ephesians 5 helped me to go: "Be subordinate to one another in reverence to Christ."

On December 25th, 2001, Christmas Day, at midnight, we were off. On the plane ride to Medjugorje, I wrote in my journal:

> Hello Mary,
>
> I've never written to you before, in fact, I haven't thought too much about you until my wife, Christine, your daughter, introduced me to you.
>
> I know perhaps it's not fair of me to request a miracle, but I pray that you will show me a sign when I visit you in Medjugorje..

I want to be able to share in my wife's faith, but I have so many doubts. I don't care (too much) if people call me crazy. I want to be on fire with the faith.

I would be thankful if you could grant this selfish request, but if it is not the Father's will, I pray that my faith will continue to grow.

Mary, pray for my faith, bless my marriage with Christine, and protect us from evil.

No matter what, do not let me stray from your Son, My Lord Jesus Christ.

Thank you, Mary.

Amen.

Medjugorje was both very difficult and amazingly transforming for me. I feared our pilgrimage there might rock my faith which, by that point, felt so life-sustaining I could not imagine living without it.

My first challenge came suddenly. Our pilgrimage leader told our group on our second day that she had a surprise in store for us. That evening she walked us over to the visionary, Marija's house and said we were going to be present for a small, private apparition in a tiny chapel attached to her home. I became quiet and terrified.

That night, after the apparition, on December 28, 2001, I wrote in my journal:

> I was afraid that any relationship that I might develop with Mary might interfere with my relationship with Jesus. Of course, I had heard the arguments given by those who prayed to Mary. They would say that Mary always leads one to Jesus, but the risk was too great.

I liked going directly to Jesus. Even if Mary interceded by praying to Jesus for us, I wanted to take my prayers directly to him. I found it difficult to believe that praying with her might lead me straight to Jesus. How was this possible? Sure, she was the Mother of Jesus, the Mother of the Church, but how could I talk to Jesus through her in the same way as talking to him directly? The explanations, no matter how logical or articulate, could not fully explain it. Faith was required. Fear was the enemy.

Anyway, we were granted a special visit with Marija, who is one of the visionaries who receives daily apparitions at 5:40 p.m. every evening.

> I was afraid. I wanted to believe these visionaries. I wanted to grow in my faith, but I didn't want to risk what I had

> in Jesus. I worried that the experience would rock my faith and create a fundamental doubt in my head. Furthermore, what if nothing happened? Suddenly, I realized that I was afraid of this as well. What if I was praying only a few feet from the Virgin Mary, the Queen of Peace, and I felt nothing? What would that say about my faith? What should I do? As I sat and prayed in the chapel, my anxieties and fears slowly began to build and build. Just moments before the apparition I panicked and thought, "Run! Get out of here!" Then a soft voice from inside me said, "Go to Jesus." Of course! I had always been able to go to Jesus. He was my rock, my salvation. I could always trust in him. So I got down on my knees and prayed to him. I felt safe, and I knew that nothing could harm me if I stayed close to him.
>
> At 5:40 p.m., in the middle of a communal rosary, Marija had her vision. I stayed in prayer, but nothing extraordinary happened for me.
>
> Later, I reflected on the experience. Where did that voice come from? I wondered. Perhaps it was Mary. After all, she always takes us to her Son. I was still troubled, but I held to that thought.

I did not tell anyone about hearing the voice, and my angst continued. The group kept praying the rosary. I liked to pray to Jesus and read the Gospel. The rosary was not my thing, and I still felt very disconnected from Mary.

By the third day of the pilgrimage, I began to wonder why I was there. I felt like an outsider among a group of devout, wonderful faith-filled people. They had accepted Mary's gift of motherhood, but for some reason, I could not shake my distrust of her. Humbled, I realized perhaps my faith was not so strong. While at adoration that night in Saint James Church, I prayed to Jesus, my friend, and asked him to help me understand my doubts about Mary. I read from Scripture, and I felt the peace of God coming back to me. Jesus did love me. I could trust in him to answer my prayers. I felt happy until I read Paul's words:

> "Therefore, whoever eats the bread or drinks the cup of the Lord unworthily will have to answer for the body and blood of the Lord. A person should examine himself, and so eat the bread and drink the cup. For anyone who eats and drinks without discerning the body, eats and drinks judgment on himself." [1 Cor 1:27-29]

Then I felt God's hand on me. The church was packed, and I panicked. I had to get out. I had to confess my sins. I told Christine I had to leave, and I went to Reconciliation with a priest named Father

Stanton and shared with him my doubts, my fears and my struggle with Mary and the rosary. The priest said that God had blessed me and not to worry, not to force anything, that I should be thankful for my relationship with Jesus. He said, "It is Jesus who saves, and Mary who takes us to Jesus. You don't have to pray the rosary for salvation. If you don't feel comfortable with it, don't do it. Let Jesus take the initiative of introducing you to his mother." I felt a holy peace come over me, and I began to cry.

Jesus healed me of my angst in that Confession, and the priest comforted me. Afterwards, I resigned to take things slowly. Perhaps the rosary still was not for me. Perhaps I was not blessed with this gift of prayer from God. Still, as my wife pointed out to me, maybe praying the rosary was not simply about feeling, but about obedience. If I believed what the visionaries were saying, which I did, then I was called to pray the rosary. I decided to ask Jesus to help me to get to know his mother Mary, and to help me to understand her whole purpose.

No, my dear one, this is how you hold my Son.

That night two women in our group, Natalie and Alicia, invited me and Christine to hike up Cross Mountain early the next day. Apparently, Mary prays to Jesus at the foot of the cross on top of this mountain in Medjugorje at 5 a.m. each morning. Initially, I declined, and then I thought to myself, "I might not have a good relationship with Mary, but one thing I have in common with her is the desire to pray at the foot of the cross to her Son."

The hike itself was incredible. Christine, Natalie, Alicia and I set out early in the dark morning, about 3:45 a.m. As we started the climb, my companions, as I expected, pulled out their rosary beads and started praying. I kept my hands in my pockets and began praying quietly to Jesus. It was clear to me, almost from the beginning of the rosary, that my wife was wheezing and would not be able to continue praying out loud. I picked up my rosary and decided to pray it on behalf of my wife—just this once.

For the first time, I felt engaged. The rosary had a purpose for me now. Since Christine had a relationship with Mary, I knew Mary would like me to pray it for her. With my love for Christine in my heart, I prayed each mystery of the rosary; and as the other two women became tired, I tried to pray the rosary even harder for them as well. At one point, I even began to lead the rosary.

An incredible energy surged through me as I bolted up the mountain. I felt amazed by Alicia and Natalie's faith and commitment. Tired and out of breath, they continued up the mountainside, gasping out the prayers, intent on reaching the summit. As we neared the top, time was running out. We had to keep moving. Still tired and overwhelmed with fatigue, Alicia and Natalie continued. Christine and I passed them. I felt inspired.

Reaching the cross exactly at 5 a.m., I fell down at the foot of it and prayed to Jesus and Mary. Christine stayed ten-feet back. She was, as I learned later, praying that Mary might intercede before God and show me a sign. Since our pilgrimage began, I had been asking Mary to show me a miracle; but once I reached the cross, I retracted that request, thinking it too selfish. Instead, I asked her to help my little brother who was struggling. Bent over on one knee, I felt a sense of serenity surround me. Then I saw a sudden flash of light brighten the sky and illuminate the mountainside. It looked similar to a bolt of lightning, except that it was a straight vertical line amidst no clouds, no rain, and no thunder.

Christine saw the flash of light, but with her eyes closed in prayer. She opened her eyes just after it happened and asked me, "Did you just see something?" I could not answer her because I was starting to cry. The miracle had taken my breath away, and through it, I sensed that Mary was saying to me, "I'm here with you, and I am inviting you into a relationship with me."

Natalie and Alicia arrived at the top of the mountain five minutes later. They had not seen the flash of light.

On the way down the mountain, I began to reflect on my experience on the mountaintop. Christine had seen the flash, but through her closed eyelids. No one else had seen the bolt of light illuminate the sky. Awestruck and humbled, I realized that perhaps the sign was meant just for me, that Mary, who knew my doubts, might be reaching out to me. In reflecting on the climb up the mountain, I also realized how Jesus had answered my prayers by giving me an insight into Mary's role. I understood that just as I prayed for my wife when she could not pray, Mary prays for us and with us when we get tired, distracted or unfocused in prayer.

On the same day as our hike up Cross Mountain, Christine and I went to another apparition. It took place at night, in the freezing cold, on Apparition Hill. When we arrived at the apparition sight, a sea of people covered the hillside. Just before the apparition, I started feeling angst once again, so I got down on my knees and clung to Jesus for a sense of peace. Growing more uncomfortable as I clasped my hands together tightly in a crouched position, I placed my hands down on the ground, and just as I did, I heard a voice say, "Don't let go." Obeying this voice and feeling guided by a gentle force, I put my hands back together and noticed I was no longer clinging Jesus, but poised as though holding a baby in my arms, in a soft, gentle embrace.

Coming down the hill, I pondered what had happened. Mary, it seemed, was teaching me that I do not need to cling to Jesus for fear he will leave me, but that I should be gentle with him and hold him like a baby. This was my first experience of Mary helping me to understand better who Jesus was. I had actually heard her and felt her guide my arms to embrace him as if to say, "No, my dear one, this is how you hold my Son."

Jesus, stay close to me

The day before we were scheduled to leave, I smelled roses on the cross that I wore around my neck, and no rose perfume roses or roses were present. I had never smelled Mary's mystical scent of roses before and kept bringing my cross up to my nose to test if I had imagined it.

I received so many graces in Medjugorje that Satan was going to make sure I did not come home with them. At the airport, I began to doubt everything—the scent of roses, Mary's messages to me, and the miracle at the cross. When I arrived home, I was not sure what I believed anymore. Christine wanted to me to give a talk with her at our parish about our pilgrimage, but I wanted nothing to do with it.

I wanted to hide and deny my beliefs because Jesus was leading me to the cross where I met up with my greatest fear—the fear of being disliked, rejected and abandoned. He was asking me to reveal to the world who I really was, a Christian.

I also sensed Mary in my prayers telling me I was holding back quite a bit of my whole self from Jesus. I knew I would have to go beyond my quiet prayer and my church group and bring Christ into every part of my life. In my marriage, Jesus had an open invitation, but I kept my Christian faith hidden from the rest of the world. Around my family and my high school, college and work friends, I acted like a chameleon character, becoming whatever they wanted me to be in order to be liked.

As I revealed more of myself to others who did not know Jesus, I met with their indifference and judgment. My fears were raging.

January 15, 2002

Dear God,

I'm falling apart. I'm on the verge of collapse. I am poured out, broken, emptied. If I don't get help soon, I am afraid I will go crazy. Fill me with your Holy Spirit. In your mercy, hear my prayers. "My soul is cast down within me, therefore I will remember you. . ." [Psalm 42]

Thankfully, I have been here before. I know that you will not abandon me. Thank you for befriending me. I wish I was stronger, but you made me as I am. I'm thankful for my beautiful wife, Christine. Thank you for blessing our marriage. She is my strength. Her faith gives me courage to carry on. Thank you for blessing our marriage. I know I can be a real pain in the you know what, but you have continued to stay by my side.

Thank you for my faith. You have given me signs and wonders, but I manage to still have many doubts. Protect us, Lord, from Satan. I am growing tired of his divisiveness.

Right now I almost feel like giving up. This is just the beginning, I know. I will need your help to get me through this dark time. I am afraid, Lord.

This is the lowest I've felt in years—abandoned by my old friends. They all think I'm weird. Half my family thinks I'm about to run off to some cult. My classmates think I'm weird. They think I'm crazy for believing in Jesus and Mary.

A couple weeks after coming back from Medjugorje, I braced myself for a trip to Aspen, Colorado where I would visit some of my old college buddies. I feared I would be tested there, that I would have a heightened expectation of being more myself, but then revert to my old behaviors. I counted on Mary's prayers to help me pick up the cross I did not want to carry.

Knowing that Mary would continue to support me, even when I faltered in my faith, gave me new hope that I could confront fears I had not battled before. Yet, at the same time, I still did not completely trust her. My experiences thus far had confirmed my mental understanding of her as the Mother of God who would lead me to Jesus, but I still feared that by praying to her I would lose Jesus who was everything to me. My spontaneous prayers to Mary consisted of a quick, "Take me to Jesus," as if to say, "I don't really want you too involved in this." I was willing to take her prayers, especially through the rosary, and I wanted her to be my intercessor in Aspen, but I was a lot less willing to hang out with her and get to know her on an intimate level. That I reserved only for her Son.

Going to Aspen was difficult. One of my friends, at the start, said something condescending about my being Christian. "So I hear you've really gone off the deep end with this Christian stuff," he said. "It looks like you've gone kooky on us. I'm expecting a halo to float out of your head any moment now."

He became the protagonist of the four-day trip. At every opportunity, he verbally attacked me in front of others and made snide comments. Every single moment I had free, if I was walking to the car or to the bathroom, I said the rosary. To my amazement, I did not feel afraid. I was very sincere and responded thoughtfully to his insults. I did not become defensive, nor respond as I normally did by downplaying my faith and my involvement in the Church. At one point, he became very aggressive and asked me one question after another, trying to put holes in my faith; but I felt filled with the Holy Spirit. Gradually, one, two, then three people sat around our table. Then finally, the whole group sat and listened as I preached the Word, challenging this or that person gently, and talking about my own experiences of faith. "That might have been you," he said, "but stuff like that wouldn't happen to me." "If you want these experiences," I told him, "you're not going to get them by talking to me about it. If you want a relationship with God, with Jesus, you'll have to ask him to be in your life, and then you'll find him there. In fact, he's already there."

Then he backed down and said, "You know what. I'm afraid. I don't want to change my life."

I had feared that by sharing my faith I would find myself alone with no one to understand me. But I found that by being true and bringing out the light, I had split the room. I could see very clearly that half the people there were already searching for God, and half were trying to avoid God, but that God was working with all of them. While stating who I was in my faith did cut me off from some in one respect, in another, I started to have a more authentic relationship with every person in that room. I did not have to hide anymore. Some of them were even amazingly thankful. At the end of the trip, the host, who was not Christian, said, "In the many years we've been doing this, we've never had this type of spirit in the group. This was the first real conversation we've had that cut through our surface level talk. And that's thanks to you."

God continued calling me to being authentic. I took that into my family, and I took that into my work place. I began praying with the homeless teenagers I work with and risked getting in trouble with my employment, recognizing the importance of inviting God into all my relationships. I gave a parish talk with Christine on Medjugorje, and it went well. Transformations began happening everywhere in my life, and I became more fearless in my faith. This can be accredited to two things, my trust in Jesus, and my extra assurance that Mary would always be present for me, even if I didn't fully trust her. My primary drive to be liked by people had kept me in a prison. Without the love of Jesus and Mary, I would not have had the confidence to risk being unloved, to risk being free.

My son would be eleven now. I named him Joshua

After a year of marriage, my wife, in her prayers, sensed that Mary was calling me to a Rachel's Vineyard Retreat[18] for further healing around the abortion. I wanted to believe I had moved past it because I had gone to Confession and felt that it was resolved. I never thought about my child or the incidence. Why should I dig up the past and create a situation to make myself feel bad, I wondered, when I've put away the abortion and don't have to deal with it anymore? I also feared I would be in a room with a bunch of weeping women and feel very out of place. I struggled against it. I dragged my feet and did not want to go, but in my prayer, I got a subtle sense that maybe I should. Once again, Saint Paul's line, "Be subordinate to one another in reverence to Christ" helped me submit to my wife. Perhaps God was using her for his purposes.

The first day of the weekend retreat I felt awkward, but my awkwardness turned into grace. Shocked to discover I had any emotion at all around the abortion, I found that a great sadness was present inside of me, and I turned out to be the one crying more than a lot of the women. Asking for forgiveness and asking the child to be in my life again greatly healed me. I named my child and discovered I could relate to him, even ask him, from time to time, to pray for me. My son would be eleven now. I named him Joshua.

I went from the denial of my own parenthood to the recognition of who and what I am, not only as Christine's husband, but also as Joshua's father. I was allowed the opportunity to begin grieving the loss of a child who was mine. Healing from the abortion, I learned, was going to take more than just the confession of a sin. I had to find out I had lost my son. A precious life that was a gift to me, that I was a steward for, was never allowed to live.

By denying the child's life, my part in creating it and taking it, and by simply talking about the abortion as a sin, I had been disconnecting from my true identity. This is something I see with other men. Women do grieve abortion more because the act is part of their body. For men, it is easier to deny the act and any responsibility for it. And when we men do that, we deny part of our humanity and suffer without even knowing why we are in pain. Problems like my anxiety disorder, my outbursts of anger, and my having to take Paxil came after the abortion and were tied to it. We cannot disconnect from our feelings of loss and feelings about others without disconnecting from who we are as human beings. That is the price we pay. We lose part of ourselves. My child is part of who I am. During the retreat, I reconnected with Joshua by writing a letter to him. By being able to grieve in this way, I was able to retrieve part of my humanity which was tied to this child. It was a mistake to kill my child. I wrote a letter to him to apologize.

> My dear little Joshua,
>
> You are probably wondering where I've been, why I left you behind to die, and why I didn't even bother to think about you these many years. The answers to these questions do not come so easy. The truth is that I was a coward for not speaking up for you twelve years ago now, and I have continued to be a coward—running away from my sin, my own involvement in our ultimate decision to abort you. It gives me comfort to know that you might be with Jesus right now as I write this letter to you, but it saddens me to know that I will never see you in this lifetime. I know that you would have been a special boy, a beautiful gift from God. I'm sorry that I did not see that then. I was afraid, afraid of what people might think if they found out that your mom was pregnant, afraid of your mom's anger if I questioned her. I put the guilt of our sin on her, and I was wrong for that. She was young and afraid like me. Like me, she did not want to believe that she was killing her own son. We were both at fault. I'm sorry for my part, and I'm sorry for blaming your mom. I pray that she may also one day see you in heaven.
>
> As for me, I humbly ask for your forgiveness. How could you forgive me? I would understand if you didn't. I hope it is not too late to turn things around for us. I have been a terrible father. How could I contemplate bringing more children into the world without first reconciling with my oldest son?
>
> I don't know if there is any gift that I could share with you that could compare with the gift you have received in being with Jesus for all eternity, but I would like to reach out to you, to hug you as my son, to share my heart with you. I would like it if you could give me a second chance to be the father that I wasn't for so many years. I missed seeing you as a baby, seeing your first steps, comforting you in your fears, laughing with you, disciplining you, teaching you, loving you.

God willing, I would like to see you. Maybe God would grant me this request before I die. To be able to hold my oldest son in this lifetime would be a great gift. If you would like to see me, ask Jesus. I'm sure he will grant you this request. I know he loves you very much. Please ask him. It would mean a lot to me.

I promise I will continue to pray for your mom, and I hope that you will keep me and my wife in your prayers. I know I wouldn't have had the courage to try to contact you if it wasn't for her. She means the world to me. We are both hoping that we can have children one day, God willing. We would like you to be included in our family. Please think about it, and let us know.

Love always.

Your dad,

John

Mary, this is who I am

My last relationship that still needed repair was with Mary. Despite all of the help Mary had given me, I continued to fear she would get in the way of my bond with Jesus. I was obeying all her messages from Medjugorje, and I still do, by praying the rosary every day, fasting on bread and water on Wednesdays and Fridays, reading the Bible, going to Confession once a month, and receiving the Eucharist, and all of this was helping me to grow and mature in my faith tremendously; but I did all these good deeds for her like I had done good deeds for my mom, my dad and God, without engaging in a real relationship.

I believe Mary understood me. When I went to see my new spiritual director, she said, "I think that now Mary is calling you into a deeper relationship." What struck me was that my spiritual director actually felt Mary's presence as she said this. She even began to tear. Then she used the Emmaus story to say that she thought I needed to go on a retreat dedicated to Mary. "Mary wants you to come to know her and her Son through the depths of your heart," she said, "like the disciples in the Emmaus story came to know Jesus when they said to each other, 'Were not our hearts on fire while he spoke to us on the way. . .?'" [Luke 24:32]

I went on a silent weekend retreat directed by a Jesuit father, and I decided to dedicate the retreat to Mary with the intention of getting to know her better. Before my first spiritual direction session with the priest, before I told him anything about myself, he walked into the retreat center bookstore while showing me around and spontaneously bought me a book called "Hearts on Fire." I opened the book, and the very first line was from the Emmaus story: "Were not our hearts on fire?"

On retreat, I intentionally went through some of my old memories as if to say, "Mary, this is who I am," in the hope of having a deeper relationship with her. I sat in silence and listened to anything she might want to tell me, but heard nothing, just silence. I continued to struggle, and the Jesuit father helped me to see that part of the reason why I could not connect with Mary was because my vision of her reflected how she is often depicted in art, standing upright with her hands out—a powerful, sometimes stern figure, but not human. I saw Jesus on the cross and with the disciples, acting real, but I saw Mary in a blue robe, in the clouds, acting surreal. My fears had turned into nightmares in which I caught glimpses of Mary and became terrified. One night I woke up and thought I saw her at the foot of the bed. Too afraid to scream, I started thrashing around, kicking off the bed covers and cutting my hand on the alarm clock. In one nightmare, I dreamt I woke up and looked into a mirror to see Mary standing right behind me. I could not speak, nor breathe, nor turn around, I was so frozen with fear.

The Jesuit father recommended I meditate on a passage from the Bible that gave more of a human aspect to Mary. I chose one of the Gospel's depictions of Mary where Jesus gave her to the disciple John at the foot of the cross. My intent was to observe Mary in a very painful human experience of loss, and not in a powerful position at all.

I went into the meditation and saw Mary at the foot of the cross, hunched over, overwhelmed and crying. She was wearing black, and a shawl covered her head. I stood behind her watching. I saw true human sadness and felt a stirring in my heart connecting me to her. I looked up at Jesus' eyes and face, and just as I did, he said to his mother, "Behold your Son," and then he turned his head away from her to look right at me. I broke down crying. I just felt loved. I had not expected that at all. I was just there as a spectator. For the very first time, I felt connected to Mary, and I was able to suffer and to cry with her. I collapsed down by her side, put my arm around her, and we sobbed together.

When I look at Mary now I begin to weep. I begin to have an emotional response. Whereas before, I felt afraid of her, now I feel love for her, and I sense her love and support for me.

Even though she had given me many experiences that could have led me to believe she was trustworthy, it was not until Jesus himself showed me he was the one leading me to Mary that I trusted her.

Just last weekend, when I was sitting in a pew at church, terrified to get up and speak during a Mass on behalf of Catholic Charities, an overwhelming sense of peace descended upon me, and I looked up wondering where it came from. Everywhere around the church I started to see Mary. I looked up above me and saw her sculpted in the rafters, hunched over at the foot of the cross. I looked to my left and saw her in despair, holding Jesus after he had been taken down from the cross. Then I looked up again and saw yet another image of her. I began to cry. I recognized that she was truly there, and that she would always be there for me, even after I die.

When I received the Eucharist at that same Mass, I felt my heart burn with light inside my chest. This lasted for a while, giving me the most intense feeling of love in my heart I had ever experienced. The feeling even burned through my doubts that it was real.

Mary had led me to Jesus, and then, literally, my heart caught fire.

* * *

You will be happy if you do not judge yourselves according to your own faults, but understand that graces are offered to you even in your faults.[19]

PATSY

Jesus spoke from the Tabernacle

I grew up in San Pedro, California as the oldest of nine children in a traditionally Catholic Mexican American family, amidst the strong faith and daily devotions of my parents. My mother and father have always been very close to Jesus. To this day, my mom is a daily communicant and goes to frequent adoration of the Blessed Sacrament, and my dad, who died on New Year's Eve, 2002, always said a daily rosary. Dad loved Jesus and Mamma Mary. He really worked hard for years and took extra jobs to put all of his nine kids through Catholic school. This was the most important thing to him.

I knew Jesus and his mother, Mary, in my own confused way. When I was young, I asked Mamma Mary and Jesus for everything. When I had to take a test, I would ask Mamma Mary to help me pass it, and if I did not pass it, I figured I must have asked her wrong. I did not think of actually reading the books. And when I went to church, my mind was on anything but church. My mind was in the world. At Catholic school I took catechism classes which taught the faith, and you'd think I would have learned something, but I didn't pay attention in class. My mind was every place else.

So when after seventeen years of marriage, my husband left me with our three kids, I thought that since I was divorced, I was excommunicated. I did not even understand what excommunication meant and just assumed that I could not receive the Sacraments.

I was devastated from the divorce and thought, "How could this happen to me when I've gone all my life to Mass, done everything I thought I was supposed to do as a good Catholic, and my husband leaves me after seventeen years? How could this happen?" I did not see at the time that God allowed it because it was the best thing for me. I concluded that Jesus must not be in the Catholic Church. If he was, this would not have happened to me. Then I got angry with him and told him how upset I was that he had left me in the wrong church all this time.

So I went looking for him.

I went to Baptist, Lutheran, and Protestant churches, every church you could think of. I would have entered the Jewish religion, but the synagogue I went to said that I could not join because I was not born Jewish. Then I said to Jesus, "What if you are in the Jewish religion, and now you're not even going to let me in there!" I began to think, "How could they have the right religion if no one can join it? Hmm. So we're all left in the cold? Thanks a lot, God.'"

During this church-hopping phase in my life, I met my second husband and married him in a civil ceremony. I dragged him around to all the different churches until he finally said, "No more." He was fed up with my search. Poor guy. I put him through so much, and he is so wonderful and patient.

Disappointed, but undeterred, I continued my search for Jesus and ended up at a Mormon church. "Wow," I thought. "They've got family unity," which was very important to me. "Now that's a good religion. He must be in there." When I learned that they believe that only a limited number of people will get into heaven, I remember thinking, "Boy, I'd better get myself, my husband and my kids in there soon so we can make the cut."

I came home one day after visiting a Mormon church and said to my husband, "We're going to be baptized Mormon." "No way," he said. "I was born a Catholic, and I will die a Catholic." I had never heard him speak so strongly about his faith before. It startled me, and so I said forcefully, "You don't even go to Mass on Sunday. What difference does it make to you?" He rolled his eyes and walked away from me. And that was that.

Then I started thinking about how every church I went to had nothing nice to say about Mamma Mary. They either had something derogatory to say about her or simply did not want her mentioned at all. Then it dawned on me. As a mother, I sure would not want my children to think of me that way, treat me that way, or allow people to talk about me that way. If Jesus is love, then he's not going to be able to fully participate in a religion that would treat his mother that way. So then I thought, "Oh, I really did it now. I'm really in trouble now. I've got myself kicked out of the real Church where his true presence is. Now what am I gonna to do?" I thought that I would never be with Jesus again, and it tore my heart out. It tortured me to believe in the Catholic Church again, and also believe I was excommunicated from it. "I've lost him," I weeped, "I've spent all this time looking for him only to find that I can't have him. I was in the right religious denomination all along, and I've thrown it away. He's in the Eucharist, and I can't touch him."

"I can at least go to confession and ask for forgiveness," I thought. "How could they deny me an apology?" So I went to confession, and

I told the priest, "I got myself excommunicated from the Catholic Church."

"What did you do?" he asked.

"I got divorced."

He laughed and said, "Well, that's not cause for excommunication."

Then I said, "Oh, you don't know the half of it. I got remarried outside the Church, and it was a woman judge to boot."

He really laughed then. "That's not cause for excommunication," he said. All you need to do is get an annulment for your first marriage and remarry in the Catholic Church."

"How do you do that?" I asked.

"Bring your husband here with you. We'll get the paperwork started, and we'll remarry you. But you'll have to live as brother and sister until then."

"Oh no," I thought. "My husband is going to kill me now. Not only am I going to have to get him to remarry me, but he's going to have to love me as a sister. He's gonna be really angry with this one." So I told Jesus to hurry up. The annulment took just a few short months, which is unheard of in the Church.

How did my husband react to all this? He loved me. He has always been a patient person and a loving person. He just accepted it.

He was just...Love

I started to get excited about receiving Jesus again at a Mass during Holy Communion in the bread and the wine. I had a hunger and a yearning to get close to him and wanted to prepare myself so I joined a prayer group. The group I joined prayed the rosary together, and one time when we prayed the Sorrowful Mysteries, I felt like I was literally at Calvary with Jesus. I was crying, sitting right in front of him as he suffered on the cross. I was there. I do not know how to explain it, but I was there. I thought others were seeing what I was seeing, but I found out later that they weren't. It was just me.

At this same time in my life, Jesus started to wake me up at 3 a.m. every morning to pray—sometimes for hours. Words started to come to me, beautiful words. I thought to myself, "I'm really getting intelligent in my old age." I was hearing a man's voice and a lady's voice, but I did not think about who was behind the voices. I just thought they were beautiful. The words were actually coming from Jesus and Mary, but I did not know about locutions—actually hearing someone speak. I also did not know that people could see visions. One morning, when

Jesus woke me up at 3 a.m. to pray, I went into my living room, and he was standing there, glowing, dressed in a white robe, behind a clear white veil. His hands extended forward towards me with his palms up as though he was inviting me to come to him, but I could not move. I remember that his bare feet were beautiful, absolutely beautiful.

I told a friend of mine in the prayer group, Ann, that I was hearing these beautiful sayings in prayer. She assured me that such things were possible and told me to write them down. Then later two people prayed over me. Both were given what is called a "word of knowledge"—a word from God that instructs, heals, or foretells. While praying over me they said that I should go and sit in front of the Blessed Sacrament and that I would be taught. I asked, "Who's gonna teach me?" "Don't worry," they responded. "Just go sit in front of the Blessed Sacrament."

So I did, the very next day. I got up really early and caught the bus. At that time, I had to take the bus wherever I went and no church existed near me. I dropped off my son at preschool and walked from there to a church named Our Lady of Perpetual Help in Santa Fe Springs, California. After Mass, I knelt in front of the Tabernacle, the real presence of Jesus.

Then, all of a sudden, looking up, I found myself alone in the church. All was still and silent. Then, coming directly from the Tabernacle, I heard a man's firm but gentle voice say, "Little one."

Filled with love, I said excitedly, "Jesus?"

"Yes."

"Where are you at?"

"Here. Haven't you been looking for me?"

I was stunned.

"I'm going to teach you," he continued.

Thrilled, I said, "You're going to teach me? Well, what are you going to teach me?"

"The Bible," he said.

"Oh my," I responded, and I lifted my arms above me with my hands pulsating rapidly over the top of my head as if pushing information into my brain. Then, I exclaimed in between my absurd hand movements, "You're going to infuse me with knowledge like you did with the apostles, aren't you!"

"Then he laughed and said with a chuckle, "No. You'll come to be with me daily in the holy sacrifice of the Mass, and then after the Mass you'll stay with me, and I'll teach you. Bring your paper and your pen and your Bible."

Then I started writing down everything he said. He knew to teach me slowly and started off by having conversations with me. I guess he did this so that I could get to know him. We talked about everything—whatever was on my heart. He was just . . . love. Everyone asks me, "What does Jesus sound like?" All I can say is, I did not know what love was until I heard his voice.

Then I had to go home and tell my husband about all this. "Oh my God," I thought. "How is he ever going to believe this?" When I got home I told him, "Jesus talked to me." And he said, "O.K." Someone asked my husband years later, "Did you really believe that Jesus was talking to her?" "Of course not," he answered. "When she first told me I thought she was crazy, but then later I realized it was true." I have put him through so much. Oh, my poor husband.

Before Jesus first started talking to me, I checked out a book from the library at Saint Pius Church in Buena Park, California called, "Is Mary Really Appearing in Medjugorje?" I read that book, and I believed that Mary was appearing there, but I was so angry that she was appearing there and not where I lived. I said to her, "We've got gangs, divorces, children that need you, and you go to the other side of the world, a place I can never go to! We'll never get to you!" I cried. But, as it turns out, she and Jesus, in their great love, brought Medjugorje to me.

First Jesus started getting me up at 3 a.m. in my own home, and both he and Mary would speak directly to me. Then in my conversations with him, as he spoke from the Tabernacle after Mass, Jesus told me that I would travel all over the world taking his teachings which he dictated to me. He told me that I would speak his words to his children in the churches to remind them of his true presence in the Eucharist. He asked me to do a "Presentation" which consists of "Five Acts of Love" to his "Five Holy Wounds": the Holy Sacrifice of the Mass, Eucharistic adoration, the Sorrowful Mysteries of the rosary, The Divine Mercy Chaplet, and a twenty minute meditation given to me by Momma Mary about Jesus' life. He started an evangelizing program through me called, "His Teachings Ministry: Evangelizing as Fishers of Men."[20] He gave me that title. Anything done in the ministry is all done by him. I am just his secretary. I have always been his secretary and nothing more. He asked for a house of prayer and it has finally happened in Las Vegas where I now live. He dictated an entire book for the program called, "For Love, With Love, Through Love," published by Queenship Publishing.

So the ministry began, and I told Jesus that I would do it if he put holy priests along my path to teach me; and for the last twenty-two years, he has answered that request. He knew I would need priests who understood mysticism.

I needed a lot of help along the way. One day I was praying in church, and I grew very excited because Jesus was telling me, "You're going to be my bride." I was thinking "nun." I thought this because they sometimes wear a habit and a ring symbolizing their commitment or their marriage to him. Ever since I was a little girl, I wanted to be a nun because I was around them so much and admired them. Obviously, it never happened, but I wanted it so much. I used to put a towel over my head and pretend to be one. "Oh, wonderful!" I thought. "I'm going to be a nun!"

Then it hit me. "But Jesus! I'm married! I can't marry you!" I was instantly devastated. I thought he would take my husband and let him die.

Jesus laughed and said, "No, child. Go home and call my beloved Ann"—my friend from the prayer group.

"No," I said indignantly. "You're God. You tell me what you mean. He just laughed and said, "Go call her."

Then I cried. I was so angry and upset. I really thought that he was going to let my husband die. I went home and I called Mary crying, "Jesus is going to take Babes." (That is what I call my husband.)

"What are you talking about?" she asked.

"Jesus is going to let my husband die because he wants me to be his bride." She laughed. Then I really got mad. First Jesus had started laughing at me, and now she starts laughing at me. Then she said, "How many times did I tell you last year to go to Bible study?"

I got really upset, and I almost screamed, "What does this have to do with anything?"

"If you had gone like I told you to, you would have learned that at the end of time all men and women will be his bride. In the book of Revelation (21:9) the bride of the Lamb is the New Jerusalem. Everyone living there is his bride. This means he's promising you heaven!"

That is the second time I heard Jesus laugh. I tell you he has a sense of humor. He chose me, didn't he? One time I asked Momma Mary, "Why me? Why does Jesus talk to me?" She said, "Because you are so unworthy, but so willing." I thought, "Ooooh! Oh well, I know I'm unworthy. That's okay."

Whatever He asks of me, I will do

I am a normal person. We are all normal people. But, I am also not normal because how can you tell someone you have a normal life when you say that God, the Creator of heaven, the earth and the universe is talking to you?

Years ago, before the locutions with Jesus and Mary started, I stood in front of a statue of Jesus in church, and I told him out loud, "You save my husband and my kids, and I'll do anything you ask." I never thought he would take me up on it.

I have been doing Jesus' bidding for over twenty years, and I have been quitting the job every single day since I started. Everyday I tell him, "I quit." Why? Because it is painful. It is a life I would not wish on anyone. But deep down I know that I would never give up—because it is he who I love most. I always tell him I am going to quit because to get close to Jesus you have daily, constant trials—some big, some small. Getting close to him is a very painful process. Where there is God, there is the Blessed Mother, but there is also the evil one, and he is going to try to take you down whichever way he can. It is a difficult life because you are going to be persecuted. Anyone who follows Jesus is going to be persecuted. There is no way around it. But whatever he asks of me, I will do.

I always want to make sure I am talking to Jesus and not the evil one. Before Jesus starts speaking to me, I always make sure he says, "Jesus is Lord," because the evil one will never say that, and I do not want to be deceived. If Jesus is telling me something that I should write down, he says, "Praise be to Jesus for Jesus is Lord, Savior, Redeemer, Reconciler of all nations." He knows I am assured it is really him if he says this. He says this only to reassure me. There is no such thing as egotism in Jesus.

When we talk, Jesus is always so grateful, so thankful. I cannot get over it. It is so unreal. Here he is. He is God. I should be bowing to him, praying and thanking Him. But he thanks me! He thanks me for listening to him, *every* time we speak. And I leave him hanging in the air sometimes. How rude is that? I will be interrupted by people and talk to them because I do not want to appear strange or feel like I have to tell them that I am in the middle of a conversation with Jesus, which few would believe. But he is so wonderful and kind. He just comes back to me later or continues speaking with me just after I am done, if he wants to. It's as though I put him on hold without letting him know and just cut him off. He's so patient.

He is always there for all of us, no matter what. He never forces himself. He takes the background. He once told me when I asked him why others do not hear him as I do, and he said, "I speak to *everyone*, child. It's just that they don't open their hearts enough to listen."

* * *

When you pray you must feel more. Prayer is a conversation with God. To pray means to listen to God. Prayer is useful for you because after prayer everything is clear. Prayer makes one know happiness. Prayer can teach you how to cry. Prayer can teach you how to blossom. Prayer is not a joke. Prayer is a dialogue with God.[21]

ANGELA

A stripper's surprise

I lived a pretty sinful life, but it was the life that everyone around me led. I did everything my friends did. I never knew anyone who went to church. At fourteen, I met my first boyfriend who was eighteen, and at fifteen I started to have sex with him and got pregnant. I didn't want to have a child, so at sixteen I had an abortion. I just thought, "I don't want to have a kid." I didn't realize I was killing a child. I cried a lot afterwards, and I could not be around kids. Every year after that I thought, "My child would be one, or two, or three. . ."

My first boyfriend was my first true love. I stayed with him for ten years. My father thought I was too young and that he was wrong for me because he was older than I and was drinking. But I felt love, and I was happy. I wanted to do what I wanted to do. I snuck out of the house to see my boyfriend whenever I could.

Right when I got together with my boyfriend, I started having problems with my father. He started to get violent and tried to run my boyfriend over with a car. He threw me out of the house on my seventeenth birthday because I disobeyed him the day before by getting a ride to school in my boyfriend's car. He was going to give me permission on my birthday. He'd had enough of me and told me not to see my boyfriend anymore. So my mother went with me to a shelter. My brother came, too.

My father found us quickly and brought us back to our house in Massachusetts, but he still didn't want anything to do with me and only talked with me when he had to. Even though I was the cause of everything in my dad's eyes, he started using my mom as a scapegoat, and my parents began to fight all the time. This kind of behavior wasn't completely new to me. Since I was little, my father was verbally abusive to my mother, and he hit her on occasion. He was really controlling, and I was always scared when I was little. I grew up thinking that one of my parents would be dead and the other in jail from one killing the other. My mom, I figured, would probably be the one who ended up dead.

I started doing stripping acts

You could say I was raised Greek Orthodox, but I never went to church, except for weddings and funerals. I never prayed and didn't know anything about God, Jesus or the Blessed Mother. When my brother, who is two years younger than I am, converted to Catholicism, I thought he was nuts, and we started growing apart.

In 1990, when I was twenty-two, I broke up with my boyfriend whom I realized had been cheating on me and doing drugs, and my parents broke up on the same day, Valentines Day. After that, I lost trust in men. I hated guys. I had so much rage inside of me that I took up kick-boxing, spent a lot of time venting my anger at the gym, and considered taking anger management classes. For the next ten years, if I found out a guy was cheating on me, I started punching him. And I never liked having a lot of friends because I had lost trust in people. It seemed like no one had real, true love. The only person I trusted was my mom. Throughout everything, I've always stayed glued to her. Her name is Mary.

One day my mom told me my dad had cheated on her. When I heard that, I felt extreme hate for my dad. When my mom found out that he'd gotten a girl pregnant, she wouldn't let him back in the house. The girl he impregnated was younger than I, and he had a son by her. My dad was a cheater and a liar, so I wanted nothing to do with his new family. I never wanted to see his son or his stepdaughter. I felt like he replaced us, and I felt abandoned by him. I still loved him very much, but I was angry because he was so mean to us all the years I was growing up. Growing up, I wanted to spend time with him, but I when I tried to speak with him, something I said always set him off, and I got yelled at or punished for it. This made me so sad that I just stopped having conversations with my father. He and the girl he impregnated stayed together and got married twelve years later. They seem happy whenever I see them, but so did my mom and dad when company came to visit.

After dad left, I started clubbing and going out and doing whatever I felt like. I dated anyone, and I was sleeping around. I bought my own house, and my brother, my mother and I lived in it. My brother and I didn't know each other's lives, we just happened to live in the same house. At that time, I always dressed in mini skirts and sexy outfits, and I ended up working at a nightclub in Massachusetts. I started doing stripping acts at a club where I took everything off, and I liked it because I got a lot of attention. Dancing and stripping was a fantasy I'd always had. It felt very natural for me, and I loved it.

I looked out at the men when I danced at the club and didn't care about anyone there. All I really looked at was the dollar sign. I figured clubs like this shouldn't exist, but since they do, I was going to make money out of them. I figured all men went to strip clubs. More than half the guys at my club were married, and it bothered me. They often told their wives they were going shopping and then bought presents for the girls and went to the club, especially at Christmas time. I heard all the lies they were telling their wives, and it made me sick. They told me everything, saying things like, "Oh, my wife doesn't know I'm here. She doesn't understand me." Sometimes, if I'd heard enough, I told them they should spend more time with their wives, or if I wanted the money, I ignored what they said.

I had the attitude that I was going to do what I wanted to do because I didn't trust anybody anyway. I just hated the whole world. I hated the club itself, but I loved my job because it made me money, and I felt like I was an actress. I was a different person when I was in there dancing.

My mom ended up finding out about my job and told me to quit. I told her in anger, "I'm old enough for you not to tell me what to do," and then I bought another house so I wouldn't have to live with her. I planned to retire at my job. I made fifteen hundred dollars a week only working Thursday, Friday, and Saturday.

In 1997, I met a new boyfriend who owned a nightclub. I loved him, but I fought a lot with him and didn't want him going to the club where I worked. I thought my boyfriend shouldn't be in a place like that where he would talk to other strippers. I also didn't like going to his club because I fought with the other girls there. One day I got in a fistfight with a woman who was married and flirting with him. I pulled her hair, kicked her, slapped her, and called her names. The police charged me with assault and battery with a deadly weapon, and I had to go to court over it. The deadly weapon, they said, was my shod foot, which means the weapon was my shoe. I was on probation for a year.

After that I wouldn't go into his club anymore. He says he was faithful to me, but I doubt it. He always said he'd propose to me, but it never happened. I loved him a lot, but I also thought I probably couldn't trust him. I still never had trust in my heart.

The only time I was happy was when I was working because I got to dress up and look beautiful and be sexy. I also received a lot of money, a lot of attention, and I loved to dance.

So that was my life before my conversion.

God wants me to quit my job

June 7th, 2000 was the day my conversion began. As I was getting ready to go to work, an unexplainable force or feeling, like a wall, was put up inside me that said I couldn't leave the house to go to work that day. Now, I just thought that maybe God was protecting me, that perhaps I'd get into a fight at work, or into a car accident and go off the side of the road since I used to fall asleep on the road a lot. When I felt the wall inside of me, I started saying out loud, "God won't let me go to work today. God won't let me go to work today."

I cried because I was losing money and wanted to go to work, but I figured I would make up for it the next day. So, bored and restless, I sat with my mom at her home and watched T.V.

The next day came, and the feeling that I should not go to work grew stronger. This time I felt God was telling me to quit my job. I had no idea why God would want this, or what exactly was happening to me, but I just kept saying out loud, "God wants me to quit my job. God wants me to quit my job." I cried hysterically at that point. I'd taken a day off, but to quit was another thing. When I called my mom to tell her what God wanted, she said, "Good. I didn't like your job, anyway."

Then my boyfriend called, and I told him the news. He didn't believe I would quit, neither did my mom. No one believed it. And I just couldn't bring myself to call my job, so I avoided it thinking, "Maybe tomorrow I'll feel different."

I didn't feel different, and I didn't go to work. On Friday, June 9th, I got an even stronger feeling that I had to quit, so I stayed at my mother's house and just cried because now I was also missing big money. My brother was living at my mother's house at this time, but he really didn't know anything about my life. He didn't know what I did for a living and still doesn't. I told everyone that I worked at a bar.

Then on Saturday, June 10th, I felt that God wanted me to stop taking birth control pills. I don't know how I knew to stop because I hadn't read or heard anything about it being wrong or that the pill could abort a baby.[22] I didn't understand why God would want this, but I told my boyfriend I was going to stop taking the pill. At this time in my life, I started getting a sense of things, and whatever I felt, I said, and then did.

That night, I also finally got the courage to call my boss and tell her I was quitting, but I still left clothes at the club because I feared I'd be tempted to return to work there. I still had no idea why God would want me to quit.

I said I was a sinner

I left my job on the 7th, told them I was quitting on the 10th and stopped taking the pill that same day. Now I had no job. I was miserable and confused.

Father's Day was coming up the next week, on Sunday, June 18th, and I had already decided that I wasn't going to visit my father and was going to disown him. At the same time, something inside of me was telling me I had to go to church on that Sunday, but I didn't know what church to go to, so when my mother happened to be talking to my aunt who went to an Assembly of God Church, I told my aunt I wanted to go with her.

We went and sat together in the back of the church. The Reverend started preaching and said, "If you feel like you're called to be here today. . . God has a reason for it . . ." I felt like he was talking directly to me. "If you need to be cleansed," he said, "come up to the altar." I told my aunt that I felt like I needed to go up there, and then I stood up and walked forward, crying the whole way. Kneeling down in front of the altar, I said I was sinner. The words just came out of my mouth, even though I didn't know what they meant.

When I left the church, I started to read the teeny pocket New Testament that my brother had given me, and as I did, I felt that I was supposed to forgive my father. I felt so drained and sick from crying so much at church that I had no energy to see him, so I called him up, wished him a happy Father's Day, and told him I wanted to see him.

My father came over to my house the next day. I told him I'd gone to church and gave him a picture of Mary. I told him I forgave him, but he was unwilling to admit any wrongdoing. I started to feel very upset with him and realized I should have just told him I loved him and let the past go. Keeping my hurt feelings aside, I continued to have a nice, Father's Day. Before he left, I gave him a hug, said I'd come visit him and that I'd like us to go to church together.

The following Sunday my father and I went to his Greek Orthodox church with his two kids, a boy and a girl, ages eleven and eight. After that day, I began visiting my dad, even though I still had a hard time talking to the girl he was with, and I started talking to the kids—the first time I ever acknowledged them. So I welcomed my dad into my life and forgave him in my heart.

God wants me to forgive you

On the Wednesday after Trinity Sunday—on June 21st, I felt a strong pull inside me, and I knew I was supposed to call up the girl I had gotten into a fight with, the fight I had gone to court over. A year after I'd beaten her up and gone on probation, I still had extreme hate for this girl who was married and worked at my boyfriend's club. I thought of her every single day since I caught her flirting with him. As much as I'd hated my dad, I hated this girl, too. Whenever her name came up, it made me sick, and I was always mad at my boyfriend for never firing her. It was very hard for me to reach out and forgive her, but that day, when I called my boyfriend's bar, she just happened to pick up the phone. I didn't even know what day she worked, and when she answered, I felt that the conversation was meant to happen.

She was probably scared when I said who I was. "I'm calling you," I said, "because I felt like God wanted me to forgive you and to tell you I'm sorry for treating you so badly. Please accept my apology." Then she started crying and said, "Oh, no, it was my fault. I was the one that was wrong, and I deserved it."

My boyfriend called me back shortly after I hung up with her and said, "She's crying, and she told me she just talked to you. What did you say to her? Are you starting in on her again?" I said, "No. I just called up to say I was sorry," and he said, "What? What did you go and do that for? You didn't have to do that." Then I just knew and thought, "Ah, so, there really was something going on!" After that day, she ended up going back to church. I found that out because my boyfriend told me. She also ended up quitting her job at the club.

This was still just two weeks after my conversion.

Without my job I didn't know what to do with myself. My mother and I had tried country western dancing, and I liked it, so a day or two after I called the girl at the club, I said, "I'm going out dancing tonight." My brother overheard me and said, "I'll take you out dancing." So I went with him and a friend of his who was thinking about becoming a nun and she picked us up to go dancing. At least I thought it was dancing. What it turned out to be was a charismatic prayer group, and when I got there, they were praying the rosary. Then they had a Mass, and after the Mass, they got up to dance and sing in tongues. That's the dancing my brother had in mind.

During the prayer service which lasted all evening and into the night, I got hungry, but I noticed that the girl who wanted to be a nun wouldn't eat when we offered her food. I asked my brother why not, and he said she fasts on Wednesdays. "What does she fast for?" I asked. "The Blessed Mother says that she wants people to fast," he answered. "Well, I want to fast, too, then," I said and started to fast on bread and water on Wednesdays and Fridays like the Blessed Mother is asking us to. The girl had also given me a book on the rosary and told me that the Blessed Mother wants us to pray the rosary every day. So the very next day, when I was walking my dogs, I practiced saying the rosary and tried to memorize the prayers. The rosary didn't mean anything to me at the time, though. I wasn't saying it with my heart, because I didn't yet know how to pray.

I love you, Mother Mary

On July 2nd, I went to the beach with my boyfriend, and we were going to make love after we got home, but I stopped him and said, "I can't do this anymore." The thought of having sex didn't feel right, and I just knew we weren't supposed to. I'd been saying the rosary every day now for a couple of weeks. My boyfriend saw all these changes going on in me—I'd quit my job, I was dressing more conservatively, I was fasting, saying the rosary and wearing Catholic medals—and he thought I was going too far.

By this point, just three and a half weeks after my conversion, I was starting to feel a love for Mary, and began saying out loud, "I love you, Mother Mary." I bought four roses for her, two pink and two white, and put them in my room. Then I felt that God wanted me to record everything, so I wrote down what was happening to me on a calendar and started writing in a journal every day. My faith was growing, and I started getting the desire to read the Bible. I had a little pocket New Testament, so I started to read its tiny writing every day. I also started to memorize the rosary prayers, but to me, they were still just words. I didn't feel them in my heart. I felt Mary wanted me to say the rosary, so I did. It was something I could do for her.

When I was at the charismatic service, I had heard that angels like to pray for us, so I learned the Guardian Angel prayer and started saying it before I went to bed every night. Then, all of a sudden, I got the gift of joy. I started laughing a whole lot when I was in bed at night, and I couldn't stop. Something inside was filling me up with joy and causing me to giggle. It was a supernatural feeling, and I wasn't laughing at anything in particular.

For two years after that, I had an extreme gift of joy. I was always smiling and happy and talking about Mary.

Wow, that's a sin?

When the end of August came around, I had a feeling that I should sell my house. Now, I loved my house. I'd fixed it just the way I liked it and felt it was perfect for me, but I sensed God telling me, "It's time to sell your house," so I stopped cleaning my boyfriend's house and started packing up my own. "Why are you packing your house now?" my mom asked. "It takes time to sell a house." "I've got to clean it out now," I said. "If God wants me to sell the house, I know it will sell fast." I started bringing boxes over to my mother's house, and in September, I put the house up for sale. This was extremely painful for me, but I obeyed God.

In August I also decided that I wanted to become Catholic so I joined the R.C.I.A. [the Rite of Christian Initiation for Adults] program. When I learned about the sins of the flesh, I realized how lost I'd been, and I began thanking God every day, every single day, for saving me and changing my heart. Before R.C.I.A., I didn't know anything about the Bible, heaven, hell, or purgatory. I didn't realize that in the life I'd been leading, I'd had one foot in hell. When I'd gotten the abortion, I didn't know any better at the time. Finding out the truth was a painful process. A soul was meant to be born, and I didn't give it that chance. I was going to healing services, and maybe that helped me deal with it. I focused a lot on God's forgiveness.

I'm going to go to Medjugorje

I was still thinking to myself, "I'm going to go to Medjugorje" and sometimes said it spontaneously out loud. One day, when I was looking at a flyer about a Marian charismatic renewal conference coming up in October, I said, "I'm going to be in Medjugorje on the feast of the Holy Rosary." This just came out of my mouth, and I didn't even know when that feast day was. I told my mom, and she said, "Yeah, yeah, yeah. What day do you think you're gonna' leave?" "I should leave October 5th," I said. This date just came out of my mouth, too. Later, I happened to look at a calendar and saw that the feast of the Holy Rosary was on October 7th. Meanwhile, I hadn't made any arrangements to go, and it was already September. I looked through the flyer again, and I happened to see something that said, "Marian Messengers." I called their organization and asked if they knew about Medjugorje. They said, "We take people there, and we have a trip leaving on Oct 5th." "I'm supposed to be on that trip," I said. "Go ahead and book me."

My mom was shocked because the trip was on the same date that I said I was going to leave. Then my mother said, “I can’t believe you booked a trip without a passport.” “I’m telling you, mom,” I said, “Mother Mary wants me to go to Medjugorje so God will get me my passport.” I got my passport two days before I left. I had such faith. I don’t know where it came from. I was never worried.

Then I told my mother, “My house is going to sell before I go to Medjugorje.” My mom told me that houses don’t sell that fast.

“Yes, it is.” I said. “If God wants it to sell, it’s gonna sell. God wants me to sell my furniture, too,” I said—and I loved my furniture. “I’ll just include it in the price of the house.”

“People who buy houses don’t want furniture.”

“I’m telling you. Whoever buys this house will want the furniture, too, and I will be living with you by November 1st.”

My mom just didn’t know what to say at this point, except for, “Yeah, yeah, yeah.” Then she asked me, “What if they want to talk you down in price while you’re gone?”

“They’re going to buy my house and pay full price,” I answered. My house sold in one week. The people who bought it paid full price for the house. They wanted the furniture, and they wanted to live there by Oct 31st. Everything that I said was happening.

I went to Medjugorje just after the house sold, and I didn’t want to come home. I loved it there and felt like I belonged. Everyone prayed the rosary wherever I went. Everyone went to Mass. I remember how packed the church there was, how patient and loving the priests were, and how helpful people were as they helped each other up Cross Mountain and Apparition Hill. And I remember how peaceful it was.

In Medjugorje I felt that I should go to the confessional and confess all my sins from my life. I told the priest that I wasn’t a Catholic but that I was in the R.C.I.A. program, and he was patient and kind to me. Later on that day, he even invited me to join up with his tour group and give a testimony because he knew some of the girls in his group also had problems with their fathers; so I shared my testimony, and he told me afterwards that it helped them.

It rained every day I was there, so our pilgrimage group didn’t go up Cross Mountain or Apparition Hill. I decided to climb up each of them by myself, in the rain. I even slept on Cross Mountain the whole night, and I had this crazy idea that Jesus might visit me. Someone walked up the hill in the middle of the night, and I thought it might be him, so I screamed and I startled the poor person. He definitely wasn’t Jesus. Just three months after my conversion, I was sleeping on top of a mountain, across the world, in the rain, in a country where the Blessed

Mother is appearing, wondering if Jesus would show up.

After going to Confession and spending the night on Cross mountain, I felt so much love in my heart that I wanted to do penance, so I walked down the mountain barefoot. I walked thinking about Jesus and how he walked carrying the cross. I wanted to feel a little of the pain that he felt.

When I came back from Medjugorje I was inspired to teach everyone the rosary, to pray it more and to talk about it. Mother Mary says in her messages to us, "Pray, pray, pray," and I wanted to pray, pray, pray. If she keeps telling us this, obviously we don't get it yet.

Something supernatural was happening

On Thursday, Friday and Saturday, January 4th, 5th, and 6th, in 2001, I went on a Cursillo retreat weekend and finally fell in love with Jesus. The friend I'd met at the charismatic prayer group invited me to the retreat, which is like a short course in Christianity. It's an encounter with Jesus and a chance to know him better. You could see Jesus in everyone else there. It was wonderful.

Before then, I knew I was to love Jesus before all else, but I didn't know how. Even though I often looked at the picture of the Sacred Heart of Jesus and told him I loved him, I didn't feel love.

When I went on the weekend, I didn't feel anything powerfully happen until after a healing service they had. Then I sensed Jesus tap me on the shoulder, and in my heart I felt him say, "You know how you think about your boyfriend all the time? You know the love that you have for your boyfriend, the way you always want to please him, make him happy, do nice things for him? I want you to love me that way." Then it hit me. Jesus died on a cross for me. At that moment, realizing how much he loved me, how much he loves us all, I responded back with great love. And the peace that he always said he'd give . . . I felt that peace. Jesus healed my hardened heart. After that, whenever I thought about Jesus, I was happy. When I thought about my boyfriend, I didn't feel that way.

When you love somebody, you want to be around them all the time, so I started going to a Roman Catholic Mass everyday because I wanted to hear through the Scripture readings what Jesus had to say. What drew me were the Gospel readings from the New Testament because I was hearing God's Word, and the homily which helped me live it. Everything I heard, like "Love one another," or "Forgive your enemies," I tried to go out and live. Now when I hear God's Word, it still brings me such joy.

Jesus had entered my heart, and after that, he was always on my mind. I talked about him all the time and told people, "Jesus loves you. Jesus loves you."

Just after the Cursillo retreat, I decided to read a book I'd bought there called "True Life in God" by Vassula Ryden. When I opened the book, I felt good energy flow through it and through my hands. I felt like I was supposed to read it and that everything in it was true. I was so hungry to learn from Jesus and be with him that I stayed up reading until 3:15 in the morning. I felt him saying to me through the prayers in the book that he loved me and wanted me to work for him. I agreed and told him that I would do anything he asked of me. I told him I would surrender my will to him.

Then I fell asleep, and about twenty minutes after I closed my eyes, I felt electricity run through my entire body. I felt scared and thought I was being electrocuted. I knew that if I opened my eyes it would stop, so I kept them closed because I had faith that something supernatural was happening. I heard a lot of ringing in my ears and a jolt of electricity in my head, and then, with the eyes of my soul, I saw a figure in front of me, at the foot of my bed. I couldn't make out any details, but I knew who it was. "Mother Mary!" I called out. "It's really you! I see you. I love you. You came to visit me. I'm so happy." My soul recognized her easily. She was very familiar to me. Then I felt the electricity more powerfully, and I could feel and hear in my head a loud sound and a vibration that literally felt like a tape rewinding.

I saw images of people in my head. They were laughing and having a good time, like they were at a party, but I didn't recognize anybody. As the tape was rewinding, I didn't see anything of my life, although I half expected to.

Then Jesus appeared in the same place where Mother Mary had been, standing at the front of my bed. My soul recognized him, although I couldn't make out any details of his features. He extended his hand before me. I saw it clearly with my soul, a very large hand that he placed right in front of my face and over my head. Then I felt extreme heat on my face. I thought my face was on fire and burnt. This lasted seconds, but it was so painful! I thought that if I looked in the mirror at that time, I'd see a burnt face, so I didn't open my eyes. I just allowed my face to continue being burned. I thought that I was being purified by this burning vision in order to grow more holy, to be more like Jesus.

Then behind Jesus I saw a large, brown, wooden cross. The vision of the cross appeared to me and then went away, three times in a row.

After that, I didn't see or feel anything anymore. I just lay in my bed with my eyes closed, hoping to see something. I wanted it all to happen again. I didn't care what pain I went through. I wanted that supernatural feeling back. I waited and waited, but nothing happened, so I opened my eyes. I called my boyfriend and left the details on his machine and told him not to erase it, so I would remember my experience the next day. I knew it wasn't a dream.

I was so excited because Jesus and Mary had just visited me. The experience was something from heaven, and I couldn't stop thinking about it. I just kept saying, "I love you, Jesus. I love you, Mary. Whatever you want me to do, I'll do."

The next day, I couldn't wait to tell my mom and my brother. I just wanted to tell everybody, and I felt like I wanted to do even more for God—whatever he wanted. When I went to church for Mass, I couldn't hold in the news, so I ran to the priest, excited and out of breath, and told him about the vision and that I wanted to receive the Eucharist *now*—that I wanted to be Catholic *now*. I was already going through the R.C.I.A. program, but I didn't want to wait until Easter. I think he thought I was nuts, but he also said, "Let's see if there's any fruit from this." I cried through the Mass—I was still so excited.

I couldn't wait, so I wrote a letter to the cardinal and said, "I have a strong desire to receive Jesus. I feel Jesus wants me to receive him now. I feel Jesus talking to me when I am at Mass in the Roman Catholic Church, and I want to complete this feeling by receiving him. Since I feel at home in the Roman Catholic Church, and I do believe in the Pope, I would like to become a Roman Catholic as soon as possible."

On January 23, 2001, the archdiocese wrote a letter to the church where I was going to R.C.I.A. I still have it, it says, "I am pleased to inform you that permission is granted for you to be received into full communion with the Catholic Church as a member of the Latin Church in accord with Canon 32.2 of the Code of Cannons of the Eastern Churches."

On February 12th, 2001, I became Catholic. On that day at Saint Mary's Church, I stood up at Mass and said a profession of faith. In their bulletin they congratulated me on becoming a full member of their church. I was so happy. I felt like this was where I belonged.

I feel extreme joy

How I feel now doesn't compare to anything I've ever felt. I used to have so much anger that I clenched my fists during the day, but now

I have peace in my heart. I don't have hate for anybody, just love. I look for Jesus in people. I feel free as a butterfly. I never feel stress anymore. It's gone. Before I didn't trust anyone, and now I have a lot of Christian friends whom I can trust. Before I didn't know God, and now I'm in love with him. Before I never went to church, and now I go to daily Mass and love it.

Before my conversion I wouldn't even talk to my father. I am so thankful for God's graces that helped me to forgive him and to have a good relationship with him. My dad died on Halloween day, 2003. Now I can pray for my dad and have Masses said for him. I'm able to help get him out of purgatory and into heaven. Before I wouldn't have known how to help him or that I could even help him at all.

Before I wouldn't have anything to do with my dad's second family. Now I have a close relationship with them. My mother even gets along with his wife now, and everything is peaceful between our families. My mother was a non-practicing Catholic up until 2001, and now she goes to Mass with me every Sunday. My boyfriend, who is now just my friend, and who just recently started going to daily Mass, says, "I want to get married, and you're bringing me closer to God." But I don't have any desire at all for marriage or physical relations. All I want to do is be with Jesus.

I want to take care of the sick, the elderly and the dying. I do that now as a home health aid. I don't have the desire to take care of a husband and my own kids. There are so many people in need.

To be closer to Jesus, you have to carry a heavy cross, but I haven't received that yet. I don't think I have any crosses. I'm too happy—but I'll take whatever he gives me. The only thing that bothers me is when I look at the world. It saddens me because I see that people don't pray. They don't love God. We do things like go to war and kill each other over power, money and religion. I want people to just stop what they're doing. I want so much for others to know God. If it's going to take me to suffer for others, so be it. I'll do whatever God wants. I'll gladly be a nun if that's what he wants for me.

I focus on God all the time now. He's on my mind, on my lips, and in my heart. I'm constantly praising him. I go to Mass, say three rosaries, do Bible reading, spend time in Eucharistic adoration, pray the Divine Mercy Chaplet at 3 o'clock—and I fast on bread and water on Wednesdays and Fridays. This is what I feel God wants for me. Plus I tell him all day that I love him. When I'm doing all these things, I feel extreme joy.

We don't even know what makes us happy. We look for eternal joy, but nothing ever lasts. Jesus stays. His peace and fulfillment stays. It doesn't go away. It's what we've always desired. We're part of him, and we're not truly happy until we live in him, talk with him.

I have complete faith now in God. It's amazing to really feel faith and live it. Since my conversion I walk out of the house and say, "Ahhh, God's with me. I have nothing to worry about."

* * *

Dear children! Today in a special way I bring the little Jesus to you, that He may bless you with His blessing of peace and love. Dear children, do not forget that this is a grace which many people neither understand nor accept. Therefore, you who have said that you are mine, and seek my help, give all of yourself. First of all, give your love and example in your families. You say that Christmas is a family feast. Therefore, dear children, put God in the first place in your families, so that He may give you peace and may protect you not only from war, but also in peace protect you from every satanic attack. When God is with you, you have everything. But when you do not want Him, then you are miserable and lost, and you do not know whose side you are on. Therefore, dear children, decide for God. Then you will get everything. Thank you for having responded to my call.[23]

FATHER JOHN

God said, "Believe"

As a kid, I do not remember any profound prayer experiences or any call or interest in becoming a priest, but religion made sense to me. It was simply a part of life, like eating, sleeping, going to school—one of those things that we did as family. My parents were not overly pious, but very solid in their faith, and they lived with integrity what they believed. They taught me, my sisters and brother how to pray and made sure we went to Sunday Mass. I enjoyed going; at least, I don't recall ever putting up a fuss. At age thirteen, I joined a boy's choir at our church in Portland, Oregon. I joined not because I wanted to sing in church—I thought the boys looked like a bunch of sissies up there. When I first saw them in their ugly green robes, I thought, "I wouldn't be caught dead in those." I joined their choir because they got to go on a tour to Europe for a few weeks and came back with wonderful stories. I remember Father Vince, the pastor and choir director, who was Italian American but did not speak Italian, humbly admitting that when they first arrived in Italy, a guy suckered him into paying over thirty dollars for a watermelon. They were all still laughing about how he had been so ripped off. They had had a great time, and I wanted to have a great time, too, so I joined the choir.

That is how I was able to observe Father Vince, a young Franciscan priest, in his mid-thirties, directing the choir, presiding at Mass, and interacting with people. Father Vince had an infectiously joyful spirit, and through his joy, he brought a large, stodgy parish to life. Even though he seemed unorganized, very busy, and kind of chaotic, in the midst of that chaos I could sense that he was very much at peace. He was a great role model. He did not have what the world said you needed to be happy. He did not have his own money. He did not have a wife or a girlfriend. He did not have a flashy car or his own comfy house. Yet he was the most deeply fulfilled person I had ever met. He was also young, energetic, and musical like me. I could see myself in him. As I observed his joyful spirit and sense of deep peace and fulfillment, I thought, "That's what I want."

God worked through another event in my youth to call me into the priesthood. In high school, I went on a three-day "Search" retreat organized by CYO, Catholic Youth Organization, and was high on God for a full month afterwards. The retreat was directed by a layman who at one point asked us to write down all the many ways God had blessed us in our lives. As I wrote down my blessings, my list grew longer and longer. I was blown away by its length. Then, when he asked us to write down all the gifts and talents God had given us, I once again felt amazed by what God was doing in me and in my life because God had given me many natural abilities, nothing I had earned on my own. Finally the retreat leader said to us, "You see all the ways God has blessed you—with people and experiences, and all your God-given talents and abilities. Now write down how you're going to say thanks—how you're going to use all those blessings and talents. What are you going to do for God?" I began to think. Perhaps I could say thank you to God by becoming a priest.

One day I was thinking out loud and ran the idea of the Franciscan priesthood past my dad who was in his office in our home downstairs. I mentioned it to him casually as I was lounging around after school, and his first words were: "It is not a natural life." As he explained later, he had serious doubts that I would be content as a priest, and he wanted me to be happy.

I tentatively shared this idea of priesthood with various other people. No one said this explicitly, but the message I received was—if you can't do anything else with your life, then be a priest. I think that attitude is part of our modern age. My dad especially did not see why I should waste my talents on something that should be a last resort. I had always done well in school and been tops at math, and my dad is lousy at math. He could see that God had given me this natural gift, and here I was going to be one of those bozo Franciscans. He had trouble taking the Franciscans seriously. "If you're going to be a priest," he said at one point, "Why don't you do it right and become a Jesuit?" Part of my sureness about my vocation was that I was not at all pushed into it, and I was not a rebellious kid, so I did not say out of spite, "I'm gonna' be ordained, so there." It was Jesus who was calling me, not someone on the sidelines. I also approached Father Vince about my interest in becoming a priest. I wanted to ask his advice about what I should do to prepare for the priesthood because I was not involved in the Church other than going to Sunday Mass and singing in the choir. I expected he would recommend that I transfer to a Catholic high school, become an altar boy, go to a Catholic college and study religion, avoid dating, and get a job at the church or do religious work. But his advice was the opposite. His advice was to experience life as a normal young man, to stay at public school, to work, date, perhaps travel, and, meanwhile, to keep this idea of priesthood percolating in the back of my mind. Once I had my college degree, if I was still interested, then he would talk seriously with me. Surprised, I thought, "Heck, I can do that."

Ah-ha

I took his advice and did everything he said. One thing I did was to travel all over India. I spent two months working with the Missionaries of Charity in Calcutta as a way of testing my vocation. Working with the Missionary of Charity brothers was a marvelous experience, and while I realized I was not called to be an MC brother, it did reinforce my desire for religious life and fueled my growing interest in missionary work. Part of the Missionary brothers' routine in Calcutta is to go out once or twice a week and pick up people who are left to die on the streets, or people who have been taken advantage of because they are mentally disabled or deformed. There are a lot of beggar pimps in India. Here in the United States, pimps primarily work with female prostitutes, but in India, pimps often work with beggars who report back to them and give them most of what they have begged for. The pimps control the beggars through extortion. They are known to deliberately deform the beggars further so that they appear more pitiful and make more money that way. It is horrific. These are the kind of people that the brothers take care of by bringing them back to their compound, a small estate I believe someone had donated. When I was there, they took care of about 150 men and boys, all with severe mental and/or physical disabilities. The brothers' work is very similar to what a nurse's aid does in this country: they feed, bathe, and clothe the men and boys. They also give them lots of love and treat them as human beings. So I helped with this ministry.

The day after I arrived, as I walked by myself over to one of the houses in the compound where the brothers were feeding and bathing these men, a huge ogre of a man began walking towards me. I had never seen anyone like him before. He was a half-White, half-Indian mongoloid, a hulking ogre, tall and wide, sweaty and quite ugly, with teeth sticking out and feet that turned sideways, splaying wide as he walked forward with a kind of lurching waddle. On his face was a big smile, and as he came towards me, he reached out his arms to hug me. I froze up and stood there like a two-by-four—petrified. He came closer and closer, and I remained paralyzed. Then he embraced me with a big greasy hug. Remember, this was in hot and humid India where this huge, sweaty, grotesque stranger with bad breath squeezed me.

Finally he let go, and I was just grateful nothing more happened. I had survived and thought to myself, "Boy, I hope that never happens again." But the next day, guess who was there to greet me? My new friend! His crazy-toothed smile bigger than ever. I thought, "Well, here goes," and I held my breath, even managing a little hug back. Funny thing. After several days of this I actually started to look forward to his greeting. As time went on, I was even mildly disappointed on the occasional day when he was not waiting for me.

Some days after this first happened, I was praying and feeling very virtuous and proud of myself because my repulsion had faded, and I was now able to see the face of Christ in him. But something inside me did not sit right, and as I continued to think and pray, I started to feel that I was missing something. As I meditated more, I had a sudden flash of insight and realized that Christ was revealing himself to me in a deeper way. I was not the one to see the face of Christ in that ugly man. I was simply seeing reflected in his eyes what he was seeing—the face of Christ in me!

I was a complete stranger to him. I looked different, and I spoke a strange language. He had never seen me before, and yet he did not judge me. He simply reached out and embraced me. I received a great "Ah-ha!" moment in my spiritual journey. I had met Christ. He had made himself known to me in a very obvious, but unexpected way. I had been looking for Christ in Mother Teresa and the missionary brothers, and yet he came to me most powerfully in this ogre. Christ gave me a flash of insight into the way that he can reveal himself, and he gave me a lesson in focusing on the inner beauty of people.

This was my "leper experience." Just as Saint Francis of Assisi purposefully kissed and embraced a leper, I willingly began hugging this man who was, in all fairness, pretty disgusting looking. He was unbelievable.

I also learned from being in Calcutta that I could pray anywhere and everywhere. Each day, the brothers and I gathered together in a little apartment room converted into a chapel. And each day a disruptive din poured through the open windows, which had no glass because the brothers were too poor and India was too hot. Just outside those windows, streetcars clanged by, along with bleating herds of goats, shouting people, and rattling buses with no mufflers. In the midst of this clamor, we were able to pray. I learned to use the noise as a reminder of people to pray for. I still do this today. If I am praying, for instance, and someone cranks their rap music, which can have pretty ungodly lyrics, I begin to pray for any people who are misguided in the ways the songs speak of. The beat can still be annoying to me though—it depends on my day.

My experience in India confirmed my vocation and gave me the desire to work with the poor like Saint Francis of Assisi did. I could see myself living the religious life and grew more sure about my missionary vocation because the missionary brothers were so warm, fun, welcoming and cheerful, amidst conditions that might seem to others like hell. They were Christ-like, and I felt extremely inspired by what they were doing.

The place exuded so much peace

After India, I completed my last year of studies for my English degree at the University of Oregon. During my five-plus years of college, I did a lot of dating, and generally my best friends were women, but because I felt pretty sure I wanted to be a priest, I thought it would show a lack of integrity and be unfair to a young woman to get too committed. What if someone fell in love with me? So I (or God) never let that happen, not seriously. There were, of course, times in college when I doubted my vocation. One of these times, when I was in my early twenties, I went into the Newman Center chapel on campus, knelt down and prayed for God to help me with my discernment. Suddenly I burst into tears. I had not cried since I was about ten. I knew that the tears came from God because they came with a message so strong and piercing that it reverberated throughout my whole being. God, I sensed, was reassuring me that I should continue pursuing a priestly vocation.

When school ended, I joined Up With People and spent a marvelous year of travel with college-age people from all over the world. We put on a big song and dance show and did community service in each place we visited. After this tour ended, I had all sorts of adventurous travel ideas about what to do next—to sign on for another year or two with Up With People, to work with the peace corps or another service organization, to simply travel around to other exotic countries...why not? I was young and free, travel was cheap, and I was sure all these life experiences would come in handy down the road. But in the months following my Up With People tour, I had a strong sense in my prayer of God saying to me, "You could diddle away a lot of years of your life, but it's time to get on with your vocation." I chose to listen and trust that call, and I gave up my travel plans. At age twenty-six, I decided to join the Franciscans.

In my first year with the Franciscans—a year called the pre-novitiate, I got my first taste of Franciscan life, observing the lives of five priests and brothers, praying with the community, and working part time in the parish as a youth minister. Along with the Franciscans, I lived with a diverse group of pre-novitiate young men. We shared our spiritual journeys and how we wanted to live the Franciscan life. Old Brother Joe kept the home fires burning with his gentleness and inspiring stories particularly of how he entered the Franciscans with great difficulty. This encouraged us to stick it out.

When I joined the Franciscans, I was told that if I had any money saved up, not to give it all away just yet because I might find after my first several months of pre-novitiate that the Franciscan Order was not for me. "If you have some money," they said, "save it for a while. Then if you decide to take vows, you can always dispose of it later." I had a few thousand dollars saved, and I decided I would like to use it to go on a spiritual pilgrimage. So, in 1989, I decided to spend a week in Rome because it was the center of the Church, a week in Assisi because it was the home of Saint Francis and where the Franciscan Order began, and a week in Medjugorje because Mary was supposedly appearing there, and I was intrigued. I wanted to see it all for myself.

I traveled on this pilgrimage with a young woman, Caren, who was interested in becoming a sister. I had met her on a vocation retreat. First we traveled to Rome where we saw the Coliseum, the Pantheon and a number of beautiful churches, and where I had the privilege of meeting the Minister General of the Franciscans. Then we traveled to the beautiful town of Assisi, which I loved, and we visited the cobbled streets and countryside where Saint Francis had walked. From there we went to Medjugorje, which turned out to be the most profoundly spiritual place for both of us.

To get to Medjugorje, we took an all night ferry ride from Italy and then rode a bus through picturesque Yugoslavian terrain, along hairpin turns and blind corners, and I figured if we arrived in one piece it would be by the grace of God. People on our bus could not decide whether or not to have the windows up or down, because if the windows were up, the heat was sweltering, and if they were down, dust came rolling in. On our bus, I met a family from the States, a man and wife accompanied by their daughter who had just graduated from high school. The wife wanted to go to Medjugorje, the daughter came along because she had just received her graduation present—the chance to see Italy, and the father was accompanying them to make his wife happy, but he did not take Medjugorje seriously.

We arrived in time for the anniversary of the apparitions, so when we came into town, things looked completely chaotic. Medjugorje, previously a peaceful little hamlet, was now choked with buses and tents and cars and people. It looked ripe for unrest, with people piled on top of one another in hot buses, with dust blowing through the air, with only a couple paved roads at that time, not enough bathrooms, horrendous traffic, and nowhere to park. We found ourselves amidst heat and sweat, with chickens and cows wandering around, among swarms of people from all over the world speaking different languages, in a town completely ill-equipped to handle so many pilgrims. It looked like a turbulent recipe for major misunderstandings, accidents and flaring tempers. But the place exuded so much peace. It did not make any sense.

That first evening, we walked into the town church, Saint James, which was packed with people praying the rosary. I remember walking forward a ways down what was left of the center isle, and in the midst of all the hubbub and confusion, feeling so much serenity. There, in that church, I felt the power of the Holy Spirit, fully present. Amidst a crowded situation, which should have been terribly chaotic, in a hot place where strangers sat packed together in the pews, while others came and went, all were blanketed with an incredibly profound spirit of peace. I am not very charismatic, but when I walked into Saint James Church, I dropped to my knees and stayed on them, overwhelmed for a very long time.

It became clear to me during my week in Medjugorje that Mary was appearing there. Twice, she appeared to a visionary in a public apparition, and when this happened, I was near the apparition sight on Apparition Hill and again felt a divine peace mixed with a collective excitement. I also saw two miraculous phenomena on two other days of our stay. One afternoon, I could look right at the sun—without squinting, with my eyes completely open, and my face completely relaxed. People who had described this Medjugorje occurrence to me generally talked about seeing the sun spinning, but to me it looked more like a vibrating, even bobbling, illuminated, glowing host. When this happened, Caren and I were walking along a roan with several other groups of people, and I found it interesting that some of us could see it, and some of us could not. Caren could not even look up at the sun because it was so bright, and I consider her a more fervent Christian than myself. This did not ruin her day, though, because she could sense the excitement in the group; people were pointing to the sky and excitedly commenting to one another about the miracle. I looked at the sun for several seconds and looked away a couple of times, but every time I looked back, it was still bobbling. I stared comfortably into that host-like sun for a long time and didn't go blind. That was fourteen years ago, and I still have 20/20 vision.

On our last night there, Mary again appeared on Apparition Hill. I did not go up the hill with many of the other pilgrims to be near the apparition site. Instead, I stayed inside. At the time of the apparition, a lightning storm struck which I could view from the balcony where I was staying. I decided to run outside to better see the storm, and when I looked up, I witnessed lightning coming down in many different colors, all over the sky—an amazing and incredibly beautiful sight. Something miraculous was obviously happening, although it looked natural, i.e. it was supernatural but not bizarre. But of course the real miracle was Mary's appearance and God's abiding presence. The lightning, I felt, was merely God's afterthought. With both the miracle of the sun and the lighting, I didn't feel surprised. I remember thinking, "If Mary is really appearing here, then of course the universe is going to acknowledge that."

For me, the most powerful sign of the authenticity of Mary's presence and the Spirit at work in Medjugorje was the conversions that were happening. The conversion that most impressed me happened to the man I had met on the bus ride in. He was the successful businessman type, and he was only there because his wife had been keen on visiting Medjugorje and had connived him and their daughter into accompanying her. During the bus trip he had spent his time rolling his eyes, pooh-poohing the whole thing, throwing doubtful glances at his wife, and questioning her sanity. Well, I ran into them some days later, and now the picture was reversed. His wife and daughter were looking at him with bemused wonder as he preached to anyone who would listen about how Mary had turned his life around and about the importance of prayer and repentance. He was on fire. He had experienced his personal Pentecost and could not stop sharing the Good News with everybody.

Conversions such as his (and they were all around), the fervency with which ordinary people were praying, the long lines of people going to confession day and night in all languages, the good will and incredible sense of peace in what should have been a riot... in the end, these were the most powerful signs of Mary's presence, and the supernatural surprises were incidental. Medjugorje is one of the experiences I can go back to if I am having doubts about my faith, or if I am feeling down, because I know God was there.

One might think I would have returned from Medjugorje just as on fire as that man, but my response was more of cautious wonder. I can say that while I did not turn into a Pentecostal for Mary, a seed had been planted deeply in me. Thanks to Medjugorje, I began praying the rosary more faithfully and made a promise to Mary that I would pray it every day, though a good half-year passed before it became an integral part of my daily prayer. When reciting the rosary became stale and mechanical, when I resented the promise I had made, I decided to give it a rest and try opening up some other "prayer windows."[24] I think, at the time, it was a good thing, a natural part of spiritual growth. I am at a different place now, more settled and mature, and the rosary has simply become part of my day, like meals and work and rest. I try to pray it first thing in the morning, but if that does not work out, I will pray it swimming laps and biking, or while driving or riding the subway. I am not alone in this habit. I was just reading about a bishop who prays it while exercising on the Nordic Trak. The rosary for me is a stabilizing part of the day's rhythm. It grounds me. If I do not pray it sometime during the day, I miss it.

In the middle of rich people

Despite the high after my spiritual pilgrimage and a positive pre-novitiate year with the Franciscans, I felt slightly distressed over entering into the novitiate. I worried it would be hard to live as a humble brother because of the way the people responded to me as a Franciscan; I did not have a habit, I had not made a vow, I was just living with other Franciscans, and already people were treating me as though I were special. Part of my attraction to the Franciscans was my fantasy of being a humble brother and not being in a position of authority and great influence. I wanted to work on the grassroots level with people, not over people.

Because I felt an intimacy with God and in touch with the wonder of God's creation when I went hiking, I decided to hike along the Columbia gorge dividing Oregon and Washington and meanwhile complained to God about not wanting to be in a position of power as a Franciscan. I had deliberately not joined the Jesuits or joined a diocese because I did not want to be a mover and a shaker, and now people were giving me privileges and power that I did not want. I thought I should just give up religious life and live simply as a layperson. As I was hiking along the trail, I had an experience in which Jesus spoke to me very precisely, not in words, but with spiritual clarity, and Jesus' answer was another question: "So many people in the world abuse power, oppress people with power, and use power for violent means, and are you now going to avoid the opportunity to use power in a life-giving way?" I reluctantly responded, "Okay, I see your point."

Jesus wasted no time answering my question, and he also clarified an important aspect of my religious vocation.

After that little chat with Jesus confirming that I should continue to pursue the priesthood, I entered the novitiate, a year of intense vocational discernment. Overall, it was a lousy year. I ended up in Santa Barbara, California, which I found completely uninspiring because I liked natural beauty, and Santa Barbara was full of manicured beauty. I wanted to be a poor Franciscan. The year before, the novitiate house had been in East Los Angeles, in a mixed neighborhood, with gang shootings and the like as part of the normal routine. I had been looking forward to gritty adventure in the inner city, and instead, I was surrounded by movie stars and coffee shops. It was the antithesis of my idea of living in poverty among marginalized people. "This isn't what it is supposed to be about," I thought. I had been brought up in the comfortable middle class and was trying to simplify my life. Instead, I got plopped down in the middle of rich people. Some of my brothers in the novitiate saw the spiritual impoverishment of the rich who can be so insulated, lonely, and unable to see God because they are surrounded by so much stuff. But I could not see beneath the artificial landscapes and superficial lifestyles; I just spent my time sulking and stewing over the stagnation of my own spirit. I was being immature. I was not getting what I wanted. I wanted an inner-city experience. I could have gotten a lot out of that year, but I wasted it by being a baby.

My only redeeming times during my novitiate year were a couple months spent at Mission San Antonio, where I helped prune olive trees in a more primitive and contemplative atmosphere, and a couple months in the Southwest spent in Topawa, Arizona, a small village on the Tohono O'odham Reservation. There I lived simply among the Tohono O'odham Indians, surrounded by the natural beauty of the desert. The pace of life was slower. I took long walks and runs through the desert, sometimes with a few O'odham kids tagging along on their bicycles. I helped repair our roof in the blazing sun, and I got to know a few of the Indians.

My novitiate ranked as one of my worst years, but the time I spent in Topawa was graced even though one of my best friends decided to leave about half way through those two months. One day there, when I was talking with a sister named Sister Carla, I complained that it seemed like God was not giving me the kind of struggles that a lot of other people had. I felt too sheltered and babied by God. "When I look at my life," I told her, "I wonder if I should ask God for more challenges—if there's something I am not doing right." She said, "No, trust God and don't worry. Your time will come. Don't feel like you have to ask for struggles because they will happen. Enjoy your life here. Take this as a time of spiritual strengthening and grace." Then I felt a little more at peace about it. She also felt that she had not experienced the kind of tragedies that befell others, but she was finding a lot of joy in life and fulfillment in her vocation. "I think of myself as one of God's spoiled brats," she told me.

I co-opted her phrase. Looking around me, I realized that, actually, I was one of God's spoiled brats, too. I was not feeling that way at the time, but I knew it was true. I had enough perspective to realize that, although I had legitimate reasons to sulk, my complaints were very trivial compared with the trials of others. Seeing the Indians on the reservation put my petty sufferings into perspective. There, I witnessed a lot of funerals, depression from unemployment, complications from diabetes, and death from alcoholism. My perspective changed from one of resentment to gratitude. I remembered that Saint Francis was by and large joyful, and so was Father Vince, and I wanted to be like them. I also knew from past experiences that life was often a matter of perspective.

I thought back to when I was in high school, working summers in a nursing home, and aside from having to be inside, I considered it a great job. Others said to me, "How can you work there? It is so depressing, it smells like urine, all those old people dying, I don't know how you can stand it." But I did not focus on those things. Instead, I cherished the moments of human kindness and the opportunity to care for people who had amazing stories because they lived in another century. Focusing on the good there came naturally to me and made my experience beautiful.

Anyway, fast forward again to the novitiate. Although I was still trying to concentrate on the good and see my life as a glass half full, not half empty, I felt my novitiate had been overall a lousy deal. I told my provincial, "Based on this experience, I wouldn't want to commit to Franciscan life. I am asking your permission to continue, but only because I believe this past year can't possibly be representative of normal Franciscan life. It's got to get better." The provincial's response was to extend my novitiate for another six months, and shortly afterward he sent me to work with the Apaches in Whiteriver, Arizona in order to give me an experience that resonated more with what I felt I was called to do.

I wanted to do missionary work

On the White Mountain Apache Reservation, I prayed for God to make it clear to me whether I should continue with the Franciscans, and I had that prayer answered. Father Ed and Brother Tony, the two Franciscans with whom I lived there, understood my rather independent missionary spirit, being missionaries themselves. They inspired me with their prayer life, their sense of community, and their love and service among Apaches. They did things together like fishing, and rejoiced in these simple pleasures, thanking God for fresh air, beautiful mountains, autumn leaves, and a meal of fresh tasty trout. They were just very balanced and healthy, very down to earth, and also very holy men. So I felt at peace. It was easy and natural to talk about fishing, and it was easy and natural to talk about God. Living with the friars among the Apaches salvaged my Franciscan vocation.

From there, I spent a semester at the Franciscan seminary in Berkeley, California and started sulking again because I wanted to do missionary work. I tenaciously argued for permission to be part of a new formation experience and live in Guatemala for a year, and they let me go. There, while I often felt at sea during my first several months and struggled to learn the language, I made some great friends among the Guatemalans and drew inspiration from the Franciscans who thrived and worked with people in the ghetto, living very simply themselves.

That year fulfilled me in terms of ministry, prayer life, and community. Among the friends I made, I was "adopted" by a Guatemalan family that treated me like one of their own. They were very fun, they told me jokes, and they loved me.

One of my favorite pictures from that time was taken when the family and I were praying the Stations of the Cross, walking down muddy alleys past houses patched together with tin and cardboard, pausing to meditate on each of the fourteen stations of Jesus' Passion. The stations were simple depictions of the events on Jesus' road to Calvary, homemade by each family, and set up in front of or inside their little shacks. In the photograph, I am carrying in my arms the youngest girl, Melanie, who was about four years old, and she is clinging to me, just as she did through the whole thing—from Jesus' condemnation, to his falling under the weight of the cross, to his crucifixion and burial. The picture is of our faces together, cheek to cheek, looking at the camera. The image is rather haunting, perhaps because I was meditating not only on the passion of Jesus but on the passion of the Guatemalan people. Walking down those little muddy tracks in the midst of horrendous poverty, the people were walking not just the Stations of the Cross, but their own lives.

What can I believe now?

I had such an extraordinary experience in Guatemala that I did not want to come back to seminary. The seminary environment was so different from what I had experienced there and with the Apaches. I am forever grateful to my first spiritual director who told me, "Satan works hardest in the seminaries." Satan knows, he said, that if he can derail people who are being trained to be Christian leaders, then he can bring others down with them. "Be on guard for this is going to happen. He's going to try to confuse you and discourage you and derail your religious vocation." He was very clear, and he did not mince words. I heard and understood what he said and felt grateful for it. "If I were Satan," I thought, "I would do the same thing."

When I came back to seminary, I started to sulk again. It took a few months for me to realize that I was actually very angry because I wanted to be back in Guatemala; and Berkeley was somewhat similar to Santa Barbara; it was exclusive, wealthy, and I felt that some of my professors had an elitist attitude. We were living much more comfortably than we had in Guatemala, and I felt uncomfortable with that. Seminary was also a time of faith crisis, as my childhood faith exploded in Christology and Scripture classes. My spiritual director was right. It seemed that the very fundamentals of my faith were being undermined and called into question. I could no longer just say that something was true because Sister Rose Ann said so in fourth grade CCD[25] classes. My childhood faith was not holding up under adult scrutiny. At times I felt my most dearly held beliefs being blown apart. But finally I decided that no matter how clever my professors were, or how subtle their arguments, nothing could change my concrete experiences of Jesus. In the midst of my debilitating doubts, I reminded myself that I had personally experienced Jesus Christ—in Calcutta, in Medjugorje, in nature. Those remembrances helped me through my darkest, most painful hours when I felt everything had fallen apart. No amount of clever argumentation could take my experiences away from me, because they were real, and through them I knew Jesus was real.

I know people who left the seminary after their childhood faith had been shattered, and they did not come back. Many of them never recovered and became spiritually lost or ambivalent. I have seen this happen in my own family. That is why I believe a little bit of theology can be dangerous. After the initial assault, I had to follow through with seminary, stick with it for a while, confront my doubts and rebuild and strengthen my faith into something that could weather these challenges. Theology isolated from spirituality is dangerous, too. Without prayer, one can learn theology and lose God.

I prayed, and what was initially bitter became sweet. My awful doubts actually strengthened my faith. Seminary annihilated my simplistic childhood beliefs, but it helped me to build a mature adult faith that could handle questions about suffering, death, and evil—a faith that I could carry with me the rest of my life. By the end of my seminary experience, I was very grateful for it. I felt well prepared, and I was even able to come to peace with living in a privileged environment. The questions raised in my classes were questions others would challenge me with in my ministry. In retrospect, I am glad I was forced to wrestle with all those doubts, but at the time, they really turned me inside out.

Prayer was what got me through the first couple years of seminary. I avoided watching T.V. and prayed in the chapel every night, often after midnight, and just sat in the dark. I brought to God whatever struggles I had endured that day and ask him to help me through the next. That was the most important thing I did.

Believe

After two years of seminary, I received another experience of God that re-confirmed my faith; God dipped his finger into my life in a very concrete way.

I was given permission to explore a missionary vocation in Thailand. My first three months spent in Bankok went well. I was learning Thai and building a close friendship with my superior, one of the five Franciscans serving in that part of Thailand. He sometimes shared with me some of his difficulties with friars past and present who were working in Thailand, so as a show of courtesy and trust, I decided to share with him my director's most recent evaluation from my last year in seminary at Berkeley—a rather critical evaluation which pointed out my weaknesses in community life, specifically my independent spirit. Maybe because I am self-critical, I thought the evaluation was pretty fair. I had not been happy in Berkeley, and I was not surprised that others commented on it. I had been working through a faith crisis, carrying a full load of theology, and studying Thai. Disgruntled and overloaded, I hadn't been very present to the other Franciscans in the community.

My superior read my evaluation, and his response was that if he had seen my evaluation before I came, he would have told me to not even bother coming. "From the looks of it," he said, "I have doubts that you're even going to be continuing as a Franciscan." He turned off the tap on our friendship, and suddenly I lost my fraternal support. During the second three months of my stay, when I lived out in the rice fields in Lamsai and spent time talking with AIDS patients and meeting the brothers there, I did not have a good friend anymore, and that made things hard. In addition, I did not feel I was a good fit for Thai culture and did not think my gifts were being used. Several weeks before it came time to leave, I felt very strongly that I probably would not come back to Thailand because I had no desire to be there. I was spinning my wheels and counting the days.

One evening when I was sitting in chapel, trying to do a little private prayer, but actually spacing out and unfocused, suddenly out of nowhere I heard the word, "Believe." This was the one time in my life that I actually heard Jesus' voice. All at once, I felt thoroughly consoled. I knew it was his voice, and I also knew what it meant. Jesus was asking me to put my life in his hands, to trust him completely with the rest of my time in Thailand, and in fact, with the rest of my life. With that one word, he was saying, "Believe in me. If you really believe in me, let go of your worries about the future, trust that I am with you, trust that I have a plan for you, and I will work everything out. Just believe!" I felt incredible peace and the deep joy that comes from being loved fully and unconditionally. I knew Jesus really was alive and with me. It is almost impossible to put into words what I experienced. I felt a spiritual sensation that was ecstatic and also very calm and present to the moment. It opened my heart and transformed my perception of reality from grainy black and white into vivid color.

When I heard Jesus say, "Believe," nothing changed, and yet everything changed. My situation had not changed at all, yet my perspective had been completely transformed, which made my last few weeks in Thailand delightful. His word had lifted all of my stress, doubts and regrets about coming to Thailand. "Whatever happens," I thought, "Jesus is here with me," and I felt at peace. I knew on a whole new level that the life of Jesus Christ was real, not just an interesting ancient story, but the story of the Son of God who is as present and relevant to us today as he was 2000 years ago. I could accept each day and each moment and not dwell on what should be different, or worry about what might come next, but be thankful for the blessings of the present. That second of grace has become another core experience that I can always return to in my moments of doubt. It was as real as anything that I could see or touch. I know that word and that moment will stay with me the rest of my life.

My review was gutwrenching

When I returned to seminary, I felt very grateful for my time in Thailand but told my provincial that I did not sense that Thailand was the best fit for me; however, if they wanted to send me back there, I would go with my whole heart. During those next several months, I felt I was doing very well as a Franciscan. It seemed that the criticism of me before pointed to my being out of balance—too independent, too focused on academics, and not focused enough on the community; but now I was finally learning to integrate and balance my studies with my spiritual life, social life, and community life.

When I received my next evaluation, it shocked me completely. I thought I had been doing better than ever as a friar; and it said that, in fact, I was doing worse than ever. My joyful, peaceful perspective collapsed, and I was overwhelmed with shock, anger, confusion and sadness. I had been thinking and dreaming about the Franciscans since I was sixteen. I had been a Franciscan for six and a half years, and now everything was falling apart. That was the lowest point in my life. I shut down emotionally. Different brothers tried to console me and give me a sense of perspective, telling me I was a great brother and friend, but I was in too much of a funk to really listen to them and just made excuses for what they were saying. I figured they were only trying to console me.

I received my evaluation in 1995 just before Lent began, and part of my frustration came from the fact that my formation director was gone all through Lent. By the time he returned, I felt so angry and depressed that I didn't want to talk about what had happened. I had gone into survival mode, and I didn't think I could talk to him rationally at that point. I had convinced myself that my dream of being a Franciscan priest was a big mistake, that I had been blind to the reality of who I was and who the Franciscans were. I figured I had been living in a fantasy world, that I did not understand the Franciscan life, and that, very likely, I should look for a community where I better fit.

I had already planned to spend the summer away in Spokane, Washington doing C.P.E., clinical pastoral education, to learn about hospital chaplaincy and thought I could spend the time to heal and gain some perspective. I saw two possibilities: one, to leave the

Franciscans and look into a missionary order; or two, to fortify myself enough psychologically to return to the Franciscan seminary and bulldoze my way through my last year of formation. ("De-formation" I was calling it.)

As it turned out, the C.P.E. program was so intense in its own right that I didn't have the time or emotional energy to process what I had gone through after my evaluation. By the end of the summer, I realized there was no way I could come back and function. I figured I was a round peg in a square hole and felt it was time to move on and find an order that could better nurture my missionary vocation. So I let my vows expire and left the Franciscans, trying not to burn bridges, but sure this was good-bye.

Go back

I went away to Kettle Falls, Washington for one year and worked in a grocery store. I had a regular schedule, lived alone and had no homework or outside responsibilities, all of which gave me the luxury to think, pray, journal, and dialogue with God. The time away helped me to gain perspective and to feel good about myself again and about my vocation to the priesthood. And I had a new dream. I wanted to become a priest with the Maryknoll Missionary Society, and soon made contact with their vocation director. I talked with him on the phone, met him in Seattle a couple times, traveled to New York and met a bunch of Maryknoll missionaries, even went to Guatemala for a couple weeks with them. We were in regular contact over the next year and a half, and my mind became convinced that Maryknoll was the way I should go. I also found out that it would simplify my entry into Maryknoll if I completed my Master of Divinity degree since I only had one year left. So I went back to the Franciscan School as a layman. It was a fun year, my best year as a student. I had time to hang out with the other students, and my schedule was my own since I was not constrained by community schedules and events. I graduated, which brought me great relief, and now I was ready to join Maryknoll.

But when I had the forms to send in to actually apply for admittance, I heard my heart whispering that I should consider giving the Franciscans one more chance. I felt a little annoyed. I told God I did not want to spend the next ten years of my life looking into different orders, and I did not think that he wanted that either, and so I prayed a very specific prayer: "God, tell me quickly and clearly what you want me to do—to either go forward with Maryknoll or some other outfit, or to come back to the Franciscans. Whatever it is, I want to get on with my life and not waste my time here."

Several weeks later, as I was running across the Fruitvale Bridge in Oakland, I received a sudden flash of illumination. It was not a voice, an image, or a word, but a split second of sublime peace and clarity through which God was communicating "Go back with the Franciscans." "Okay," I replied and had absolutely no doubts as to what I should do. I then talked with one of the Franciscan friars and said that I had been planning to go to Maryknoll, but I was feeling drawn back to the friars. He told me, "Well, how about if I arrange for you to live at our friary in Oakland, California for a few months on probation, and we'll see how it goes?" I accepted.

After my experience on the bridge, I let go of any worries. My vocation to the Franciscans was in God's hands. I still needed to work through forgiveness, and it took me about six years to come to it. I did not feel ready for it, but I finally decided that I needed to forgive anyway if I was going to move on. "I have to do this," I told myself. "I'm tired of holding a grudge." Part of my unwillingness to forgive was tied to my unwillingness to forgive myself for my stupidity, naiveté, loss of perspective, and self-centered navel-gazing in my reaction to the evaluation and in my decision to leave. I think true forgiveness always involves forgiving oneself, too. And I suppose my unwillingness to forgive God for all that had happened also delayed the process, because if I were God, I would have worked out things more comfortably for me. "Okay God," I'd say to him, "I know you have to teach me some things, but do you have to teach them to me this way?"

After I finished my time on probation, I went back into simple vows and continued to live in Oakland while working with the homeless in San Francisco at Saint Anthony's Foundation. After a year there, I was transferred to Tularosa, New Mexico to do music and youth ministry. Two years later, I was sent to a parish in Tucson, Arizona where I served as a deacon and later as a newly ordained priest. From there, I was sent to live and work on the Mescalero Reservation among the Apaches. In each of these places I felt greatly privileged to serve the people, and I felt the grace of God in my life. This was what I was meant to do.

I truly am God's spoiled brat

I feel very grateful to be a priest. Even my dad who was initially discouraging is now openly enthusiastic "because obviously you're happy." (He also likes to joke, "Of all my kids, the one who's the most financially solvent has the vow of poverty!") My life has evened out in the past few years, and lately I have been feeling like God's spoiled brat again. I am up for a good challenge. Now I am off to Siberia where I will not know the language, or the culture or anyone there—only fifteen Franciscans are spread out over all of Russia. God has given me a missionary spirit and a missionary heart. In my life as a Franciscan, I find myself in a different place almost every year, which means I am constantly saying "Goodbye" to people. So I have learned to focus on cherishing the time I have together with others, rather than bemoaning the fact that I have to leave. And knowing that we will see each other again, if not in this life, then in the next life, it is not really "Goodbye," it is always, "See you later." "Goodbye's" aren't that hard, if you really believe.

* * *

Dear children! Also today I call you to give thanks to God in your heart for all the graces which He gives you, also through the signs and colors that are in nature. God wants to draw you closer to Himself and moves you to give Him glory and thanks. Therefore, little children, I call you anew to pray, pray, pray and do not forget that I am with you. I intercede before God for each of you until your joy in Him is complete. Thank you for having responded to my call.[26]

CHRIS

A homosexual man's new life of courage

I began as the by-product of an adulterous relationship. And that is exactly how it felt for the most part of my early life: a leftover item, a misfit, something to be passed from home to home. If my father's story can be believed, I was almost aborted. My mother denies this. There was a long stretch of my life when I wished abortion had been my destiny.

I was two weeks old when my mother, through force of circumstances, gave me up and handed me over to my father. Although the surname appearing on my birth certificate is my mother's, dad took responsibility for me and legally adopted me.

In retrospect, I am glad I never grew up in my mother's home. The sight of me would have been a constant reminder to her husband of the betrayal he had suffered from his wife and closest mate. It could have been an unbearable childhood at his hands.

There were no scanners in those times, so my gender remained a mystery until birth, but during my term in the womb I believe my mother's husband was constantly saying he hoped I was a girl. His idea of a perfect family was "one boy and one girl, and they already had a young son. Experts in spiritual healing say that the stresses and sins of the parents can have a psychological impact upon the baby's development, that their expressed thoughts and desires during pre-birth formation can even affect gender identification, so I am left wondering about that. Gender confusion has played a large part in my life journey.

Dad eventually found it impossible to raise me with the help of live-in housekeepers, so I became the Hand Me Down Kid. Before I turned ten years old I had gone through six foster homes. All the stand-in mummies and daddies who offered to take care of me soon realized that, although I looked the picture of an angel, they'd inherited a problem child, a real little handful, precocious, gifted, a fair little devil. For no reason ever properly explained to me, I was hurriedly and regularly shuffled sideways to newer pastures.

From time to time in my childhood I woke up crying during the night, and was never really sure why. Through my teenage years I was repeatedly accused of being sullen or moody, but, really, I had trouble verbalizing my thoughts and recognizing feelings. I'd learned to burrow away inside myself because adults didn't like the real me when they saw him. Winston Churchill's "black dog" of depression became my deadliest enemy, overshadowing much of my adolescence. Often disguised, never recognized, the black dog crept up on me and offered frequent notions of ending it all.

There's a photo of myself at thirteen where I look utterly dejected, a real "misery guts" as someone nicknamed me. The only thing which saved me from abject loneliness was a special friendship with a very macho boy who lived around the corner from me. I met Tony while potato picking during the school holidays, and although he was three years my junior, he seemed more mature in many ways and most advanced in the science of pursuing and chatting up girls. He was solid, blond-haired, of Swedish descent, and had the looks to go with the personality. Before long Tony and I became inseparable. I grew close to his large Catholic family as well, and his mother looked on me as her "other son." Tony taught me how to have better dress sense, the latest hairstyle, more pride in my appearance, and the discos became our happy hunting grounds where he coached me in his methods of picking up girls with sweet-talk and funny lines. I had several girlfriends. But I was play-acting. It was him whom I adored. I thrived in Tony's company, felt so comfortable with him. We would open our hearts to one another, talk about the most private things, while also joking and being silly. I liked being crammed into the couch beside him, limbs touching, the warmth of his presence communicating physically.

Definitely, I was on the prowl for love and security by my late teens. Anxious to marry, to settle down, to have all the normal prerequisites of adulthood, to meet the soul-mate with whom I was "fated" to share the rest of my life. That was the script, the formula, the way things were expected to happen, wasn't it? I'd heard all those wry comments about men in their thirties who were still unmarried and were "real mummy's boys," and that wasn't my future. Anyhow, when I met Anna at a nightclub during my eighteenth year I knew immediately she was the one. She was of tiny stature, red-haired, pretty, and I was drawn to her in so many ways. At sweet sixteen she had a wisdom and sophistication beyond her years, a delicious earthy sense of humor and an artistic creative mind.

As with Tony, I could explore anything and everything in our conversations. By the time we were engaged three years later, I had lost contact with Tony and embraced this new family of future in-laws, Catholics, too, like Tony's family. I'd noticed that Catholics had this indefinable "x" factor. Anna's mother, Sylvia, was full of highly entertaining stories with insights into human nature and its frailties—obviously Anna had been schooled at her mother's feet. To be accepted into the heart of her warm and close-knit family satisfied the deepest longings in me. At last I was beginning to BELONG somewhere.

I almost died

I had agreed to get married in the Catholic Church so I attended marriage instruction classes with Anna. I remember sitting through these sessions with the local priest, thinking how it was one big intellectual yawn. I just couldn't credit that anyone still subscribed to such antiquated beliefs and superstitions (this was the nineteen-seventies, for heaven's sake!), and when I heard how Catholics believed it's the REAL body and blood of Jesus they consume in Holy Communion, I was equally shocked and amused: these people practice cannibalism, I blinked. By age twenty-two I had become the most hardened cynic, skeptic and scoffer. I had long ago rejected all possibility of the existence of God. It was just a myth invented to keep the populace happy. In the broadening horizons of the 'sixties world in which I had grown up, Christian religion with its "these and thous" and "thou shalt nots" no longer seemed relevant to everyday life.

Our early days as man and wife were crazy times, quite literally. I felt lost at sea in suburbia, in this new role I'd taken on. I had no idea how to cultivate the emotional intimacy of marriage. Closeness was a real problem for me. That's when I started sinking, the black dog dragging me under again. I had everything I ever dreamt of, and now something inside of me was pushing it all away. I was suffocating. I felt hemmed in by in-laws on all sides who were constantly on our doorstep.

And at work, new pressures. I had been promoted beyond my level of competence into a managerial position in an advertising department, and the gut-gnawing feeling of "not belonging" was rearing its ugly head again. I just didn't belong in this world, neither at home nor at the office. And the giddy, empty feeling of NOT WANTING to belong began nudging at me…

At that time, Anna returned to Catholicism as a regular church-goer. My reaction was one of horror for I felt she had a more questing and freer spirit, like mine, unbound by convention. Well, I wasn't going to join her as a victim of the "narrow, oppressive, simplistic views of Christianity" so I reacted with my own individual form of religion. I gorged myself on fast-food spirituality, ferreting down dark alleys of occult, antiquarian wisdom of Egypt, reincarnation, eastern beliefs, wacky mysticism, secret knowledge of Masonic brotherhoods—all the hallmarks of what is now known as New Age—and the outcome was far from enlightenment. It concluded in the absolute pit of depression with two serious attempts at quitting this world.

I survived the first suicide bid of swallowing sleeping pills while alone in our house because Anna had a mysterious, urgent impulse to leave work mid-morning and drive home. As small as she is, she leapt over a six-foot fence to the next door neighbor's to get help after she found me. I hadn't counted on her rescuing me.

After my stomach was pumped I found myself back in the gray vacuum of nothingness with the further discomfort of a psychiatrist probing me: "You're newly married and should be radiantly happy. Why aren't you?" "I dunno," I thought, "you tell me!" The gray vacuum was worse now because everyone knew something was wrong with me. Nothing would ever come right again. Nursing staff had no time for me, treating me like rubbish. If I wanted to die then let me die, was their attitude, adding to my heavy burden of worthlessness. I was prescribed anti-depressants which only made me feel worse, more alienated. Three months later I took mouthfuls of them, along with sleeping tablets and tried a second overdose. This induced a massive stroke. Fortunately, I was inside the hospital when this occurred and doctors were able to act immediately. I almost died; was considered beyond help. The slim chance of recovery meant permanent damage, doctors said. Miraculously I pulled through, suffering loss of limbs only briefly. I have only vague memories of that time, but I recall pushing myself around on a walker trying to get my legs to function again.

Unknown to me, Anna was down at her church with others praying the rosary for me. This I only learned some years later.

Life was one big party, and I was one big headache

To escape death twice was an enormous coincidence. Something or Somebody was not letting me quit. I began to think God may be real, after all. Or was it spirit guides helping me? For some reason, unknown to me, this Supreme Energy Force valued my existence even if I didn't. Maybe I was worth more than I cared to believe; maybe I'd been saved for something…? I began to see that I was, perhaps, a unique person, as special as every human being is special and a "one and only" never-to-be-repeated individual. A friend of mine who had been the best man at my wedding came to visit me at hospital and said, "You've fallen as far as you can go. When you hit the bottom there's only one way... up!" and his words really connected and registered for me. There was hope. And although my code of beliefs was pretty hazy, I did believe that there was an underlying pattern to life, nothing was haphazard, nothing was coincidence—there was a plan, after all, and some guiding light in the background was looking after me. Out of the blue, I felt lifted by a rush of spiritual adrenalin… managed to bridge the bottomless gray hole I had slid into…picked up the threads of my life and soldiered on. I tossed all the remaining medication down the toilet.

Around this time, I became captivated by Saint Francis of Assisi. When I saw the Franco Zefferelli movie *Brother Sun, Sister Moon* I felt a great affinity for the youthful Francis, identifying with his simplicity, his pure idealism, joy of life and respect for nature. When he was misunderstood by his materialistic father and rejected his father's wealth and status by shedding every last scrap of clothing, walking off with nothing but his birthday suit to pursue his dream, my admiration knew no bounds. So intrigued by this 13th century saint was I that I bought a book about him and looked to him for my inspiration.

I was turning a new corner in my life, and the outlook was brightening, but my life did not follow a steady climb towards the light, rather it became a roller coaster ride of moving towards and away from God. Encouraged by a friend, I sat a copywriter's audition at Christchurch's top radio station and passed. I switched to a career perfectly tailored for my temperament: on the fringes of showbiz, writing and producing ads and jingles, even spoof soap-opera serials. It was a new and glamorous world which, in time, extended to after-hours drinking, necessary to relieve all the creative pressure. At a special bar reserved for us, I would mix 'n' mingle with the celebrities of radio and television. A friend in the pop-music industry told me broadcasting had a reputation for having a "gay" element—"So watch yourself!" he warned jokingly. As my capacity for alcohol expanded, my inhibitions and natural shyness loosened up. Slowly, inevitably, I got caught in a web of social irresponsibility: partying, marijuana, LSD, sex and debauchery. One Friday night after a session of drunkenness a sports commentator helped me unbolt the basement door to my long-denied homosexual inclinations. I didn't need much coercing. It was the mid-seventies and "do what you feel" was the philosophy in vogue. The experts reckoned the odd extra-marital fling improved one's marriage. I never questioned it.

So…from a sincere, introspective and idealistic twenty-five year-old, I soon degenerated into this abominable person who drank and caroused, hell-bent upon physical gratification.

Life was one big party, and I was one big headache. Anna, wisely, chose to remain aloof from most of this socializing; she didn't like the superficial circle I mixed in, preferring to stop at her parents' place or stay home with our two baby sons, Reuben and Nathan. This period was typified by a return to my contemptuous dismissal of anything Christian. We had two pictures hanging in our home, lovely Byzantine-style images of the Sacred Heart of Jesus and the Immaculate Heart of Mary, and I hated them. I ripped them from their antique frames and used the pictures as backing for surrealistic Dali prints. There was only one thing I hated more: Anna said she put God first in her life--and I insisted that surely I should be her number one?!

The unforgiveable

In 1975 we moved to Auckland. I knew I'd messed my nest during those last days in Christchurch—Anna almost left me. Pregnant with Sarah, she finally agreed to move, and I assured her I'd start afresh in Auckland. Resolutely, I became this brand new sanitized family man who set new boundaries, not permitting radio social life to intrude on time devoted to wife and children. It didn't last long. After two years of sober living I was right back into whisky, grass and hallucinogenics. At a rock festival I was busted and charged with possessing marijuana. When our Station Manager gave me a formal warning I was incensed. In defiance, I accepted an offer with a rival "pirate" radio station. With a new high stress job and with our fourth child on the way, stress levels were rising on all fronts. I was insisting on abortion.

One night, with a belly full of booze and dope, I did something I never thought I was capable of doing. Arriving home absolutely "out of it" I was trying to share some "divine enlightenment" with Anna. I'd been side-tracked with alternative spiritualities again, scouring the back streets of the occult, constructing astrology charts and reading up on the Illuminati, a secret European brotherhood in the Masonic style and a sworn enemy of the Catholic Church. I had bought a hemp-woven wallet decorated with the emblem of a red dragon, and I was showing Anna. "This is the symbol of MY god," I told her. "I can't figure out why people have this unfounded fear of dragons—if only they would realize that god is a seven headed dragon!"

Naturally enough, she resisted my weird notions, and when she did I interpreted her resistance as rejection. So maddened was I, so frustrated at her refusal to "believe in me," my protest escalated in ferocity to a primal scream. All the years of stored-up rage at my mother's rejection were transferred onto Anna, and at the height of my physical outburst I experienced what psychologists call "disassociation." I saw myself from a removed position, like an overview, and was shocked to the core. Next I was trying to murder the one person I loved the most. Releasing my fingers from Anna's throat, I was overwhelmed by the realization of my actions. Sobs shuddered through me as I collapsed on the couch, dissolving into hot tears of remorse and disbelief. Anna was traumatized. I was inconsolable at what I had done.

The next day, returning home from work, I found my home empty. A goodbye note from Anna explained everything. I was shattered. That is when I finally turned my life over to God. Any remaining shred of self-reliance had run aground. How many times had I promised to reform myself and failed miserably? I needed help. Real help, and not from psychologists. My problems were of spiritual origins. Something inside me knew that a battle was going on for my soul. And I recognized it would take more than mere human resources to rectify matters.

The day after I found my wife and children gone (they were staying at a woman's refuge camp, I later discovered, before they flew back to Anna's family in Christchurch), I sought the help of the "gray institution" as I had cynically referred to the Church. The local parish priest, Father George Marinovich, had once impressed me as a "sweet old bloke" so I paid him a visit. He listened to my long and tangled story and then told me of a "charismatic healer" at the Franciscan friary in Three Kings, a monk who turned people's lives around with prayer-healing. The next weekend, I went to meet him. I was expecting a Padre Pio character in brown habit with supernatural powers, but instead, there was just this ordinary and unassuming chap dressed in a mountain shirt and overalls. Perhaps I'd been given the gardener by mistake? We settled down together, Brother Ray and I, on a park bench in the extensive friary grounds as I spilled out my life history to him. He was about fifty, I guessed, and he had a gentle non-invasive manner. Opened on his lap was a Holy Bible, and he drew my attention to several passages. I recall him telling me that the heart of my problems was the chronic pain of rejection, a deep-seated wound which needed the healing touch of the Risen Lord. I agreed to let him and another "charismatic" friend pray over me and invite the Spirit of Christ to enter the painful hot spots of my past and heal them, one by one, starting from the womb right through to present day. All I wanted to know was HOW SOON. There seemed an urgency, and I had this terror that Satan himself was hot on my heels.

The following Wednesday night, I went to Brother Ray and his friend. At first I resisted. When I saw the door being locked on this little room I wanted to flee like the devil, escape from the clutches of the two men with me. Prayer was something foreign to me—creepy. And Brother Ray was in his brown habit which scared the living hell out of me. Eventually, I settled down and let the two men begin. An emotion-charged and life-changing hour later—or was it hours?—I was left weak and exhausted, cleansed by the continual stream of my own tears. Time had stood still. A warm glow had flooded through me with the sweetest peace, and all the while this electric "presence" filling the room which left me in no doubt about the resurrected Christ. I was so conscious of this other unseen person. When I returned to work the next day, one of my workmates commented, "You look like a great burden has been lifted off your shoulders!" And my best friend's mother said, "I've never seen you looking so relaxed before!"

The evening before my prayer-healing session, I saw Anna for the last time before she and the children left Auckland. I spilled the beans about my homosexuality and previous infidelities, and it was the final straw for her. We lived apart for nine months. In the ensuing turmoil I lost my job at pirate radio. When Benjamin was born in a Christchurch maternity hospital I journeyed south to visit both him and Anna before returning to Auckland ahead of her and the children. I vacated the family homestead and moved into an apartment in St. Mary's Bay where I went through an interlude of "finding myself" and "coming out"—assuming a new and flamboyant identity as I gave in to the inclinations I had refused to openly acknowledge for thirty years. I wrote to my father telling him I was gay, and his reply surprised me. No condemnation, but rather, a tone of encouragement and support: "Follow your own star. Be true to yourself."

During this time of separation, I received a greeting card on my 31st birthday from my mother-in-law. A ten-dollar bill was tucked inside and the card was signed simply "To Chris… always loved, Sylvia." To think Sylvia remembered me with such affection when I had been such a brute to her daughter… I couldn't comprehend her generosity of spirit. I wept.

It was all extremely hush-hush

During my time in St. Mary's Bay, preoccupied with a same-sex lifestyle, the reality of the experience at the friary diminished. I began to suspect it had all been an emotional high, Christ's presence just a figment of my imagination—the aftermath of my last LSD trip. The

Bible that Brother Ray had given me got buried under piles of dubious "spiritual" books like *God is Gay*. The black dog of depression moved in on me again. I grew steadily more and more disenchanted with the supposedly "gay" subculture after some harrowing experiences, and descended into a kind of self-loathing. In the name of pleasure I had allowed myself to be used and abused when, really, promiscuity was not my style. What I had wanted was not mindless sex, but a special relationship with a heart-to-heart basis: the impossible, I supposed—a male soul-mate. I was sick of all the frivolous bitching and backbiting so typical of the gay scene. I was a mess, and I missed my kids. Then a promise I had made to myself at age twelve kept coming back to haunt me: "If ever I have children, I want their upbringing to be different than mine: I wanted them to have two parents and a normal life."

In September of 1980 Anna and I reunited. There seemed to be a power beyond my control driving us back together. I was sure that people were praying for our reconciliation, and I couldn't resist the forces at work. But I felt my wife had re-admitted me to the family home like some wayward child.

Time, however, is a wonderful healer. Despite all odds, the decade that followed our separation was a period of relative peace and enrichment. While Anna and I somewhat shakily resumed our marriage, I also resumed contact with my Franciscan mentor, Brother Ray, who gently drew me, step by step, closer to the Catholic faith. By 1982, I was developing a new fascination with the supernatural, but this time in the form of visionary encounters with the Virgin Mary. Over the first three years back with

Anna, the Lord was filling the void left by my birth mother with a Heavenly Mother.

One night at the school my children were attending, I watched a short documentary film on the believed appearances of Our Lady of Mt. Carmel at a remote mountain hamlet in Spain from 1962 to 1965. Unlike Lourdes and Fatima, these events had happened in my own lifetime. I was gripped by the revelations of Garabandal. I bought a book called *O Children Listen to Me: Our Lady Teaches at Garabandal*, and it made a huge impact on me. On the front cover were the reported words of the Blessed Virgin: "What God loves above all is humility. What displeases Him above all is pride."

Those words touched a raw nerve. I felt convicted. I knew I was guilty of pride. Little did I know that I was soon to be humbled. Just admitting that the Catholic Church might be RIGHT, and I was possibly wrong was humiliating enough. Worse still my darkest and deadliest secret: I was now reading Catholic literature—and heaven forbid!—

reading the Bible, even praying!

One thing which really impressed me about Garabandal was the way the Virgin Mary reinforced so many of the Catholic Church's teachings by practical demonstrations and lessons give to the four young visionaries. She upheld all the fundamental virtues like modesty and purity, the social virtues like working and serving. She spoke of purgatory, heaven, hell, original sin, the sacraments, baptism, marriage, prayer for the dead, the importance of having religious objects around us and upon us, and she gave special emphasis to the Eucharist.

All of these basic Catholic matters began to gradually make sense to my disbelieving mind. I was becoming more and more intrigued with the Catholic Church, especially as its origins could be traced right back, through the unbroken lines of popes, to the apostle Peter himself. Even the Encyclopedia Britannica conceded this fact by listing every name in the papal succession. In my follow-up reading, I began to realize there was a consistent message from the Virgin Mary: "Pray the rosary." What was more, in the places where she appeared, there was already great devotion to this age-old prayer. Always Catholic places, I noted.

Just after my thirty-third birthday, late one afternoon in June, I approached Father Marinovich about becoming a Catholic. I disappeared from home for ten minutes and slipped around the corner to the church of St. Francis where he pastored, not wanting anyone to know where I'd gone. It was all extremely hush-hush. Anna told me months down the track that this move of mine coincided with her ultimatum to God: "If You don't do something about Chris, I'm leaving him! I give up on him. He's all Yours. Only You can save him." The very next day when I announced that I was joining the Catholic Church, she was dumbfounded. Nevertheless, she was reserving her judgment. Over the years, she'd heard a good few broken promises from my lips.

By August of 1982 I was rising an hour earlier, at dawn, sharing the first hour with the Lord. My prayer life grew daily as I poured out my heart to Jesus, meditated, asked, listened. There was an almost tangible closeness to Him, and the Holy Spirit took me on a guided tour of Catholicism, revealing many things by numerous means: questions instantly answered by books I opened at random, through people who "happened to cross my path." Brother Ray and Father Marinovich had an uncanny knack of providing answers before I voiced the questions, and this impressed upon me how the Holy Spirit was directing the very words to their lips. The more I learned the more I was able to straighten out a whole backlog of misconceptions I had held against Christianity.

When I commenced faith instruction I was very fortunate that our parish priest had a special devotion to Mary. Fr. Marinovich was a stickler for doctrine, and some local Catholics said he was "the old school," but for me he was perfect. I connected with him immediately—we were both writers and artists—and when he explained the basic tenets of Catholicism to me it enveloped a sweet fervor for "Our DEAR Mother" as he called Mary. "She's Mum," he chuckled, hugging a life-size statue of her.

Whether Father sensed in me a motherly absence or I'd told him about this, I can't recall, but he certainly wasted no time in quickening my spirit to an awareness of our Heavenly Mother. Before long I was praying the rosary daily, consecrated to the Immaculate Heart and enrolled in the Brown Scapular. Since then, nearly all the milestones in my life have occurred on Marian feasts, anniversaries, and First Saturdays—just to remind me, I'm sure, that my Mother cares.

Sundays soon became my Scripture reading day. I would put aside an hour and vanish into the bedroom. Highly embarrassing for me, this new habit. Wasn't this the same man who'd once taunted his wife at bedtime every time he found her studying her Bible? I used to level Anna with black looks and shake my head—"Fair go! You're NOT reading that damn book again are you? Can't you read something else for a change? It's time you broadened your mind a bit!"

Come September I was going to Mass every Sunday, each attendance an emotional time of repentance with surges of understanding. Old truths I had previously rejected, such as the virgin birth, all made obvious sense now. Before long we were at Mass as a family. Often I'd feel "touched"—anointed by the Holy Spirit—like a pulse of electricity through my body at poignant moments, triggering tears. Frequently it would happen during the consecration of the host, although I had no conscious idea that Christ becomes truly present in Holy Communion—I'd long ago forgotten my remarks about cannibalism. When I was later instructed on the divine nature of the Eucharist, it came as no surprise but was confirmed by the memory of those early spiritual glows.

Around that time, I hung a picture of the Holy Family on our lounge wall, and encouraged by the promises Jesus made to St. Margaret Mary—that "Sinners shall find mercy, tepid souls shall become fervent, fervent souls shall rise speedily to great perfection"—I also placed a picture of the Sacred Heart in an honored position. Definitely out of character for me was the defense I launched when the picture prompted an old friend to make a blistering attack on Christianity. Previously we'd shared this pastime together, both of us very vocal in howling down such "myths of medieval fantasy," so I'm not sure who was the more startled by my new stance, she or I.

I can finally live

It is difficult to explain now, but the closer I got to the Church, the more conscious I was of the devil breathing down my neck—not literally, but his reality was apparent. A fear, perhaps, which magnified as I awaited the day I could come into full union with the Lord at the Eucharistic feast. Spurred on by this fear, I hurried around to the presbytery in a disturbed state on October 14th and begged Father Marinovich to give me the safe custody of the Church. "Please, I want to join, straight away!" There seemed to be fingers at my throat, trying to choke back the words. I was gasping, my voice barely audible. The genial old Croatian priest made me repeat my request more clearly and loudly. Gradually, as he spoke to me, the heaviness and tension faded away. A perfect peace descended upon me as he blessed me. I nearly floated out of the presbytery. The next day I was received into the Church, and the following day, Saturday October 16th, was a day of rejoicing, my first Holy Communion on the feast of Saint Margaret Mary, the visionary of the Sacred Heart.

A few days before Christmas I was confirmed in a private ceremony with the Bishop of Auckland, taking the names Francis John as my confirmation names. I helped paint a host of angels and the Jerusalem backdrop for the crib scene before the altar, and it was the most perfect, deeply significant Christmas I had ever celebrated. I had this overwhelming sense of belonging. I had "come home".

The old black dog

In the years that followed, Anna became convinced my faith had genuine roots and was not a passing phase, and I began to believe God's grace was healing me forever of same-sex attraction, little realizing that my associated feelings and emotions had been pushed underground, sublimated by the more pressing needs of providing for and raising a family. In 1986, with great moral indignation, I voted against the Homosexual Law Reform Bill: an uptight, squeaky clean, little Christian who could not recognize his own hypocrisy.

Things came to a head in 1990. The issue I didn't want to deal with just would not go away. I found myself taking second looks at attractive men, studying handsome chests, feeling aroused by certain thoughts. I went to Confession and confessed my temptations, but didn't elucidate any details. To the priest in the confessional it sounded like I was referring to women. "Maybe," I offered at the close of our discussion, "I just have a heightened appreciation for the beauty of God's handiwork?" The priest chuckled and I thought, "Oh dear, you wouldn't be laughing if you knew what I was really talking about!"

The relentless, lengthening shadows of the old black dog were back on my horizon. The black dog began circling and closing in on me. I couldn't hold it at bay any more than I could halt the approach of winter. We had moved back to Christchurch four years earlier when Anna had a debilitating illness because there we could count on the wider support of Anna's family. I was now working as a nurse-aide at an elderly people's hospital just around the river, but it was grueling work with inhumane rosters. Often I would work eight days in a row with one day off, and the pace was stressful, the constant lifting of heavy patients physically demanding. I transferred to a nearby hospital, doing lighter work as an orderly, but my spirits were sinking. I became progressively unhappier, and my rumbling depression kept getting subverted into angry outbursts at inappropriate moments at home. My family was constantly tiptoeing around the rim of a volcano.

After injuring a knee cartilage, I quit the tedious orderly's job. Three temporary jobs—scriptwriting for television, freelance copywriting for an old radio friend, and nurse-aiding again—brought in the necessary income, but there was no reliability, no regularity. It made Anna uneasy, never certain of how much money she would have to budget each week. It was tricky when there were six mouths to feed and six bodies to clothe. After several months of this, sometimes toiling from sunrise to midnight, I reached burn-out point. I retreated to the Redemptorist Monastery for a quiet week away from everything, and with me I took a twenty-two year-old street kid whom I had met through our early morning rosary at the Cathedral and whom I had been supporting in his attempt to overcome an addiction to glue-sniffing.

It wasn't until a year later that I discovered Anna had suspected I was "on" with this young man and back into my "old ways" (not true). When she phoned me at the monastery and told me she wanted a legal separation, I was devastated. I was also angry—justifiably, I thought. For ten years now I had been a good husband and father. I had done everything in my power to make up for the previous eight years as the miscreant… and this was the outcome of all my efforts!

Today I can understand Anna's frustration with me. I was far from ideal husband material. Always I'd been a free spirit, and my attitude—I see clearly now—was more single-minded than married. She needed a regular type of guy who was straight up and down, solid, dependable, who would bring home the weekly pay packet, who didn't suffer from all these inner tensions that frequently immobilized me, whose burdens of stress didn't weigh down her own effectiveness. In truth, I was the fifth child in our family: a forty year-old man-boy.

When Anna insisted that, please, I do not return to the family homestead, I obliged somewhat unwillingly, agreeing to her terms with a terse, "If that's what you want, then that's what I want too!" As far as she was concerned there was no room for reconciliation. A quick clean cut was what she wanted—"no post mortems, please." I was dumbfounded to find the next day that she had lodged a Separation Order, and there was even a trespass order built-in. Alternating between anger at the injustice of it all, and grief, I cried and sobbed and bawled for days, absolutely gutted. Eighteen years of married life—gone—just like that! My devastation was immeasurable because I had built my whole sense of belonging around Anna and the family. Now my home-made insurance against a legacy of insecurities had been blasted from beneath my feet, leaving me dangling in mid-air. I had been so proud of the tight-knit family unit I had headed and nurtured, so proud of the triumph over my own dysfunctional family background. Without warning, that perfectly framed picture of Home Sweet Home had fallen and smashed.

It took marriage collapse and divorce to force me to face the truth about myself, to confront with honesty my own limitations, my inability to cope with stress, my issues of abandonment by both parents, and paramountly, my re-closeted sexual orientation. Undoubtedly the most terror-stricken moment of being a father was when I revealed the dark secret of forty-two years to my four children in the presence of a family-court counselor. My second eldest son, fifteen years-old at the time, sprang to my support and moved me to the brink of tears. When the counselor asked, "how do you feel about dad now?" Nathan didn't hesitate. In a very matter-of-fact tone of acceptance, he said, "He's still dad."

A damned fine loving!

It was months after Anna and I were legally separated that I crossed the line I thought I'd never cross again. Hardly surprising really, considering that I was still hanging onto this old pet notion of mine, that one day I'd find a male soul-mate. At a city bus shelter one evening I met Matthew.

We fell into talking, and when he caught the same bus as I and then alighted at the same bus stop, I was amused by this coincidence. We talked some more before heading to our respective homes and found we had much in common, particularly creative writing and music. I agreed to get together with him for a coffee the following evening. This was the man with whom I would share the next ten years of my life.

Significantly, one of our first conversations was about the "so-called fairer sex." Like me, Matthew was just recovering from a break-up with a woman he'd been living with, so together we seethed about how western females had become so aggressive and domineering, poor imitations of men. Sweet-natured and sensitive, Matthew has a generous spirit and a heart of gold—warm, funny, intelligent.

My world totally caved-in during the first year of our relationship. As I "came out of the closet" and gradually admitted to friends and family the new direction my life had taken—that Matthew and I were a male couple living together—I swung between gay-pride and self-effacement, soaring emotions and despondency, heartache at my losses. A Christian counselor who prayed with me commented that I was like someone who'd lost a great treasure. He was right. I was stretched on a torture rack between heaven and hell. Spirituality and sensuality are not compatible bedfellows, but I wanted "life in the Spirit" with God, and I wanted Matthew as well because I felt so loved. My arguments went like this: "My lifelong desires are being fulfilled. Why should God want to come between me and this man? We're made for each other!" But the eternal tussle continued. I had to explain away those convicting passages of Scripture. "The Old Testament references to fornication and the abomination of man-to-man sex are about promiscuity," I'd protest, "Not about loving gay unions as we know them in modern times." I even began writing a whole book called *A Damned Fine Loving!* to justify my lifestyle. "If you read the story of Sodom and Gomorrah," I wrote, "you'll see it's about violent and inhuman gang rape. The men of Sodom were animalistic, their behavior an offense against Love. And St. Paul's remarks? Let's be honest, he's homophobic, probably homosexual himself..."

And so it went on. For a short spell my conscience would be quieted, and then it would start up again. Scott Hahn, the great convert theologian, says if we do not repent of our sins, God lets us have our own way and abandons us to our sins, allowing us to experience the natural consequences of them. Illicit pleasures usually leave us feeling empty, dissatisfied, and as we persist, we form a habit, a vice, which darkens our intellect and weakens our will. This happened to me.

It was only a matter of time before my anger spilled over onto the Church. When I found a letter from our cardinal urging all Catholics to vote against the upcoming anti-discriminatory segment of the Homosexual Law Reform Bill, I was livid. Furiously, I wrote letters to Catholic newspapers deploring the "red-necked bigotry" and lack of tolerance. I walked away from the Catholic Church for two years.

Despite my own spiritual struggle, Matthew was attracted to Catholicism. He was fascinated by the richness of its culture and had great admiration for Pope John Paul II. Right from the start, though, I vowed I would never foist my beliefs on him, that I'd only speak about the Faith if he asked questions. Which he did. Many.

Roses

Off and on for years, Matthew toyed with the idea of becoming a Catholic, but our co-habitation was always, for him, an obstacle to that goal. He even told me that God had spoken to him and said He did not approve of our physical relationship. But neither of us wanted to rock the boat as we had developed an emotional co-dependence, and around us we had gathered a network of loyal and supportive non-gay friends. It was often remarked that our love outshone the love of many heterosexual relationships.

A major turning point for me was reading the first of five volumes of The Poem of the Man-God by the Italian mystic Maria Valtorta. The reading is recommended by the Blessed Virgin herself in her messages at Medjugorje.[27] From the confinement of her bed, Maria Valtorta wrote over 15,000 pages of visions on the untold life of Christ. She saw at a place called Clearwater, Jesus healing a young male leper who, in the years prior to contracting the disease, had committed adultery with someone's wife. Unlike the tender compassion shown for the woman caught in the act of adultery, Jesus was most severe: "I prefer to touch the putrefied flesh of a corpse," He cautioned him, "than go near anyone who smells of lust. Lewdness disgusts me."[28] Our Lord was visibly pale and shaken as He acknowledged the youth's mother who had wept and pleaded on her son's behalf. "It is only for the sake of your mother," He concluded sternly, "that I am healing you."

That story left me reeling. If God was disgusted with heterosexual adultery, what were His feelings in regard to me…? The uncanny part was that the event took place at Clearwater, and our house was situated in Ngatea Road—"Ngatea" translated from the Maori means "Clearwater."

At this point I will let a testimony I wrote in 1999 explain the next stage of the journey. It was written for the newsletter of a Catholic movement called *Courage*[29] which Matthew and I joined—a worldwide spiritual support network for those who experience same-sex attraction but desire to live chaste lives in accordance with the

Church's teaching.

The story of how my male partner and I chose chastity and became members of *Courage* is one of startling suddenness in its initiation. It was an immediate answer to prayer. During Advent last year (8th December, the feast of the Immaculate Heart of Mary, to be precise) I came across a leaflet in the Catholic bookshop concerning *Devotions to Jesus King of All Nations*. The promise of "powerful and unprecedented effects" was attached to a novena of Holy Communions in honor of Jesus under that title. The very next day I went to Mass and began to pray the novena firstly for myself, naturally enough. It was during that time—nine consecutive communions but not necessarily nine calendar days in a row—that I was inundated with more doubts about my lifestyle. As a homosexual Catholic who has lived the past eight years with a non-Catholic man in a loving, caring, committed relationship, I had previously had doubts—so had he—about the sexual aspect of our union but both of us always managed to shut out these nagging thoughts. A week before Christmas I went to reconciliation (a condition of the novena) and timidly confessed, without being specific, to "sexual sins." Once I'd done this I began hoping I'd "stay clean" for Christmas, which happened, and a very special Christmas Day it was. From there on, my doubts multiplied. I began wanting to stay clean longer, and this put me in a very problematic position with my partner, Matthew. How was I to tell him I'd started thinking differently about things?

On the sixth day of 1999 I began a second novena of Holy Communions, this time for Matthew, and I asked the Lord to help me to solve this whole complex situation. Somehow, please, could He change Matthew's heart, get him to approach me and say, "I want us to give up sex!"—not because I was afraid to broach the subject myself but because it was such a thorny issue: I didn't want to be enforcing my Catholic conscience upon him, nor did I want to put him off the Church he'd often shown signs of interest in by insisting the physical side of our love cease. After all, it was our devotion to each other—unrelenting against every obstacle over eight years—that had bought so much healing for him. He had suffered deeply through childhood abuse, and we had always believed this healing came from God through the love we shared.

After my second Holy Communion for this novena (Sunday Mass, January 10th) I was in for the surprise of my life. Later that day Matthew told me he had something serious to discuss with me. "I want to become a Catholic," he said.

"I want to go for instruction and be baptized." I nearly fell over backwards, especially at the next piece of news: "I also want to receive Holy Communion, and that's the tricky bit. I'm sorry, Chris, but we'll have to end our sex life. I couldn't possibly go to Communion and be sexually active. It had to come to this eventually, anyway—my childhood has ruined that part of me. So how do you feel about celibacy?"

I remembered all the times I had been to Communion while sexually sinning and admired Matthew's stand. He's got more integrity than I, I thought ruefully. Three days later I went to a full and proper Confession. On the way home I called in at the Cathedral and found a newsletter saying Confession could be arranged by appointment. Heart in mouth, I wandered over to the presbytery, hoping I might bump into the priest I'd met there a couple of years ago who had really impressed me by his holiness and doctrinal precision. He opened the door of the presbytery! He agreed to hear my confession. Thankfully, he didn't sound judgmental when I spoke about my homosexuality, but instead acknowledged mildly, "So you've sinned with another man."

After going to Confession, I began to have a deep yearning to attend daily Mass, whenever I could, and with each succeeding Mass I was gradually regaining my spiritual eyes to see that homosexual sex was wrong; I wept from time to time before the Lord in the Tabernacle; I began to experience a profound and moving sense of union with Jesus at communion time; I began to recall how wonderful it had once been to be so close to Him eight years ago, and to realize I was able to resume this spiritual intimacy with a clear conscience. It felt so amazingly good to be pure, to be chaste, to "recover [my] innocence through the Sacrament of Penance." (to quote the words of Jesus to Sr. Josefa Menendez).[30]

Over the days and weeks that ensued, I half expected Matthew to change his mind and recant his wish for chastity. But he didn't. By the end of January he was suggesting we establish separate bedrooms, which we did. Over four months later, our celibacy continues, though we have had two slip-ups. Both of us felt so dirtied and terrible afterwards so we vowed never to break the celibacy ruling again. What has helped us tremendously in our ongoing efforts, of course, is *Courage* which does not ask its members to change their orientation but simply encourages and supports them in their walk with God to live chaste lives and develop their spiritual commitment to the Catholic Faith. The priest I'd approached for confession at the cathedral—unbeknown to me—was chaplain of the diocese's first chapter of *Courage* which was just starting to

> find its feet. He gently suggested I consider joining. Taking home the *Courage* handbook to study, Matthew and I studied it together and both agreed to start attending the following Wednesday. Today Matthew also goes to private instruction with the same priest, preparing to become a Catholic, and I sit in on sessions as his sponsor. Now firm in his conviction that acts of "gay" sex are against God's will, he has found peace for the first time in thirty-one years and eagerly looks forward to baptism and Holy Communion.

They say a mother's prayer moves heaven. Well, I knew, unshakably, that my arrival at this new threshold was through the tears and intercession of my Heavenly Mother. In all the years Matthew and I had been together, I always remained faithful to praying my daily rosary, and, I know now, that a mother's love never gives up on her children. I believe it was Mary who obtained for me the same privilege granted the young leper at Clearwater—a second chance. "It is only for the sake of your mother" were the cautionary words of Jesus to the youth, and those words were also applicable to me. Something had awakened in my memory, something I'd almost forgotten. Eighteen months earlier, there had been a sign of the Mother Mary's presence with me when I made my first unsuccessful bid for chastity: Matthew and I had been separated for ten weeks, and I had thought we were breaking-up, so tearfully one night at bedtime, I surrendered my sexuality to God. "I'm all yours," I said. Then I fell into the deepest, most sound sleep I'd had for ages. I had been taking pills to help me sleep, I was so distraught, but that night—June 15, 1997, the night after my birthday—I slept the sleep of angels. As I drifted off I could smell this most beautiful perfume of ROSES. "Roses," I thought, "that's odd." I had been burning oils, but I didn't have Roses among the fragrances.

I can't go back

I wrote my story for the Courage newsletter when Matthew was taking up faith instruction and we were attending Courage together. Then in January of 2000 he said he wanted us to resume our full physical relationship as before. Uncannily, he chose the anniversary of my return to Holy Communion (one year to the day) to say he no longer wanted to be celibate. I stalled him as I prayed and prayed for nine days, not knowing WHAT to do. It was the most difficult decision I've ever had to face, yet I knew all along what I must do. I got up before dawn on the tenth day and handed Matthew over to

Jesus: "I surrender him to you, Lord. I'm sorry, I've been trying to hold onto him, and he doesn't belong to me, he belongs to you." When Matthew awoke I told him I had decided to continue along the path of celibacy/chastity I had chosen.

I knew, as I was telling him this, that I was sounding the death knell for our relationship. My tears were unstoppable, washing down my cheeks as I tried to explain that the last twelve months had been a time of spiritual progress for me, of ground recovered which I could not relinquish so easily; that to perversely pursue what I now knew to be wrong was to throw God's love and graces back in His face. "I can't go back,

Matt," I told him. "In the last year I've rediscovered that pearl of great price I lost ten years ago. Now I've found it again. I would give up EVERYTHING, if I had to, to hold onto it." I cried and cried, and he held me and said he understood—that he didn't want to come between God and me.

Nowadays I realize that the only way God can rebuild us in his image is to first demolish every last prop and support, and then clear the ground of the building site. The clearing, in this instance, was gentle and gradual. In March 2001 I reached my second biggest decision, to sever what was fast becoming a torturous situation. For a year, Matthew and I had tried to hold together the crumbling foundations of our ten year union with our lives and beliefs now sharply divided. While I had been stumbling along the narrow way of celibacy, he had veered off down the wide and sensually-inviting avenues of the world.

Our house went up for sale, and I made decision number three. With my share of the equity I was going to make reality something I had dreamt of doing for twenty years. I was a youthful fifty-one, but time was marching on. If I didn't do it now, I'd never do it. There were two back-to-back package deals with Harvest, the Australian specialists in pilgrimages: a fortnight in Italy, the country I had always yearned to see, followed by a tour of Marian shrines—Lourdes, Fatima and Garabandal—with a week's extension to Medjugorje. But! It was due to depart in ten weeks' time. "If You want me to go on this pilgrimage," I told Jesus and Mary, "if it's God's will for me, then help me sell the house in time." Despite the slump in the real estate market at that time, we had a buyer inside two weeks.

My journey with two parties of like-minded Australian pilgrims was full of blessings. It brought home to me two important things: that I could go to the other end of the earth and connect on a deep level with others, making true friendships, and that I belonged to a worldwide family of believers regardless of culture or nationality.

In Medjugorje, in particular, the faith of believers was palpable. I went there during a youth festival and witnessed hundreds, perhaps thousands, of young people who couldn't get enough of singing praying, praising, going to Mass, going to adoration. Hundreds of them were on their knees in the forecourt of the church at 11 o'clock at night, and lots of them young men—all given the gift of faith. Everywhere you go, young and old are proud of wearing their crucifixes and religious medals. In retrospect, I would also say that the fruit of my journey to Medjugorje was and remains a real and abiding PEACE in the very core of my being, and it is commented upon by others. I used to be someone who fretted a lot about the future. In the last two years since my pilgrimage, my entire focus has shifted. The future—as well as the past—no longer have a hold on me. Each day of my life is now precious, to be lived to its full. I feel very blessed to be alive at this moment of history in such extraordinary times. Finally, I understand Christ's words: "I come to give you life, life in all its fullness!"

No longer a slave

I still see Matthew. He lives a few blocks away. Last year he became a Catholic. He was baptized and confirmed in a private ceremony and Mass at the Cathedral of the Blessed Sacrament, achieving at long last his goal of receiving Holy Communion. Around the same time I succeeded in getting an annulment for my marriage to Anna, an important closure for both of us. Nowadays she and I can relate much better than we ever did. She is remarried, and our four wonderful children are in their early to late twenties.

As for me, I have entered a new season in my life. Recently, after a year's novitiate study, I was professed as a Lay Franciscan in the Order of St. Francis. I work today as a community carer in the inner-city suburb where I live, helping the elderly, the sick, the disabled, and those with psychiatric conditions by cleaning, shopping, doing household tasks, sometimes cooking for them, so that they can remain in their own homes rather than be admitted to institutions. It has been an uphill battle learning to live with same-sex attraction, but I am no longer looking for miraculous cures. I am resigned to God's will that, like St. Paul's unnamed thorn in his side, this condition is to remain with me to keep me humble. After five years I am still attending *Courage* each fortnight, and although we are a small group we hope to grow as others become disenchanted with the gay lifestyle. I prefer to see myself as "having same-sex attraction" rather than wearing the political label "gay" which suggests sexuality is the axis of my identity when, in fact, it is just a fragment of who I am. I couldn't care less if anyone thinks chastity is an old-fashioned concept, weird or geeky. There is real empowerment in my non-sexual commitment because I experience absolute freedom. I'm the freest I've ever been in my adult life—no longer a slave to my body's appetites, no secrets to weigh me down, no old baggage, no guilt. Regular confession and daily Mass are a big part of my ongoing healing, and prayer has a special priority early each morning and evening; the rosary daily, fasting twice a week, praise meetings once a week. The craving for love which got me into so much trouble in the past doesn't snare me in its sticky web any more. I am fulfilled by an ever-deepening intimacy with a God of Love who lives not "way out there somewhere" but as close as my own heart. In Him, I belong.Thanks to God's grace, I have defeated depression in the last ten years, and for someone who used to be a quitter, I have actually quitted on quitting. Best of all, the Good News is that the profoundly destructive effects of rejection no longer have such power over me.

Back in 1993 a personal word of prophecy was given to me by a friend: "The Lord is giving back to you the years the locusts have devoured." That time is now.

* * *

Dear children, I am your mother and I warn you this time is a time of temptation. Satan is trying to find emptiness in you, so he can enter and destroy you. Do not surrender! I will pray with you. Do not pray just with your lips, but pray with the heart. In this way prayer will obtain victory![31]

MARYBETH

She told God to go to hell, and He rescued her from it

I was raised Catholic. I went to church on Sundays with my parents and older brothers, but I didn't pray and didn't understand faith. Not until high school, when I grew loosely attached to a Catholic youth group my first year, did I become more involved in my religion. I felt happy then, and in my freshman year, two supernatural experiences, in particular, surprised me and gave me a taste of heaven. The first occurred when I stayed at home on a school night while my parents were attending a Mass. As I sat in my parents' bedroom, a physical feeling came over my entire body, particularly my torso, and took my breath away. I was drawn into a state of ecstasy, a feeling of such intense and perfect pleasure that it left me paralyzed and stunned, afraid to move should it stop. "Please don't end!" I wanted to shout, but before I could say those words, the sensation was gone.

At that time, I didn't know God, I knew of him. I didn't yet understand that God could communicate personally and draw me towards him, so I simply thought of my experience as heavenly. When my parents came home, I ran to them and said, "You're never going to believe what happened. I think I experienced heaven for a split second!" We realized this happened when the priest held up the host during the Mass. My mom was also praying for me at that moment. This same mysterious gift happened again a few months later, on another school night, when my parents were at Mass and my mother was praying for me as the priest elevated the host. Both times the feeling took my breath away, and both times I did not want it to end.

The happiness I felt in my first year of high school slowly faded and disappeared by my senior year when I began to feel lost. My fleeting moments of ecstasy, my involvement in the Catholic youth group and my belief in God hadn't solved one problem: the reason for my existence. Hit by a combination of low self-esteem, a sugar addiction, and an existential sadness, I wondered, "Why am I here? What's the point of my life?"

I went to college only to please my mom with whom I had a strained relationship. I hated going. If I didn't like a class, I simply wouldn't attend nor bother dropping it. I remember distinctly wanting to be invisible. This desire worsened in each successive year of college. Graduation was a shock and a relief.

I went to church occasionally my first and second year in college due to a sense of obligation. In that small chapel, packed to its brim with people, I cried openly. The music and the homily pierced my heart, although I never prayed and shuffled through my college days in despondent misery. Normally, I didn't feel a part of anything, and Mass was the one moment when I didn't feel lost or alone. I didn't know it then, but I felt God for that one hour.

How sick is God?

One day, in April of 1984, when I was a college junior in summer school, my sister-in-law went jogging with my brother who rode his bike just next to her while carrying their three year-old son on the infant seat in the back. A man they knew stopped my brother to talk to him while my sister-in-law continued jogging forward along with their dog. When my brother started biking again to catch up with her, he could not find her. At the intersection of two streets in their small suburban neighborhood in Utah, my brother found only the dog standing in the middle of the intersection barking. She had disappeared.

When I came home from college for the summer, my mom sat me down and said, "There's something I have to tell you." She then proceeded to say that my sister-in-law was missing, that she was presumed dead, and that investigators were trying to find out what had happened. My mom's words fell upon me like a ton of bricks. My mind exploded, and I became instantly hysterical. My brother was left devastated, and he had a little boy to raise.

Four months after my sister-in-law's disappearance, they found her body in a ravine. She had been abducted, and her head had been smashed in with a baseball bat. That is when my whole concept of God switched from on to off. My hatred for him was intensely sharp and biting. "I know you exist," I told him, "but I have no idea why anyone could care less about you or even love you because you're evil." I despised him with such passion because my brother is one of the sweetest and gentlest of men—so sensitive, loving, and incapable of hurting anyone. For that to happen to him, of all people . . . and his wife, so sweet and innocent as well . . . for that to happen to her! "How sick is God?" I wondered.

My life fell apart. Our family did not talk about it. It was something too tragic to talk about. I could talk to my friends, but they could not keep me from plummeting deeper into my depression. I had a lot of rage—a lot of rage.

After my sister-in-law was murdered, a friend of mine from high school who went to a nearby college called me. I felt surprised to hear from her since I saw her once a year at most, and our relationship had grown apart because she was doing drugs. She told me after few introductory words that she was pregnant. I knew exactly why she had called me; she wanted me to talk her out of getting an abortion. She knew me from my high school days when I was very Catholic and talked about not approving of having sex, getting drunk, choosing abortion, etc. I knew God wanted me to tell her, "Abortion is wrong. You can't do it. You'd be killing your child." But I didn't want to tell her. I hated God so much that I just didn't care. Instead, I thought incredulously, "How dare you call me. How dare you expect me to save you, because that's not going to happen." I was not the person she expected me to be. I was dead spiritually did not want any kind of involvement. After a bitter internal struggle, I told her the decision was hers to make, and I felt my heart turn further away from God.

After she had her abortion she called me and said, "You've changed. I can't believe you've changed." Her words elicited a violent internal reaction from me. I felt justified in how I was, without a trace of remorse, and the screws of my anger turned more tightly away from God. She told me about the abortion and said her children were twins. In high school she was Catholic. Now she is an atheist.

I continued to stew in my anger. When I came home for the summers, my parents asked me on Sundays if I wanted to go to church with them, and I always answered, "No." Humbly and sweetly, they simply said, "O.K.," and went themselves without pressuring me. I know they wanted me to go, but they never got angry or made me feel guilty as they walked out the door. If they had acted any differently, my relationship with God would have grown even worse. As it was, I stayed home watching T.V. or reading the paper, feeling tremendous guilt.

After one summer break, as I stood in my parents' driveway, ready to get into my car to go back to college, my dad said, "Oh, you don't have to worry about anything, Marybeth. I pray a rosary for you every day." He held his arms out to hug me goodbye, and I felt a violent reaction towards him stir in my gut. "Ugh! Get away from me!" I wanted to scream, and I pushed him away in disgust. As I drove away, my heart turned firmly against him and revolted even more angrily against God.

My period of darkness lasted for three and a half years, from my junior year in college until I went to Medjugorje in 1987. Looking back, I am surprised I was never suicidal. I slept all the time, anesthetized myself with food, and dreamed of disappearing. I was experiencing very deep grief. I thought about my sister-in-law's death quite a bit, shocked that such a thing could occur. It seemed like a sick and twisted premeditated plan on God's part. "You're so evil," I often said to God, "because this scheme didn't happen to a jerk. It happened to my sweet brother. You can rot in hell for all I care."

Walking into God

Toward the end of my college years, I traveled to Europe with a friend of mine. While my normal escape mechanisms were eating and sleeping which left me depressed and listless, my newfound way of escaping became European travel which I found exciting and life-giving. Our escapades through Europe helped me to know that I could feel happiness again which had eluded me for so long, but when I came back home, I noticed nothing had really changed. I still hated God with a vengeance.

On the advice of a friend, I considered seeing a psychiatrist my first year out of college. I had reached a point at which the depression was more than I could bear. Until my friend suggested I get help, I lived with the assumption of being miserable and hopeless for the rest of my life, never realizing there was a possible option for me to feel differently. I went to see the psychiatrist, and he put me on antidepressants. It had no effect.

After working at a secretarial job for a year, I yearned to travel again, ready to escape into my new passion. I took off for Europe with a college friend for a four-month tour.

We traveled to eight countries on the continent. In Austria, where churches stand everywhere, beautiful and ornate, covered with artistic paintings, stained glass windows, marble columns and elaborate gold Tabernacles, something miraculous started to happen to me. As I walked from the outdoors, away from the hot sun, the sweat, the traffic and the noise, into these dark, stunning, quiet, peaceful, cool churches, I walked into a different world. Each of my senses was assaulted in a positive, exhilarating, and transcendent way. I felt as though I were walking into God. I felt as if a mist of God's presence came to envelope me from all sides and imbue me with a very comforting, peaceful and pervasive joy. I insisted to my friend that we go into every single church I saw in Vienna and in Salzburg, grateful my quirky desires mimicked the touristy thing to do.

When I walked into those churches, I understood for the first time that God was personal. I felt him embrace and welcome me, and I fell in love. My hatred towards him dissipated and could no longer rear its ugly head. Because I was stepping into God, I stepped easily out of my old self.

At the entrance of each church, I had noticed a picture of Mary's face above words written in German. I didn't know of Mary's importance in the Church nor of any devotions to her, except for the rosary which to me meant only a babbled bunch of beads. One day, I pointed to Mary's picture and asked, "What is this?" and my friend who could read German said it concerned Medjugorje. Then she said spontaneously, "You should go." As a Lutheran, disinterested in Catholicism for herself, she encouraged me to travel to Medjugorje, and I haven't a clue why. In that moment, I didn't give her suggestion a thought because I didn't know where Yugoslavia or Medjugorje were, much less the significance of traveling there.

Not until I decided to go to Mass one Sunday in Vienna, did Medjugorje cross my mind again. The inspiration to go could only have come from God because I hadn't attended Mass for a couple of years and remained ignorant of its power and grace. On my way there, on a rainy and cold day, I got lost. "What am I doing?" I wondered and almost turned around, but then found the church. To my disappointment, I arrived as a Mass was ending, but to my surprise, it was being said in English. As I stood in the back of the church, wet, freezing and frustrated, but enjoying the fact that English-speaking people lived in Austria, a man started advancing down the isle towards me. Without a premeditated thought, I walked up to him as if compelled by an outside force, and suddenly unexpected words flew out of my mouth. "How can I get to Medjugorje?" I asked, surprised and confused by my own question. "Oh, come talk to my wife," he answered, then introduced me to her: "This young lady would like to know how to get to Medjugorje." His wife smiled at me with confidence and said, "Oh, Our Lady must be calling you." A familiar sense of scorn and disgust returned instantly to my heart, and I thought, "Yeah, whatever, Mrs. Holier-than-thou." Then she said, "Well, we actually have a bus going in two days, and I'll see if I can get you on it."

Wanting to go to Medjugorje, but not knowing why, I ran back to the hostel to tell my friend. She encouraged me to go, even though we had only traveled for a month and this ruined our plans to travel with a two-month travel pass. When I spoke to the lady again she said, "Sorry, I can't get you in on this trip, but if you come back in a month, I promise you, I'll get you on the next trip."

Fortunately, this meant that we still had an entire month remaining on our Eurail passes, so we traveled from Austria to Rome, another place I knew nothing about. One day, as we walked around Rome in complete ignorance, we ended up outside in the audience of the Pope. I knew the Pope as a title—head of the Church—but I didn't know his name, history or character. He passed right by me, and I froze. My friend pushed me towards the front of the crowd and said, "Shake his hand! Take a picture! Do something!" And I just stood there in shock. I could not do anything. "What's wrong with you?!" she asked. "I couldn't move," I answered. I had unexpectedly felt something in his presence I had not sensed in anyone before. I felt his holiness.

Before long, I was on a bus. Looking back, I think, "How bizarre. What kind of idiot was I, riding on a bus with a bunch of Austrian strangers, going to a place I didn't know anything about?" Unbeknownst to me, I had embarked upon a bus ride seventeen hours long. I did not know about apparitions, nor did I care about Mary. The words, "The Blessed Mother is appearing in Medjugorje" meant nothing to me. I knew only that I would spend a couple of days in Medjugorje and then return. On the bus ride there, everyone, excluding myself, prayed the rosary for what seemed to be much of the seventeen-hour trip. It was dreadful to hear. I wanted them to stop. I wanted to get off the bus, but I was stuck.

The moment we arrived, however, a joyous feeling similar to the one I experienced in the Austrian churches came over me. It was the presence of God.

There's no way I can leave

I walked around Medjugorje in awe, spellbound, and fully aware that the delight and peace I felt came from God and this holy place. A big, genuine smile glued itself to my face, and before long a spring inside of me bubbled up, and I found myself praying the rosary. I stayed at a local family's home along with a girl from Vienna named Maria who spoke English very slowly, and because I knew nothing about where I was, I followed her around like a puppy dog. If she climbed Mount Krizevac (Cross Mountain) at night with no flashlight, I climbed Mount Krizevac at night with no flashlight. If she went into Saint James Church, I went into Saint James Church. When she knelt on the church's stone floor for three hours, so did I. Maria also found a couple books for me in English about Medjugorje, so I began reading those and little booklets of Mary's messages.

My first day in Medjugorje I thought to myself, "There's no way I can leave," and I panicked. After two days, when we were scheduled to leave, my anxiety quickened. I wanted to stay but didn't know how to: I didn't know where I was on a map, I didn't speak the language, and I didn't know how to get back to Austria on my own. Maria decided to stay with me for another week and then said, "I'm going to go home, but don't worry about staying longer. When you decide you want to go, talk to someone in the church about going back to Vienna. Buses come here often from Austria." So I continued to stay with the family in Medjugorje and ended up staying with them for five weeks.

In Medjugorje, I prayed more than I had in my lifetime. I prayed climbing up Apparition Hill. I prayed climbing mount Krizevac. I went to the English speaking Mass every morning and to the three hour Croatian evening program every night. At that time, the evening program consisted of the Joyful and part of the Sorrowful Mysteries of the rosary, then a pause in silence when Mary appeared to some of the visionaries, then the remainder of the Sorrowful mysteries, followed by Mass, and then the Glorious Mysteries.

Little "Ah-ha" moments filled each of my days. Shortly after I arrived, as I was walking around Medjugorje on a sunny day, with no traces of clouds, rain or sprinkling, I looked up and saw a gigantic, full, double rainbow painted across the sky. I felt ecstatic and began jumping up and down, far too excited to remain on the ground. I somehow knew this glorious rainbow came from God and thought, "You did that for me. I can't believe you did that for me."

There I was, in a village where the Blessed Mary was appearing every day. I knew no one; I didn't speak the language; I was basically alone in a distant, unknown land amidst strangers, and at the same time, deliriously happy. It made no sense.

Each day, I learned more about my faith from Mass and the many talks given by the visionaries and priests. I had been a thirsty sponge, parched and tired of walking in the desert, and now that someone from heaven was giving me water, I couldn't stop drinking it all in. The temporary joy and peace I felt in the Austrian churches became a constant, enduring surprise. In the few weeks I spent there in 1987, I was completely healed of my depression.

Stirrings of repentance

As I learned more about my faith, I also began to feel powerful stirrings of repentance, and when I saw lines of people outside the church going to Confession, I stood in line to see an English speaking priest. A certain memory weighed heavily on me, and with great seriousness, I said, "One time, I was really mean to my saintly Italian grandmother." "That's it?" he responded. My old anger immediately returned, and I thought, "How can you minimize the torturous depths of contrition for what I've done?" I attributed all my heartfelt repentance to this one instance. The priest probably saw that I was only confessing the tip of the iceberg, for I was only beginning to thaw out. I couldn't see into myself further than one sin. I didn't yet know how to probe my own heart.

Then I met Father Philip, a priest of both American and Croatian descent who talked to the English-speaking pilgrims every day in the afternoon after the English Mass. He was sweet and wonderful—very fatherly and gentle, with the face of a doll. I adored him and wanted to jump into his arms. He anchored me in the faith and appealed to my sense of logic by speaking about very serious matters in a contemporary and understandable way. One could see his love for the Blessed Mother in his eyes and hear it in his voice. Through his wise, intelligent and loving preaching, he helped fulfill my longing to know more about God, more about the Church, more about the Blessed Mother, more about life.

I made an appointment to speak with Father Philip in his office, and initially he planned to just pray over me, then as we talked more, he encouraged me to do a general Confession. With gentleness, compassion and great insight, he traveled through my whole life with me, helping me to see where Jesus had been present, and also where the devil had been working. When he made a strong point, he looked into my eyes, took his index finger and gently touched me with it for emphasis. The experience amazed, enthralled, and saddened me, as my eyes opened to see the spiritual dimension of my life. I told him how I could have done my part in trying to prevent my friend from aborting her twin children but did not. I told him I had hated God so much that I hadn't cared about her cry for help. I told him how repulsed I had been by my parents. I also realized I had lived in mortal sin for years due to not going to Church and hating God intensely. My heart melted open, and I felt forgiven. I had been in terrible grief, and Satan had had a tremendous opportunity to influence me because instead of blaming Satan for ruining my brother's life, my sister in law's life and her family's life, I had blamed God.

As I continued to listen and learn from Mass, talks, and vocalized prayers, I felt moved and inspired in my heart to confess often. Nearly every other day, I saw Father Philip for Confession and spiritual direction. My inner darkness was slowly melting away. I was no longer angry with God in Medjugorje. I didn't hate him, and I didn't blame him for my sister-in-law's death, but I could not forgive my sister-in-law's murderer. I still had fantasies of finding, torturing and killing him. Whenever her death came to mind, I wanted him to suffer the same fate he had made her suffer. It has taken years since then for me to let go of that rage. Only over time and with the help of prayer and Confession did the intensity of my anger dissipate.

People's lives are changing

During my five-week stay, my sense of scorn returned at times. When I met Americans, they often shared their excitement about the common miracles that occur there, asking me questions such as, "Oh, did you see the sun spin or see a rosary turn gold?" I felt repulsed by their pursuit because it seemed to me they were focusing on trivia. Looking back now, I understand it and do not ever want to disparage anyone who delights in the miracles of Medjugorje, but they seemed so unimportant at the time. "Why are you focused so much on that?" I wanted to say. "People's lives are changing! They are having tremendous conversions, and the Blessed Mother is really here!" My life had changed so dramatically. God had removed my misery and depression that had colored much of my life and given me a profound serenity and joy that I was experiencing for the first time. Just walking around Medjugorje, somewhere, anywhere there, I felt such depths of peace and happiness inside that it made me giddy. Rosaries turning gold and the sun spinning seemed anti-climatic and irrelevant.

People's lives can change dramatically when they go there. Addicts can be healed there of their addictions. I met a girl from Australia whose brother struggled with a cocaine addiction. He was stealing money from his job every night to support his habit, and his priest even told him not to come to Confession anymore because he did not seem able to change. His family and his friends, everyone gave up on him because of his helpless state. Then someone in his family found out about Medjugorje, and he traveled there with his sister. As soon as he got on the plane and realized he was not turning back, he was healed miraculously of his addiction. He never once suffered any cravings or side-effects—nothing, and has been off the drugs ever since. Before then, when he had tried to give up cocaine, he had become gravely ill. Medjugorje transformed him, and when he returned home, he entered the seminary.

After five weeks in Medjugorje, I did not want to leave. As I boarded a bus back to Austria, a painful sorrow came over me. I felt as though I were being ripped out of the arms of God. I met up with my new friend Maria, and then returned reluctantly to the states. When my mom, dad, aunt and uncle greeted me at the airport, I walked out the gate and began sobbing hysterically as my aunt came forward to hug me. I hadn't realized until then how much I didn't want to be home. Home was now the place I had left behind. My heart and senses had experienced a foretaste of heaven, and now I had to return to earth.

Gradually, I assimilated to life in the states and started going to graduate school to study theology because I wanted to learn everything about my faith. Once I learned a little, I wanted to learn more, and once I learned more, I wanted to teach others in order to share the incredible beauty of the Catholic religion. In college, I thought of Catholicism as a ridiculous joke; and after Medjugorje, I saw it as a precious jewel I wanted others to have. With a sense of excitement, I taught high school religion for a year, then graduated from theology school. For the last eight years, I have worked for the Church in different capacities, and since Medjugorje, I never suffer from depression and harbor no malice towards God. When I think of him I only feel love.

I am truly living now

Medjugorje was my life-saver. I do not know how to describe my conversion other than, I feel like I have my pre-Medjugorje life and my post-Medjugorje life. I was a closed flower bud that slowly opened up in the Austrian churches and fully bloomed in Medjugorje. I am truly living now, whereas before, I simply existed. My depression is completely gone. I don't remember exactly when, but at some point while in Medjugorje, I sensed God's intense sadness and pain over my sister-in-law's death. I realized that God never wanted my sister-in-law to be murdered. Against his will, a life that he created was snuffed out before its time. It wasn't that he had a perverted, twisted, sick way of doing things. A good parent suffers when his or her child suffers. It hurts me tremendously to think of how mean I had been to him and how blind I had been. He wanted to comfort me, and in return, I cursed him. I had felt so burdened by my sister-in-law's death for years, in part, because I couldn't talk with my family about it, but when I was in Medjugorje, I sensed God saying to me, "I know. I know how you feel."

I know that God allowed my sister-in-law's death to happen, but he did not want it to happen, and there is a vast difference between the two. I know, technically, that everything happens for a reason, but at the same time, God does not want us to suffer. We suffer because of sin. We were not created for suffering. We were created to be loved by him and to love him, and because he respects our free will, and we can choose to sin, suffering is going to happen. But he can bring good out of it. He brought good out of my pain, and I have always said, "If I had to go through all my troubles to experience the peace and conversion in Medjugorje, then so be it. It was worth it."

My point is . . . I suffered a lot growing up because of my own issues. If I had been happy, who knows if I would have traveled, or gone into churches and felt God's presence, or ever ended up at Medjugorje. I now see God's hand in all of those moments. If I hadn't been miserable, would I have tried to escape by traveling? Probably not. It says in the Bible that God works things out for the good for those who love him. Well, he also works out things for the good for those who hate him, because I hated him. I didn't deserve what I received. I didn't deserve the many gifts God gave me, and this showed me God's unfathomable mercy and love.

* * *

If you would abandon yourselves to me, you would not even feel the passage from this life to the next. You would begin to live the life of heaven on earth.[32]

PETER

A sex and pornography addict embraced by mercy

My first major run-in with God happened when I was fourteen years old. I was sitting on the front doorstep at the house of my then best friend, and as we were talking, we saw a frog hop by. Frogs were a commodity in the East Coast suburbs where we lived and provided instant entertainment for two, bored high school boys. My friend picked the frog up, and we began to play with it. As we amused ourselves at the frog's expense, we found that its legs looked funny when it flew through the air. We began to toss the frog higher and higher into the air, laughing at the way it looked as it fell. Amazingly, the frog didn't die, not that we were trying to kill it. The fall just didn't seem to hurt it when it hit the grass. I remember thinking that we were being cruel, but I didn't care.

Higher and higher the frog went. Finally my friend tossed the frog very high, and as it fell back to the ground, it hit the handlebars on my bike, bounced off them, and fell on the grass motionless. We looked at the frog for a while and realized that we had killed it. We instantly felt terrible. My friend, who felt responsible since he was the one who had tossed the frog into the air, said he thought we should say an "Our Father." I thought it was brave of him to suggest, because I was also sad that we had killed it, but I was too embarrassed to say an "Our Father" with him out loud. I doubted that God could or would do anything, and I thought it was foolish to pray together out loud for the sake of a frog. My friend was relentless. He insisted, and finally I told him to say it alone. He put his hand on the frog, closed his eyes and began saying the "Our Father."

When he first started to pray I was uncomfortable, but gradually my feeling of discomfort disappeared. When he finished the prayer, the frog, which lay on its back and had been dead for a few minutes, twitched once, squirmed over and hopped away. We looked at it in amazement and disbelief. We had seen a miracle. From the unknown, an immense power had suddenly and inexplicably revealed itself to us, a power able to restore life. God showed us that he truly existed. He said, "Look! I do exist! And I can do anything!" I had not truly believed. I distrusted in his power and had been embarrassed to call on him, and yet he revealed himself to me anyway. His message was simple, "I am always here, and I love you, even when you are at your worst." It was a reassuring and prophetic message, as I was later to learn.

God loves you, Peter

I was born into an extended blue-collar family of recent immigrant workers—butchers, barbers, and the like—and grew up in the suburbs of a large East Coast city. From a very young age, there was something painfully apparent to me that I found difficult to explain: I did not fit in. So many children who grow up in dysfunctional families feel the same way that I did - confused, unwanted, and unloved.

On the outside, my family life was one of idyllic splendor. We were, and still are, very close. I was an altar boy with a love of the Church. My brothers and I played sports and did well in school. I became involved in the arts and did community service.

By my early teens, I began to unravel as the first cracks in the façade of family tranquility appeared in my fragile psyche. There was simply no communication at home. I was never heard. My parents fought often. They also enforced seemingly arbitrary rules without offering the least bit of an explanation. By fourteen years old, my relationship with my parents, my frustration with their denial and lack of communication, became so great that I eventually became suicidal. Once, after a particularly frustrating argument, I attempted suicide by trying to stab myself in the stomach and then trying to slit my wrists with a serrated steak knife. The attempt was a cry for help, and except for a few bruises, I was fine. I could not actually go through with the act because I was afraid of the physical pain. Needless to say, I was desperate for someone to listen to me…someone to understand.

Then I discovered girls. At age fifteen, I met Anne and learned about the beauty of intimate conversation with a member of the opposite sex. Here was everything I had ever wanted! Anne was an attractive young woman who spoke softly, looked me in the eyes, told me that I was special, shared her feelings, and listened to me while I shared my own. I instantly fell in love with her. Unfortunately, although my friendship with Anne was strong, she did not share my desire for romance, and I quickly fell into despair. I simply could not tolerate the rejection that I was once again feeling. One night, in a moment of teenage angst, I wrote a love poem (a thoroughly bad love poem, but heartfelt.) In the poem I asked anyone out there who might love me to tell me so.

A short time later, I dreamed that I was floating in darkness. I felt compelled to turn to my right, and as I did I saw a bright light in the distance. My body was unexplainably drawn to the light, and as I approached it I wanted to move into it to see what was there. My desire made me move faster. As I got closer I saw two people standing in the light. I instantly realized that they were Jesus and Mary, and I was seized with an insatiable desire to draw close enough to see their faces. My supreme desire was simply to know what they actually looked like.

Jesus was standing in the distance in a rust-colored loincloth, with a crown of thorns on his head. He had long, wavy brown hair and a beard, and blood ran down his face; his whole body was covered in blood. He was, in a word, pummeled, and he was suffering tremendously. He looked as if it pained him to stand. On his left stood his mother, the Blessed Virgin Mary. She was shorter than he, had long dark hair, and was wearing a white dress and veil trimmed in a deep, rich blue.

When I got close to them, it was Mary who finally spoke. Jesus remained silent, although his presence next to her was all the evidence I needed to tell me that he was witnessing to her words. "God loves you, Peter," she said. Then again, "God loves you, Peter." And again, "God loves you, Peter."

I awoke by jumping into a sitting position saying out loud, "God loves me, God loves me, God loves me!" My mouth was saying the words, but I was not. My soul was speaking to me, and I was listening. I was in a cold sweat and my body was soaked in perspiration. I was burning up, yet chilled. I remember thinking that I must have a fever. After a moment, I lay back down in exhaustion to go to sleep. I felt completely drained, relaxed and content.

I know now that the dream was both a consolation and a warning. God was telling me that he loved me and also warning me not to make an idol of women. If I loved God first, then everything else would fall into place.

The dream, while captivating and inspiring me, profoundly haunted my imagination. God was trying to help me, heal me, and save me from the path where I was headed. But I did not have the tools to understand it correctly. I was Catholic, but my family had stopped going to Mass, and I would not go back again for several years. I was lost, and women were quickly becoming my god and my savior, even as I repeatedly found myself rejected by them. But they were real, and they were close, and I understood them better than I understood God.

At the time, my relationship with God was modeled by both my relationship with my parents and by their understanding of God. In the world I inhabited, God was demanding and authoritarian, vengeful and vindictive. He made demands, not conversation. He was an angry and spiteful God out to test me at every turn, always eager to punish, smothering and guilt-inducing, and merciless when I failed. God used love as a weapon. He tolerated no rivals and so would not stand for any competition from a woman. Due to my culture and upbringing, I simply viewed the two as adversaries, with God as the predetermined winner. This caused me to fight bitterly with him and to misunderstand his call to love him first as a beckon to the priesthood, which I did not desire.

Nevertheless, the dreams kept on coming. God was working overtime to get me to listen, and in my case dreams were his *modus operandi*. One of my favorite dreams from this time gave me an insight into God's own emotions. In the dream I was standing near a marshy swamp on a humid, southern summer night. Peering through a warm haze, I noticed a light blue mist hovering over the water. I stood admiring the beauty of the sight, and especially the sounds. There were frogs croaking and crickets chirping, and the noise was amazing. I had never thought that frogs croaking and crickets chirping could sound so beautiful. As I pondered and listened, God spoke to me. "Listen to the frogs," he said. "They are so beautiful, and you want to hold on to them. But when you try to catch them, you can't. They won't let you. They squirm and jump, slip out of your hands, and hop away. You can't hold onto them as much as you want to. That is how I feel when dealing with people."

Despite the dreams and the fascination with all things spiritual, at sixteen I started to squirm out of God's hands. I never prayed, regarded spirituality as a secondary passion, and put all of my effort into pursuing women.

I had no idea what I was getting myself into

At seventeen I became sexually active with a young woman named Ashley. I truly believe that it was at that fateful moment, when I lost my virginity, that women became an idol and a disaster for me. I often say that if I could take back one decision in my life, it would be the choice to give away my virginity. I had no idea what I was getting myself into. I accepted the lie that so many people fall into, the lie that my parents had mistakenly taught me—that love, without a binding commitment in the Sacrament of marriage, is enough to permit sexual activity. Since neither Ashley nor I had ever been sexually active before, and since we desired to be married, we thought that the stigma against premarital sex was null and void in our case. Time and again I had seen couples in love, even couples who were engaged to be married, have their relationship break off at the last moment, but in my naiveté, I figured that my situation would be different. Besides, love felt good, better than anything else I had ever known. At this point, despite the dreams, God had become a remote concept, at best an object of detached fascination, at worst an ogre in the sky. I had no tolerance for what I perceived to be his authoritarian rules about sex or anything else. I clung instead to my idealized concept of sex and love which was based on Hollywood movies. Little did I know how much else went along with this idealization. Like many others, when I "did" before saying "I do," I sold myself and my partner short.

My intentions with Ashley were not entirely ignoble. Although mired in the ignorance of youth, I loved her, and I wanted to be with one woman all of my life. Unfortunately, my decision to have premarital sex doomed my romantic notion. Ashley had been gang raped shortly before we started dating. I had no idea that she had been abused when we became intimate and did not find out until after we broke up. I did not make her situation any better with my insecurities or by pressuring her into having sex. We were far too young to deal with the can of worms we had opened. I needed communication and affection. She needed time and space. I hurt her by pressuring her. The relationship, my first, was a disaster of lies, arguments and cheating that lasted three years. It ended with Ashley becoming a lesbian and my beginning to question my ability to find happiness with women. I even began to question my own sexuality. But by that point, at age nineteen, I had already chosen my path.

I was now in college in Arizona and my desire for sexual activity was quickly starting to take over. I had developed a sense of powerlessness around women and sex. I desperately needed to regain the control that I felt I had lost with Ashley. I had been robbed of my immature dream of marrying the unspoiled, perfect woman who would complete me by loving only me, and I was determined to get it back. If I could not get it back, I was determined at least to have a sexual relationship that I could control, with a woman who made me the center of her world. It never dawned upon me that being sexually active was only furthering my inferiority complex by introducing me to women who were already sharing themselves with other men—the exact thing that I was trying to avoid. And the fact that Ashley was sharing herself with other women was almost too much to bear. In addition to feeling like the ultimate male failure, I also felt (and to this day still feel) partially responsible for her choice. I treated her very poorly.

When I was twenty I began dating Sarah, an attractive young woman who was the talk of the college residence halls. Sarah was beautiful, and I felt like a million bucks. My self-esteem went up, and I mistakenly began to think that I had regained what I had lost. But my relationship with Sarah was fleeting. Sarah and I had sex, and shortly afterwards she cheated on me with a close friend. Then she repeatedly lied to me to cover it up. Instead of getting angry with her, I accepted the pattern, became numb to it, turned off my emotions and broke up with her.

At about this time, I made two decisions which would have profound consequences later in my life. The first decision was to return to Church. A Catholic friend from college who had witnessed my breakup with Ashley had been urging me to return to Mass for some time. The church she suggested, Saint Stephen's, had a vibrant young adult community. I began attending their Mass regularly and began reconverting to the faith of my childhood. The second decision was to begin looking at pornography.

Don't you feel crippled?

I was first exposed to pornography at three years old. My parents had left a magazine lying around the house, and like any inquisitive child, I soon found it. The discovery I made on that day is one of the earliest childhood memories that I have. I cannot say what it was that captivated me so much, but the pictures, even at that young age, had a profound psychological impact on me, one that sowed seeds of destruction. As I grew into adulthood, pornography became a time bomb waiting to explode. When my relationships with women became unmanageable, there was always the prospect of pornography to get me high and make me feel good. At last I had found the control over women that I lacked. In my dysfunctional mind, pornography was about women who wanted to be with men. In reality, pornography is all about power, the power men have to make women do what they want and thus feel good about themselves. It should be no surprise that several serial killers of women have been obsessed with pornography.

It wasn't too long before I realized that pornography was becoming a problem for me. One night during this time Jesus came to me again in a dream. In the dream I was walking through a field. I was approached by a young deer which I fed out of my hand. This made me very happy. The deer turned suddenly into a lamb and stood on its two hind legs, walked towards me and began talking to me. I don't remember what it said, and I feared that it wasn't from God, that it was evil, and I felt the need to test it. With great drama and fanfare I yelled, "Arise, O Lord, and scatter thine enemies!" As soon as I was finished a voice from the sky said, "Peter." I ignored it and again said, "Arise, O Lord, and scatter thine enemies!" Again, the voice said my name, this time more emphatically, and then added, "It is me." I said a third time, (for some reason I was compelled to say it three times), "Arise, O Lord, and scatter thine enemies!" At that, the voice said, "Mine is my Father's and my Father's is mine." With those words Jesus identified himself. I was overjoyed—nearly paralyzed with joy. Jesus said to me several times, "Don't you feel crippled?" "Yes!" I exclaimed, "Yes!" But I thought that he meant, "Don't you feel like the crippled man in the Bible who has just had an encounter with Jesus and is overjoyed?" But then he said to me, "Do you know how easily I could concoct a medicine to cure you?" Again he said, "Don't you feel crippled?" And the dream ended. When I awoke I realized that he was talking about sex, that I was crippled by giving in to my desires. I began begging Jesus in prayer for his "medicine," although I had no idea what it might be.

I also had a couple of dreams at this time telling me that I had to go to Confession. On one occasion, I saw Jesus in a white robe telling me to go. On another, I saw Saint Teresa of Avila, and she, too, told me to go. This time, at age twenty-one, I listened to what God was saying. I began attending Mass more fervently, began making Christian friends, and became involved in a chaste relationship with a young woman named Cecilia. It was through this relationship, and the spiritual discussions and experiences we shared, that I finally mustered the courage to receive the Sacrament of Reconciliation. On the day that I made up my mind to go, at the precise moment I said "yes" to God, I looked up and saw a huge rainbow coming out of the sky and landing on a cross atop a distant church.

When my relationship with Cecilia ended, I was as confused as ever, but I was also acutely aware that our break-up was the easiest I had ever experienced. I knew that because Cecilia and I had not been sexually active, the parting had come much easier. At this time, the spirituality of sex finally started to make sense to me. God gave me a dream in which I saw blood cells flowing through veins, and as I looked, God said that it was sex. It illustrated "one flesh" to me quite literally. Looking at it, I felt clean, bright, divine, pure, happy, love. It was sex as God intended it to be in marriage. I realized that the physical act of sexual intimacy carried with it a power that I could not fully understand and could not control. I knew Jesus said explicitly in Matthew 19:1-

6 that in sexual intimacy the two become "one flesh," that when the sexual act is complete, our souls and our bodies are inextricably linked to the other person. My soul had become bound to all of the women I had been intimate with (and not only with them, but with all of the people they had been intimate with as well), because I had become one flesh with each of them. When I became sexually active, I took on the demons of others, both literally and figuratively, whether I wanted to or not. That is why I ultimately lost my sense of self and well-being when I became promiscuous, and why things really started to spiral out of control with each additional sexual encounter that I had. That is why it was so painful when things did not go well in my relationships, and I broke up with the women that I was dating. By walking away from those women, I was ripping my own body and soul in half.

I have seen this truth in friends who profess no belief in God. There is simply no way around this reality. The only way to heal the rift was to be reconciled with God through the Sacrament of Reconciliation, which alone brought me comfort and peace. I also began thinking seriously about the priesthood, a combination, I think, of my misunderstanding God's demand for all my love, and my desire to avoid my own growing sexual dysfunction.

Am I really gay?

I went to a young priest, Father Rick, at Saint Stephen's for advice. I had met him one Saturday afternoon in the confessional. When I told him of my possible vocation to the priesthood he encouraged me to contact him. I was afraid but finally relented and called him. I had a million questions and was desperate for answers. What did God want from me? How could I discern God's call in my life? Did I have to become a priest if God wanted me to become one, but I didn't have the ultimate desire? Why were my relationships always a mess? Why was I always craving sex? Why couldn't I control my desire to look at pornography? Fr. Rick took me to dinner, introduced me to the vocations director, brought me to the seminary, and welcomed me into the world of priestly ministry. He never answered any of my questions, but I felt special. We eventually became friends and even went on vacation to the Grand Canyon together.

While I don't doubt Fr. Rick's initial concern with my possible vocation, it soon became evident that he had an additional motivation for our friendship. One night Fr. Rick, who had been transferred to a new parish some distance away, was back in town visiting friends and stayed the night at my apartment. As a recent college graduate living in a studio apartment, I did not have a spare bedroom or a couch. Since my bed was large, I told Fr. Rick that I was fine if he slept in the same bed as me. This was my first mistake. I have slept in the same bed with male family and friends on many occasions during my life, and it never occurred to me that this might be a problem. It quickly turned into one. Fr. Rick suddenly stripped to his underwear and asked if it was all right if he slept that way since that was how he slept every night. Uneasy, but trusting in his priestly vocation, I said, "Sure." Then Fr. Rick became very upset. He was reliving a bad experience from his past and needed comforting. Would it be okay if I gave him a hug? More uneasiness—hesitation. Well, guys can hug each other for comfort. Besides, I knew that Fr. Rick had been abused, probably sexually, and I wanted to comfort him as a friend. And he was a priest! "Uhh, sure." And as I reached out and hugged him he made a pass at me.

I backed away from him in shock and confusion. What had just happened? I told him that he had made me uncomfortable, that I wasn't gay. And then I got angry, although I tried not to show it. I tossed my pillow on the floor and told him that I wasn't sleeping in the same bed as him. The next day I asked Fr. Rick if he thought that I was gay. He said that he thought I might be. Again, I was shocked. By this point, I had graduated from college and was working professionally in the entertainment industry. Could this be the reason Fr. Rick thought that I was gay?

I quickly forgave Fr. Rick, although every time we went out for a drink, or to get something to eat, it was at a gay bar or a gay restaurant. One night, on another visit, while getting out of a cab, Fr. Rick, who was very drunk, kissed me on the lips. More disbelief. I was trying to be understanding because he had been abused in his past, but it became too much to bear. A few days later I exploded at him. "How dare you assume that I am gay," I told him. "If you weren't a priest, I'd knock you out." Here I was, at a vulnerable point in my life, on the verge of an addiction to pornography, taking infant steps in my faith, trying to change learned behaviors, trying to stay chaste, considering a vocation, discerning my problems with women, and a priest I sought for counsel, a priest I had met in the confessional was making passes at me, taking me to gay bars, and making me think, "Am I really homosexual? Am I latent and in denial? Is that why I have problems with women?" I had questioned my sexuality before, when I couldn't find satisfaction with girls as a teenager. But after considering it then, I knew that I was straight. I knew my problem was that I liked women too much, and in the wrong ways. But now I wasn't sure… Fr. Rick turned the whole situation on its head. I wanted to complain to somebody, but a mutual friend of ours, a layman named Jake, himself a gay man who was very much in love with Fr. Rick, swore me to silence. "You'll bring trouble and shame on the priesthood and the entire Church if you say something," he said.

My heart became sick, and now at twenty-two, I felt more screwed up than ever. I kept going to Church, but my soul was no longer in it. I drifted away from my friendship with Fr. Rick until we finally lost contact, but the damage was done, and it had a drastic and lasting impact. Fr. Rick's breach of trust and his crossing of proper ministerial boundaries turned the Church from a place of refuge and hope into a place of desolation and despair. I lost all of the joy that Mass had begun to bring me. Attending Church now became a laborious emotional and psychological process. The feeling that God was a vindictive ogre in the sky also returned, and my anger at him started to become vicious. Every negative thought I had about God had been reinforced by Fr. Rick's behavior. I screamed and cursed at God regularly. Because he was in control, it was easy to blame him for everything. At the time, I did not know that Satan was real and that he would stop at nothing to block my conversion and my return to Jesus. I also had no idea that God permits free will and that our negative decisions have a negative impact on our lives. I saw only an arbitrary and ambiguous puppet-master bent on making me miserable. "I finally try to change my life, and this is what you do?!" I roared at God. Along with my anger, my former desire for power and control returned in spades, and now it was fueled by a desire to prove to myself that, in addition to being acceptable to women, I was not gay.

The Devil's lair

I decided to move to Los Angeles, where I continued my career in the entertainment industry. At twenty-three years old I was making good money. The glitz and the glamour of L.A. were tremendously appealing, and I was successful at what I did. In time I realized why I loved the entertainment business so much in the first place. There was attention and there were women…lots of women. And since the entertainment industry is fueled by good looks, most of the women were very attractive. It felt like heaven.

I had been prepared for this moment years before. God had given me a dream, a premonition, to show me where I was headed, but I didn't heed his message. In the dream, I somehow walked into barbed wire and got stuck. I had to peel myself free. At the time I had been reading about Saint Francis of Assisi rolling in thorns to stop his lustful temptations, but I didn't associate the barbed wire in the dream with my own lustful temptations. When I was free of the barbed wire, I went to a place where I applied for a job as a sound effects technician, a field in which I had no experience. The position required the sound effect of a person screaming as he or she fell into hell. I was masterful at creating the sound effect, and as I played it for those listening we all thought that it was very funny. I got the job. When I awoke I was clueless as to the dream's meaning. It was a warning which connected lust, the entertainment business and the loss of my soul, but I did not understand.

Fr. Rick's actions had radically stoked the fires of my promiscuity. Of course, my promiscuity was saturated with conflict and guilt. I knew I was a hypocrite and that I was going against everything God had showed me about sex and marriage, and the pornography only exacerbated the problem. I was holding women to pornographic standards, expecting them to look, think and behave like the women I had seen in the pornography I was watching. When they did act that way, I was repulsed because the behavior conflicted with my ideal of "the pure and unspoiled angel." But when they failed to act that way, it only increased my dissatisfaction. This inner-conflict sometimes affected my libido, and the loss of libido further stoked the fires of my inferiority complex, which furthered my desire for more sexual contact. I found myself in a Catch-22 at every turn and entered deeper into the devil's lair.

Then one day at work I met Lindsey. By this point, physical beauty had become an obsession with me, and Lindsey was very beautiful. Like Sarah, she was the talk of the town. All of the guys stood around on break at work and talked about dating someone like Lindsey. She was energetic, smart, playful and fun. She was always smiling, and she was very talented. To add fuel to the fire, she was also a burgeoning Catholic. She spoke about God with passion and desire. She admitted she had secretly considered becoming a Catholic sister. Lindsey quickly captured my attention and then my heart. I was shortly infatuated. Then I was in love. There was only one problem. Lindsey was fifteen years old, and I was twenty-four.

I switched jobs to work near Lindsey. Soon we became good friends. We spoke about God, vocation, and life, and thoroughly enjoyed each other's company. Lindsey quickly became the unspoiled "angel" I had been looking for. She was young and innocent and full of potential and possibility. I thought I had found my soul mate and was convinced that God had blessed our union. I had never felt so strongly about a woman in my life. I was beside myself with desire for her. I would do whatever it took to be with her forever. I had never completely stopped going to weekly Mass, but now I was attending with renewed vigor. I stopped looking at pornography. I became chaste. Lindsey and I soon began dating. We decided that we would wait until she turned eighteen and then get married.

The problem with Lindsey, besides her age, was that she had been raped, horrendously, and often. The problem with me, besides my age, was that I continued to remain blind to the long-term effects of sexual abuse, both with Lindsey and, to a lesser extent, with myself and with my own emotional and sexual dysfunction. In addition, Fr. Rick had helped to obliterate any final sense I had of maintaining healthy boundaries. It was a matter of days before Lindsey and I kissed. It was a matter of weeks before we began having sex. Both sets of parents knew what was transpiring, and though hesitant at first, in time they were not concerned. Meanwhile, I had become a statutory rapist.

At this point in my story, all hell broke loose—literally. If I was a somewhat misguided but good-willed person before Lindsey, I became a monster during and after my relationship with her. As our relationship progressed, Lindsey started to tell me her full story, and I was not prepared to deal with what I heard. She was not the angel I had supposed her to be. To be honest, even if she had been, I do not think I would have been satisfied with her. I was fighting a hopeless battle against myself. Lindsey was only the excuse I used to cover for my own short-comings.

Lindsey, whose parents were divorced, had been molested throughout her childhood by her sister. Lindsey's father knew about the abuse, but he was involved in organized crime, and was a criminal of the worst kind. I think he was afraid to step in and stop the abuse lest his family turn against him in a court of law, so the abuse went on. At fourteen, Lindsey lost her virginity. The next day her boyfriend came back and raped her. And then again. And then again. He raped her almost every day for months. He broke into the house to rape her while she was home alone. He beat her while he raped her. He attempted to drown her while he raped her. He made her bleed. He nearly knocked her unconscious. Almost broke her jaw. Sodomized her. Threatened to kill her. She wanted to tell her father, but she knew she could not. Her father would kill the boy, so she said nothing until one day she stood up for herself and the abuse miraculously ended. Then she was abused again by two other men in the short time before we finally met.

Lindsey's ex-boyfriend, with whom I had been friends and from whom I had "stolen" her, started stalking me and threatened to have my fingers and legs broken by "family friends." In the meantime, Lindsey began pressing charges against her family and moved in with her father, who by this time was a drug-ruined, paranoid schizophrenic, who slept with guns and watched specials about Hitler on the History Channel all day. Sadly, he was an exceptionally intelligent man with a large heart and great faith that had been sorely misguided. I stayed over the house with Lindsey many nights, and Lindsey's father began confessing crimes to me, crimes I shudder to repeat to anyone. When Lindsey went to confession and told our parish priest some of the things her father had done, she said the poor priest's eyes opened wide, and he looked shocked.

Lindsey and I were both Catholic and faith-filled, and we went to Mass together every Sunday. But we were having sex and leading unfaithful lives. With all of the pressures, our relationship started to unravel. Eventually, Lindsey and I started cheating on one another and lying about it. We fought bitterly about everything. I was usually the one who instigated the fighting. Because of my history, I was jealous, controlling and manipulative. I started ranting and raving like a lunatic. I was emotionally and verbally abusive. On one occasion I raised my fist to hit her. I am thankful to this day that I did not. Instead I punched and kicked anything that got in my way when I was angry – walls, mailboxes, garbage cans, even my car. On another occasion I was so consumed with rage that I wanted to rape her just to make her hurt, to take from her what I wanted and thought she would not, or could not, give to me. My faith prevented me from doing it. Instead of raping her, I calmly stared at her and told her how, and why, a man decides to rape a woman.

It was not long before Child Protective Services contacted Lindsey's father. What did he know about the sexual abuse? He might have to testify against his family. He knew that if he testified they would sing like canaries about his violent past. He got scared and switched into fight or flight mode. He chose to fight. He threw Lindsey out of the house by piling her belongings on the front lawn and blamed me for instigating the case and for encouraging her to talk about her past with people. My parents, with whom I was living at the time, felt sorry for Lindsey and allowed her to move into our house. Lindsey's father soon began calling the house and threatening me. One day he called up and said, "You want to play hard ball with me? I got two words for you buddy: statutory rape." These were the words I dreaded hearing. They meant several years in prison and they were not coming from a healthy man. I called his bluff because I knew about his past—I held the upper hand. I spent several hours on the phone debating with him before he eventually backed off. But I was deathly afraid of his mental instability and began to fear for my life.

I began to lose control. Lindsey and I never told anyone that we were dating, although it must have been obvious to everyone concerned that we were. I was living a lie and was paranoid about being caught, paranoid about what Lindsey's father would do, and most of all, paranoid about all of the cheating. In addition to dating Lindsey, I was dating another woman, whose boyfriend was a friend of mine. She lied to her boyfriend, and I lied to Lindsey. And Lindsey, who was also cheating, lied to me.

My façade of sanity was breaking. I was diagnosed as clinically depressed, then as a manic depressive. I was put on all sorts of medications, first anti-depressants and then anti-psychotics. There was no rhyme or reason to my mental state. I was in a mental fog. Nothing made sense. I was utterly confused and saw no way out. I wanted to love Lindsey, but I could not. I was so mentally and physically infatuated with her that the thought of living without her was worse than the thought of living in torment with her. I could not keep my job and began missing work. Then I just quit. I wrecked my car. I fell into bankruptcy. I stopped taking care of myself. I ate fast food three times a day, if I ate at all. I drank coffee and chain-smoked cigarettes day and night. I began drinking alcohol and smoking pot. Strangely, as I headed toward oblivion, I listened over and over again to the song, "Amazing Grace." It was my only comfort.

Finally, one night I snapped in public. I had been out drinking and smoking pot with friends, and the marijuana, which may have been laced with something, reacted poorly with my medication, which caused me to go ballistic. The experience brought me to a place of evil there are no words for. My friends attempted to bring me to the hospital but were too far gone to drive safely, so they quickly turned around and took me home with them. I knew I needed to go to the hospital so I left my friend's house and ran to the nearest pay-phone and called an ambulance by myself. When the police came instead of an ambulance, I told them to put me in handcuffs because if they did not I would "do something stupid." One of the cops asked me what that "something stupid" was, and I told him that I was so angry that I would take his gun and start shooting. I was quickly handcuffed and escorted to the psych-ward at the local hospital where I was strapped down and detoxed until morning. Throughout the night, which I barely remember, I screamed like a fiend because I was so drugged up that I thought I had died and gone to hell. I confessed my statutory rape to the police (who didn't seem to mind as long as Lindsey's parents didn't press charges), told everyone concerned that I was gay (I really doubted myself and started to think that I might be latent), and I think, but don't remember for sure, that I may have divulged Lindsey's father's secrets. I am sure that I said countless other things as well.

The next morning one of the nurses came in, sat down on the bed, looked me straight in the eyes and said, "You said some crazy things last night." She was waiting for an answer. When I told her that it was all true, she looked surprised. She told me that I needed to get help, and she meant it. She was the first benevolent person I had come across in months. I was released from the hospital when my parents came to pick me up. There were no words. I had stopped talking to them months before about anything of substance, and our silence simply codified in practice what had long ago been decided in theory.

A few days later I returned to the hospital psych ward. I had crossed a line that afternoon and decided that I would kill myself. I had written a suicide note, gone into the kitchen, mixed together a bunch of pills, put them in my mouth and was about to drink some water to swallow them when my hand froze, and the fear of hell crept into me. I truly believe that my guardian angel stayed my hand. I felt his presence and decided not to go through with it. At that moment a profound sense of peace came over me that I had not felt in months, and I sensed a heavy burden leaving my soul. It was nothing I could have caused myself. More than anything, I sensed that God was still with me and that there was still some kind of hope. I was hanging on by a thread.

A week later Lindsey told me she had slept with one of our mutual friends. Up until that point, I did not know the specifics of what she had done. Everything was suspicion and accusation in both directions. We were still trying to work things out, and when she told me the truth I felt set free. I disappeared on a road trip for several days without telling anyone where I was going. When I returned home, I checked myself into the psych ward for the third time and cried for three days straight. When I was released from the hospital, I packed a small suitcase and left the next day for a friend's wedding in Arizona.

I was still violent and unpredictable. On the plane to the wedding I had an anxiety attack. I would have several more over the next several months. During the attacks I was overcome with rage and felt the urge to kill somebody. I began to hear noises and sometimes voices that were not there. I heard the devil telling me to kill people on at least two occasions. I had so much rage inside of me that I was petrified of what I might do. I know and understand what goes on in the minds of killers. While I had enough God in me to retain my sense of self, I can see how some people don't, and how that rage is released.

After the wedding, I decided to stick around Arizona for a while. I managed to keep my promiscuity alive in the first few weeks of the trip. It seemed wherever I looked women were available. I was now twenty-five, and it was all becoming too easy. I visited Ashley, my first girlfriend, who was still a lesbian. I had found out through old friends that she recently contracted a rare disease and had come very close to dying. I think I needed to see her for closure. I had also gotten back in touch with Anne, my very first love, who had moved to Arizona a few years before. It took me no time to pursue her in an effort to prove that I could win her after all these years. Chasing her added to my desire to stay.

Peter, God loves you

One afternoon in Arizona, as I sat in absolute despair with the destruction of my life lying all around me, Fr. Rick's old friend, Jake, put on the John Michael Talbot version of the Magnificat called "Holy is His Name." The music and the lyrics mesmerized me. It was a beautiful song of redemption. As I listened to Mary's famous words from the Bible, "My soul proclaims the greatness of the Lord, and my spirit rejoices in God my Savior, for He has looked with mercy on my lowliness…" I felt that Mary was saying the words directly to me and telling me that everything was going to be okay.

And then it hit me—the Blessed Virgin Mary, my pursuit of Anne, the poem I had written—I had been here before. I realized at that moment that roughly ten years earlier God had warned me through Mary and numerous other dreams where my life was headed. I thought back to when I was fifteen years old, suffering from unrequited love for Anne, and had written a poem one night asking someone to love me. I remembered the dream I had that night when I saw Mary, the Mother of God, standing next to Jesus, who looked bruised and beaten and was covered in blood, and I heard her say to me, "Peter, God loves you." I was back where I had been so many years before and God was giving me a second chance. My life had come full circle. As I listened to Mary's words gently calling out to me through the song, I realized that God was still there, and that he was saying exactly what he had said in the beginning. And, most importantly, he was not saying, "I told you so." In that moment, when God came again, there was no accusation. There was no guilt. There was no shame. There was no condemnation—none of the things which had tainted my image of God and brought me to despair. There was only, "I still love you. I'm still here." And that is what finally saved me, that unconditional love, that unconditional forgiveness. It was at that moment that I finally fell in love with God, and I wept bitterly.

I'm in hell, and I can't stop

I decided to dedicate my life to God, but I did not get better overnight. I discovered a graduate program at a local university in Arizona that had openings, and I applied. To my surprise, I was accepted. I had always wanted to return to college some day, and the prospect of earning a master's degree was exciting. But I had been unemployed for some time, and it was financially very difficult to get started. I lived with Jake for a while, but as I spent more time with Anne, he became jealous and possessive and threw me out. I ended up on the street with two small suitcases. I had no money and nowhere to go. Anne's family, with whom she lived, was gracious enough to let me sleep on their couch. But I was still unhealthy. I still wanted to prove to myself that after all these years I could "conquer" her. To my surprise, Anne did develop an interest in me. Eventually one thing led to another and we had sex. Afterwards, I felt nothing. We kept having sex, and I kept feeling nothing. I ended the relationship and moved out of Anne's house. It would be the last time I would have sexual intercourse.

In total, I moved six times in that first semester of school. I ended up in the "ghetto," staying in tenement hotels for a while, and for the first time in my life I was completely isolated. That is when my conversion finally kicked into gear. One night, while alone in my tenement hotel room, God exposed the lie I had been living as I wrote in my journal. I realized that I had been saying I was a Christian my whole life, but that I was not really a Christian at all. I was just playing a game with God to see how much I could get away with. I was paying it all lip-service. I used Christianity to puff up my ego because my self-esteem was so low. I needed to be better than everyone else because I felt so poorly about myself. Though I believed it all, religion had become a great charade for me. I had to admit that I was manipulative, jealous, spiteful, proud...all the things nobody wants to admit of themselves. It was a sobering moment. I decided, come hell or high water, that I was going to be honest about myself and to give my life over to Jesus once and for all.

It was not easy. Though I didn't know it at the time, my initial conversion would take a few years and would be a *very* difficult process. To paraphrase Saint John of the Cross, "When you rub out old stains, you use strong soap." God began applying some serious elbow grease to my soul, and it wasn't until he began exposing my heart that I realized how weak, helpless, and lost I really was. At times it seemed like the purging I experienced during my early conversion would kill me, and in many ways my behavior got much worse for a time. But while my behavior may have been worse, my understanding had changed because my desire had changed. Through an internal conversion of the heart, God was rebuilding me from the bottom up, from the inside out. On the outside I was as sinful as ever, but on the inside, where my soul resided, a profound shift was occurring. In the past, my prime concern had been finding a woman and having sex, but now my prime concern was changing my life and finding God. I did continue to go through severe temptation, and many times I fell, but I stopped making excuses for myself and tried to change. When I look back on that period now I realize that the darkest moments of my early conversion were never as dark as when I was in the throes of agony with Lindsey. My whole world was crashing down around me, but I had finally found hope. His name was Jesus Christ.

The first thing God purged me of was my pride. This was an extremely difficult spiritual process, and it was not pretty. He did it by leaving me to my own devices so that, despite my newfound desire to change, I could do nothing good. I literally descended into a pit of sin. With Saint Paul I began screaming, "What I do, I do not understand. For I do not do what I want, but I do what I hate." [Romans 7:15] My behavior was also a last scream against letting go of my bad ways. It was an ugly scream, a horrible bellow of despair.

One night, while walking home from a friend's house in a drunken stupor, I passed a strip club and walked in. By the time I walked out, I had done the one thing that I swore I would never, ever, do. I had engaged in sexual activity with a prostitute. I knew that it was wrong, and I was very sorry. There were no excuses this time. The immorality of it all was very clear, and I felt horrible. It made my body and soul ache with mental and physical pain. But I had no self-control. There was something alluring about the ease of it all. Pay the money, get what you want. Despite my desire to change, I started to visit strip clubs and pay for prostitutes. I looked at pornography. I spent hundreds and hundreds of dollars.

When I was having sexual contact with prostitutes, I could never go all the way and have intercourse with them, partially because I knew it was wrong, and partially because I was afraid of contracting AIDS. Sometimes, despite my desires, I couldn't even get aroused. I realized that I craved the sex, but that I was repulsed by the situation at the same time. My conscience was awakening.

One day, while walking home from work, I again fell into serious temptation. I began to pray and told God that I was weak, that if he did not do something quickly I would surely sin again. The temptation was far too strong for me to resist. As I prayed, for some reason my guardian angel popped into my mind. I asked him to "please pray for me" because I needed his help to avoid sinning. I also told him that he should thank God that he had never known sin. I told him how awful it was and how lucky he was to have never experienced it. At that moment my guardian angel spoke to my heart with clear words. To date, it is the only time I have actually heard his voice. He told me that he was "terrified of sin," and that the thoughts he had of it, or of ever sinning himself, were horrible. He communicated to me that he simply could not imagine sinning against God's goodness. In a very real way, his innocence and his desire were like that of a child terrified of hurting or offending someone he loves. At that moment I began to realize that sin was not wrong because it randomly proscribed certain actions, but because it destroyed our relationship with God and with each other.

Yet my desire for sexual contact was maddening. I desperately craved sexual experiences; I needed them like an addict needs a drug. When the temptations came I felt wrenched and tortured in my own skin, and often wanted to jump out of myself. Late one night, while battling with my desire to go back to the strip club, with my shortage of money, and with my guilt, I was walking down a city street swirling in temptation and confusion and I thought, "I'm in hell, and I can't stop." Finally, God revealed my soul to me. I didn't know there was such a thing as sexual addiction, but I felt overwhelmed by my own helplessness, and for the very first time, I saw that I was utterly lost. My soul was screaming in desperation and despair. Mentally and physically, the weight of evil pressing upon me was so great that I could barely see. I mean this quite literally. As I stumbled down the street in a drunk-like stupor, I thought I was going blind. I was petrified by the thought of going to hell, but my desire for sexual release was so great that I would deny everything and anything, even God, to get a fix. The only rational thought I had, the only thing that I knew for sure, was that my soul was teetering on the edge of damnation. I saw that without God, there was nothing good inside of me. But I could not choose God. I went home and wept like an infant that night. As I lay in bed, I repeated out loud as I wept, "I'm going crazy." The loss of control effected a profound and painful realization. The pride which had hitherto informed my sense of self began to melt away. I was nothing. I could do nothing. I could be nothing but sin.

A few weeks later I went home for Christmas, and when I returned to school, I moved in with a friend. I had been absolutely alone for several months up until that point, and the social contact was good for my soul. My desire for prostitutes gradually disappeared. I had weathered a serious storm.

Sin never satisfies

Early in the spring semester, when I was twenty-six, I was invited to volunteer as a minister at the Catholic chapel at the local state prison. It just happened to be one where executions were carried out. It was my penance. I often say that it is a miracle I did not end up in jail, and I truly believe that my prison ministry experience was the payment of a debt that I owed to God. God did not send me to prison, which I think would have probably killed me, yet in another, more gentle way, he did.

The first time I went to the prison was on Good Friday. On the day of Christ's passion and death, I participated in the Stations of the Cross, which the inmates reflected upon and read out loud: Jesus is arrested, Jesus is tried, Jesus is convicted, Jesus falls, Jesus is crucified. Sitting in the chapel, just a few hundred yards away from the gas chamber, I shared the moment of human salvation with men who knew more about the power of the cross than I ever could. These murderers, these violent criminals, had been saved by the love of Jesus. The insight I had into the magnificence of the crucifixion and the power of the redemption at that moment brought me to tears. There was nothing and no one who could not be forgiven, including myself.

Twice a week for the next two years, sometimes with sweaty palms and the fear of being exposed as a statutory rapist, I went through the prison gates and taught religion classes, led prayer services, and counseled the men who were incarcerated there. These men were murderers, rapists, drug dealers and gang members who had, through the grace of God, managed to transform themselves into some of the holiest human beings I have ever met.

In graduate school I began to meet fellow Catholics around my age. For the first time in my life, I had a true Christian community. I was blessed to have these friends enter my life when they did. Some of them had had difficult pasts, some had become chaste after being sexually active, some of them were virgins, and our conversations together proved therapeutic all around. For the first time in my life, I was surrounded by good people, and we all learned from and strengthened each other. Time and again these friends told me that they loved me for who I was, not what I was, or what I might yet become. Because I could trust them, and because they did not judge me, I was able to be honest with them about my past and my current struggles. For the first time, I was not leading a double life. It made all the difference in the world. Daily, we went to Mass together as a group, then spent an hour in prayer in adoration of the Blessed Sacrament. And we ended each night by praying the rosary. We shared our lives, our fears, our failures, our hopes and our faith.

We also talked about Medjugorje and began encouraging each other to live Mary's messages in earnest. I had discovered Mary's apparitions in Medjugorje years before by reading Wayne Weible's, "Medjugorje: The Message." Though I was fascinated by the story at the time, I did not heed Mary's messages because I was still afraid of God. Yet because of my early dream experience of Mary, and the way God sang to me through her Magnificat, the whole prospect of Marian devotion became so interesting that I finally became receptive to her.

Around this time, my friends and I drove to a Marian Conference in San Rafael, California for the Jubilee Year 2000. At the conference I remember Ivan, one of the visionaries from Medjugorje, saying, "We are all in the school of Mary." I also remember him saying that he asked the Blessed Mother in an apparition why she was so beautiful and she responded, "I'm beautiful because I love." It was a profound and beautiful statement of truth. But it was Wayne Weible who had the deepest impact on me. After Wayne's speech, which was a magnificent story of a prostitute who had found her way to Medjugorje and converted, he read a poem called "Love Me As You Are." The poem, which brought me to tears when I first heard it, provided the spiritual release I needed to begin getting over the shame I had regarding my sexual dysfunction, and to see God for the mercy which he is.

Mary's messages in Medjugorje were part of God's process of making me realize the tools that I needed in the fight for my own soul: daily prayer—especially the rosary, regular Confession, frequent reception of the Eucharist, Bible reading, fasting, and continued conversion. After the conference, conversions happened left and right among my group of Christian friends. One woman, an agnostic, converted to Catholicism. Two of the men began discerning vocations to the priesthood. Another woman became a nun. My conversion was also moving forward at full speed, but my sexual desires did not disappear. I was still looking at pornography. During this period a close friend of mine related a vivid dream she had in which she saw me sitting across a small dinner table from an attractive woman. The woman and I each had a plate of food in front of us. As I reached across the table to touch the woman in lust, her face became chopped up, old, spoiled meat. The food in front of me was then taken away, and I was left with nothing to eat. I knew the dream was another warning from God that lust would lead to my destruction. I begged God for mercy, and I prayed for hours, weeks, months on end for him to remove my temptations. But the desires remained. I became aware of Saint Paul's thorn in the side and God's promise that, "My grace is sufficient for you, for power is made perfect in weakness." [2 Cor. 12:9]. Was this to be my thorn?

One night, in desperation, I had a friend pray over me for hours. That night a tremendous amount of evil came out of me. I know it did because the event was accompanied by physical phenomena which we both witnessed. During the experience the room turned frigid, and though we tried twice to turn up the heat, the room just kept getting colder and colder until finally it became an ice-box. Before that moment I knew that evil existed. I had heard the devil's voice once before, as clear as day, telling me that Sarah was cheating on me. When I confronted her, she was bewildered that I knew the exact day and time in which she had been tempted. But after this new experience I had an even deeper sense of evil's reality in the world. That night much of the residual anger I had repressed against God left my soul. After the experience, with the weight of my friend's dream pressing upon me, I decided to try with all my might to save sex for marriage.

I continued to pray fervently, but my sexual desires and my need for pornography remained. I started thinking, "It's demons. It's the devil tempting me. There must be something inside of me that won't leave." But I was just objectifying the problem, putting it outside of myself and continuing to make myself into a victim. I had gone from the one extreme of blaming God to the other extreme of blaming the devil. With difficulty, I came to the conclusion that, yes, there were evil influences acting on me, but that I had also made evil choices on my own and was personally responsible for them. I couldn't always blame demons, the devil, my parents or the world. I also had to blame myself. I learned that evil comes and tempts us all, and that some people have the spiritual integrity to stand strong; others do not. Although I had been praying and converting, I soon realized that I did not yet have the spiritual integrity or experience to stand firm in the face of sexual temptation. I was still a religious infant taking baby steps in my faith. I needed to heed the advice of Saint Ignatius of Loyola, who told Christians to practice their spirituality like an athlete, so that when the time of trial came, they would be experienced and prepared enough to defend themselves against it.

Though I accepted chastity, I still retained the desire for a sexual fix, and pornography, which did not involve contact with a real, living, breathing woman, was the solution to the dilemma I found myself in. I could remain chaste, but still get my sexual fix in a "safe" environment. The lies, of course, in this train of thought were that pornography was chastity and a safe solution to the problem. It was neither. Sin never satisfies. It always left me craving for more. I quickly realized that I had been playing this game with pornography for years. It had finally turned on me. The fact that the addiction to pornography exploded in the way that it did, at the time that it did, during my initial conversion when I had started praying fervently and attending daily Mass, was a testament to how sick I really was. I had not properly weeded the garden of my soul, so the weeds kept coming back to the surface.

I became a full blown porn addict

I became a full blown porn addict. I was binge-eating on sexual images. I spent hours on end surfing the Internet for porn. Some days I would go over fifteen hours straight surfing online. I started to fall behind in my class work and miss deadlines for papers at school. I spent hundreds of dollars renting and buying porno movies. The desire for a fix became insatiable. Increasingly, it became obvious that it was purely a physical fixation. I had finally moved beyond any emotional need and reduced women to the lowest common denominator. I had finally arrived at the ultimate moment in my long journey of sexual dysfunction: women were no longer human beings. They were simply objects for my arousal and satisfaction.

When women become objects, anything and everything becomes possible. Increasingly, I found myself looking at more and more outlandish types of pornography in search of a greater high. When my emotions were finally ripped away, there was nothing left but the physical act. There was no mystery to give the act the sense of awe and reverence that I desired. As one image or film failed to deliver the necessary high I moved on to the next, like a criminal graduating from petty theft to violent crimes. Because I was so immersed in pornography, the darker shades of sexuality began to tint my entire world. I could view the world in only one way: sexually. I had completely lost control.

I prayed, I confessed and I wrestled. And then I prayed less, and I surfed more. Then I ran back to God and prayed, confessed and wrestled again. Over and over again the cycle repeated itself. Was there no end to the madness? Why couldn't I stop? Why was Confession, which healed others, not healing me? I knew what God was doing. He was breaking me of my pride once and for all. He was allowing me to wallow in the filth that I had wedded myself to.

I often say that if there is a sexual fetish or deviance out there, I have probably thought about it, wrestled with it, considered it, been tempted by it, or been aroused by it. Pornography inspired the deeds I am most ashamed of. It inspired the thoughts and actions I have had and done which make me run away in shame and fear of ever being exposed. These are the details I hold back when I speak with family and friends about my addiction to sex in general, and my addiction to pornography in particular. These are the things I fear that few could ever understand. This is me at my darkest hour, alone, isolated, a complete sexual deviant. This is the secret Peter.

God was bleaching my soul, and the sting was unbearable. Once again he was exposing my soul for what it was. Once again he was showing me that grace alone would preserve me and save me from destruction. Grace alone would liberate me. Grace alone would bring me joy, peace and understanding. Once again he was showing me that grace was a free gift that only came from him, that I did not merit and could not earn.

My soul was defeated. The battle I had been waging against God for the last fourteen years had been won. I was a porn addict. I was a sex addict. I was violent. I was jealous. I was needy. I was manipulative. I was prideful. I was nothing, nobody, without God's saving love. One day, I finally conceded defeat. I said to God, "You win. You win." Then the healing began.

I met Fr. George, a priest of the same religious order as Fr. Rick, on a silent retreat. I went to confession to him, and when I told him what had happened with Fr. Rick, he apologized for his religious order and, though he generally only worked pastorally with the clergy, he encouraged me to see him regularly for Confession and spiritual direction. I accepted his offer. It was Fr. George who encouraged me to join Sex Addicts Anonymous (SAA), where I learned about sexual addiction and met others like myself for the first time in my life. He also encouraged me to begin counseling with a professional therapist.

A few months later I graduated with my M.A. I then returned to my hometown for a few months and found an amazing spiritual director, a priest named Fr. John, who loves Jesus and Mary with his whole heart. When I told Fr. John about my addiction and went into all of the gruesome details, he smiled and said, "So what?" Fr. John is a wonderful priest—compassionate, understanding, educated, sincere, dedicated to the Eucharist and faithful to his vows. After years of counseling and ministering to parishioners, Fr. John had learned many things about addiction. He taught me that temptation and failure were human. It was Fr. John who told me that as an addict I was not culpable for my addiction because I had lost my free-will. My desire to refrain from sinning was good enough for God as long as I tried in earnest to avoid all near occasions of sin. I was refreshed to hear him say this. He also counseled me on the spiritual life, and, most importantly, he taught me how to pray. He told me that I absolutely needed to pray on a daily basis, preferably in front of the Blessed Sacrament, either when it is exposed during adoration, or enclosed in the Tabernacle. He encouraged me to let go of my desires while praying and to let God lead my heart. He encouraged me to read Scripture and to receive the Eucharist often, daily if possible. He invited me to a weekly Holy Hour and introduced me to the Chaplet of Divine Mercy, which I now pray daily. Fr. John also knew all about Medjugorje. He had been to Medjugorje many times, and he incorporated Mary's message of conversion so fluidly into his spiritual counsel and direction that I began to live the messages without even realizing it.

Fr. John was a gift from God. I remained at home for nearly a year, meeting with him weekly, working through many of the emotional and spiritual issues that had plagued me for so long. Under his tutelage my addiction finally became clear. He explained that I needed more than Confession to help me cope with my addiction. He taught me that in addition to Confession, prayer, a twelve-step program and professional counseling, I needed Jesus in the Eucharist. Period. He reminded me constantly of the words of Jesus in John 6, verse 56, "Whoever eats my flesh and drinks my blood remains in me and I in him." He showed me that by praying in front of the Eucharist, and by going to Mass and receiving the Eucharist daily, I have God himself living inside of me to fight the addiction. The Eucharist became the key to managing my sexual addiction.

Shortly after I started praying in front of the Eucharist, I came across a quotation from Tertullian, an early Church Father who said, "The Eucharist is the medicine of immortality." The phrase hit me like a sledgehammer. "That's it!!!" I thought. "That's what Jesus meant in my dream so many years ago when he warned me about my crippling sexual addiction and said, "Do you know how easily I could concoct a medicine to cure you?" The Eucharist is the medicine I need, the only medicine that has the power to keep me healthy and sober. I am sad that it took me so long to figure out this truth.

Today, if I pray daily, attend daily Mass in addition to Sunday

Mass, go to therapy on a regular basis, maintain healthy and active friendships, and faithfully work a twelve-step group, either through Sex Addicts Anonymous, Sex and Love Addicts Anonymous, or Sexaholics Anonymous[33], my addiction remains controllable. I rarely have the temptations that once plagued me, and when I do, I have the tools and a support network to control them. Of course, I am not perfect. I struggle often and sometimes I fail. But as long as I continue to pray, attend therapy, work my program, and receive the Eucharist, I do not spiral out of control like I used to. However, if I don't do these things, my addiction quickly takes over. It is a lot of work, and it can be exhausting. I work out my salvation with fear and trembling, because I know what the alternative is. Sex addiction is indeed my thorn, and Jesus has used it to humble me and liberate me with the realization that I have no power of my own. Through sex addiction, God has perfected me in weakness by teaching me that his grace alone is indeed sufficient. I now understand why the song "Amazing Grace" resonated so deeply when I was embroiled in turmoil. God's grace set me free.

Today I am a different human being. I have confronted my parents on the past, and my relationship with them and my siblings is stronger than it has ever been. Several of my extended family members, including my parents and a sibling, have slowly returned to the Church. After much prayer and consultation with priests, lawyers and friends, I realized that the Church has a vested interest in keeping sexually dysfunctional priests out of active ministry, and I decided to lodge a formal complaint against Fr. Rick with the proper ecclesial authorities. I am medication free, and I don't suffer from depression. I have hope where I once was hopeless. I rarely have religious dreams because I don't need them like I used to. I take care of my body physically as well as mentally and spiritually. I still love the arts and the world of entertainment, although I am far more selective in what I view. Though I often struggle with temptation during moments of intimacy, I don't sleep with women anymore—I haven't for several years. Today I listen to women and communicate with them better than I ever have. I don't lose my temper and rarely raise my voice. My career path is also doing very well. I am currently earning a Ph.D. on a full-scholarship. I actively do ministry in the community. And perhaps most importantly, I have a wonderful group of Christian friends who challenge me and support me.

I don't pretend that my story is a simple one. I was not hit over the head with a lightning bolt, nor did I accept God without a fight. Like so much of life, my conversion has been messy and complicated and marred by emotions I am still discovering, and which remain a mystery to me. So often, when I have opened the box of my heart to others, there has been so much shame, fear and confusion that I have slammed it shut again, unable, and unwilling, to let anyone see what is inside of me—who I am and what I once was. Yet I am able to dismiss the demons of my past, the memories and fears which from time to time haunt my conscience, because I know that Jesus is bigger than my sins. This is not a realization that I arrived at overnight, although the truth of it was always staring me in the face, waiting for my acceptance.

As I grow older, my relationship with Jesus grows deeper, stronger, and more mature. I cannot express in words the love that springs to my heart when I think about Jesus Christ and how much he loves me. Every day I try to love him more. And thanks to Mary's messages from Medjugorje, which I have incorporated into my daily life, I am slowly being freed of my fears and learning to cope with my addiction. Some day, when I get the time and the money, I will go to Medjugorje on a pilgrimage of thanksgiving. My salvation is for Mary's glory. It is a gem in her crown that I am saved. Thanks to Mary's wonderful intercession, the love that springs to my heart when I think about Jesus consumes me with a gentle and heavenly fire. Jesus loves me, just as I am.

Love me as you are

At the Marian Conference I attended in San Rafael, California, in February 2000, Wayne Weible read a poem written by a priest entitled, *Love Me As You Are*. He encouraged those present to share the poem with others on the Christian journey. Throughout my battle with sexual addiction, I have turned frequently to the poem for comfort and support. It continues to be a source of prayer and inspiration. According to the priest, it came from Jesus.

I know your miseries

The trials and tribulations of your soul

The deficiencies and frailty of your body

I am aware of your cowardliness

Of your sins

And I say to you all the same

Give me your heart

Love me as you are

If you wait until you become an angel before you abandon yourself to love

You will never love

Even if you are vial in the practice of your duties and virtues

And even if you fall again and again in the same sins that you would wish no to longer commit

Even still

I ask that you love me

Love me as you are

In every moment and situation in which you find yourself

In fervor or in aridity

Or with infidelities

Love me as you are

I wish the love of your poor heart

If you will wait until you are perfect, you will never love

Could I not, if I wished, change every grain of sand into an ardent seraphim of purity, of nobility, of love?

Am I not the all-powerful One?

And yet if it pleases me to leave the marvelous creatures in void

And to prefer the poverty of your heart

Am I not the master of my own love?

My child, permit me to love

I wish your heart

Certainly, with time, I wish to transform you

But now

Now

I love you just as you are

I delight in the love of the poor and the miserable

From the poorest beggars I wish to hear a strong cry lifted up unceasingly,

"Jesus, I love you"

I wish only the song of your heart

I do not need knowledge or talents

There is only one thing that preoccupies me

To see that you do everything with love

It's not your virtues that I desire

If I were to give you some more

You are so weak that they would only increase your self-love

Don't be disturbed about that

I could have destined you for great things

But no

You will be the useless servant

I will take from you even the very little you possess

Because I created only for love

Today I stand at the door of your heart like a beggar

I, the King of Kings

I knock and I wait

Hurry

Open to me

Do not enclose yourself in your misery

If you really knew your indignity you would die of sadness

That which would wound my heart would be to see you doubt me

And lose confidence

I want you to perform the most insignificant actions with love

I count on you to give me joy

Do not worry if you do not possess virtues

I will give you mine

When you suffer

I will give you strength

Give me love and I will make you capable of loving over and above everything you ever dreamed

But remember

Love me as you are

I give you my Mother

Offer everything through her heart which is so pure

Whatever happens in your life

Don't wait until you are holy

Until you abandon yourself to love

Or you will never love me at all

Love me as you are

* * *

Dear children, I have told you already that I have especially chosen you just the way you are. I am your Mother and I love you all. During times that are difficult, do not be afraid, for I love you even when you are far from my Son and me. Please, do not let my heart weep with tears of blood for the souls that are being lost in sin. Therefore, dear children, pray, pray, pray![34]

Dear children, this is the reason for my presence among you for such a long time: to lead you to Jesus. I want to save you, and through you, to save the whole world. Many people now live without faith; some don't even want to hear about Jesus, and yet they still want peace and fulfillment! Children, this is the reason why I need your prayer: prayer is the only way to save the human race.[35]

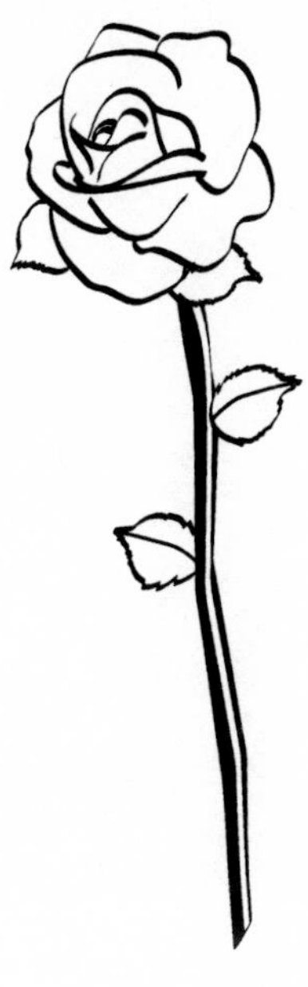

APPENDIX

The Medjugorje Story

On June 24th, 1981, in an obscure, remote village in the former communist Yugoslavia, two teenage girls, Mirjana and Ivanka, went for a walk. As they exchanged the latest news in their lives, Ivanka suddenly noticed a light high up on Mount Podbrdo, the large hill behind the village. Looking up, she saw a woman, radiating with light, hovering above the ground on a cloud and holding a baby in her arms. Ivanka said to Mirjana, "I think that Our Lady is on the hill." Mirjana, not bothering to glance up responded glibly, "Yes. Our Lady has nothing better to do than to come to the two of us." Brushing off Ivanka's strange behavior, she left and walked back toward the village, but soon felt a great urge to return. When she did, she found Ivanka in the same spot, still staring at the hill, mesmerized. "Look at it now, please," said Ivanka. Mirjana looked up and saw a beautiful woman with blue eyes and long dark hair, dressed in a gray dress and a white veil, with a baby in her arms and a crown of twelve stars around her head. Mirjana says of that instant, "All the possible emotions that exist I felt in my heart at the same time. To put it simply, I was not aware if I was alive or dead."

At that moment, a friend of theirs named Vicka was passing by looking for the two of them, and when she, too, saw the woman on the hill, she jumped out of her slippers and ran headlong back to the village. Just a few moments later, a teenage boy named Ivan passed by on his way home carrying apples in his arms, and upon seeing the woman, threw down the apples and ran away. Then Mirjana said to Ivanka, "Who knows what's going on. It's better for us to go home as well."

The next day, all four children felt drawn back to the same spot which is now called Apparition Hill. Vicka ran to get her friend, Marija, and ten-year-old Jakov, and all six children saw the beautiful woman. The following day, July 26th, again they saw her, this time with almost the entire village present. Over five thousand saw the visionaries bathed in an immense light and believed. Vicka, at her grandmother's urging, sprinkled holy water at the woman in the sign of the cross and said, "If you are Satan, go away from us." The woman just smiled with an expression of immense love. Then she spoke:

Do not be afraid, dear angels.

I am the Mother of God.

I am the Queen of Peace.

I am the mother of all people.[36]

Thus began Mary's daily apparitions to the six children, the longest occurring apparitions in Church history, which continue to this day.

Mary has chosen to appear in Medjugorje and to give the world messages in order to continue the work she set out to do when she appeared to three young children in Fatima, Portugal in 1917. Part of her message from August 25, 1991, states,

> ...I call all of you, dear children, to pray and fast still more firmly...so that with your help everything I wanted to realize through the secrets I began in Fatima may be fulfilled. I call you, dear children, to grasp the importance of my coming and the seriousness of the situation...[37]

On the second day of the Medjugorje apparitions, Marija saw Mary crying and carrying a wooden cross. "Peace, peace, peace!" she said. "Be reconciled! Only peace!"[38] Mary is appearing to a world intent on destroying itself in order to urge her children to return to the ways of God. She has said that this is the last time she will appear on earth, and we will know why. Our Lady has promised that, when she stops appearing, a visible and lasting sign, undeniably of God, will be left on the spot of her first apparition. Strongly urging everyone to "pray, pray, pray," she has given five specific means to holiness that she wishes of us: frequent attendance of the Holy Mass, monthly Confession, Bible reading, daily prayer-especially daily prayer of the rosary, and fasting on bread and water on Wednesdays and Fridays—all done with the heart. "I am not God, she has said, "I need your prayers and sacrifices to help me."[39] "You have forgotten that with prayer and fasting you can ward off wars, suspend natural laws."[40]

Since the apparitions began, the visionaries who humbly say that they are not important and no more holy than you or I, spend as many as six hours or more daily in prayer and fast on bread and water up to three times a week. Following their initial fright, the six young visionaries quickly lost their fear of the Virgin Mary. They say her love for them and all of humanity cannot be expressed in words and that to be in her presence is like being in heaven. They speak of her as "beautiful beyond anything in this world"[41] "Why are you so beautiful?" They asked her in the early days of the apparitions, and she said, "I am beautiful because I love. You, too, are beautiful when you love."[42]

As with all apparitions, the Church will not make an official pronouncement regarding Medjugorje until the apparitions there have ceased. Pope John Paul II has made several personal statements giving his wholehearted support of it. "If I wasn't the Pope," he said, "I'd be in Medjugorje already!" as reported April 29, 1989 by Bishop Paul Hnilica, SJ, Auxiliary Bishop of Rome, after having been admonished by the Holy Father for not stopping in Medjugorje on his return trip to Rome. To Monsignor Maurillo Kreiger, former bishop of Florianopolis in Brazil, he said, "Medjugorje, Medjugorje, it's the spiritual heart of the world."[43]

Since 1981, when the apparitions to the children began, between twenty and thirty million pilgrims from all over the world have been to Medjugorje, including priests, bishops and cardinals. Each day, villagers and pilgrims pray for hours in the local church, while others wait in the long lines for Confession. All day, and often into the night, pilgrims climb Apparition Hill where Mary first appeared to the children, lending their prayers to the sacred atmosphere. Nearby, pilgrims also climb Cross Mountain, upon which the villagers erected by hand a 15-ton, 36-foot high cross in 1933 to commemorate the 1900th anniversary of the crucifixion. Mary chose to appear in Medjugorje because of the faith she found in the village, and she continues to call people from across the globe to make a pilgrimage there to encounter her Son. Those who heed her call with an open spirit find themselves in a place of great peace, where rosaries turn gold, the sun dances and spins in the sky, where miracles, conversions, and healings—most importantly, healings of the human heart—abound.

RESOURCES

Videotape: *"On The Edge of His Grace"*

Mary Lou McCall conducts an in-depth television interview with Christine Watkins about her dangerous dealings with supernatural powers and the New Age movement. Mrs. Watkins tells the remarkable story of her troubled past, her conversion, her physical healing, and her miraculous trip to Medjugorje. Tape also includes a brief interview with her husband John Watkins.

Videotape "On The Edge of His Grace" is available through Focus:
Worldwide Network
106 Metarie Lawn Drive
Metarie, Louisiana 70001

To order call (504) 840-9898, or log onto focusvideos.com and fax order form with Order Number F-872 to (504) 840-9818

Natural Family Planning (NFP)

Natural birth control without the use of artificial pills or invasive procedures. NFP's effectiveness in avoiding pregnancy is equal to or better than drugs or devices on the market. For information and instruction, go to:

The Creighton Model "Fertility*Care* System
www.creightonmodel.com

Billings Ovulation Method of Natural Fertility Regulation
www.billings-centre.ab.ca

The *Sympto-Thermal Method* taught by the *Couple to Couple League*
www.ccli.org

For educational resources concerning the harms of contraception go to onemoresoul.com

Medjugorje

Recommended reading:

Richard J. Beyer, *Medjugorje Day by Day.* (Notre Dame: Ave Maria Press, 1993)

Janice Connell, *Visions of the Children.* (New York: St. Martin's Press, 1997); *Queen of the Cosmos.* (Brewster: Paraclete Press, 1990)

Wayne Weible, *Medjugorje the Message.* (Brewster: Paraclete Press, 1989)

Medjugorje Magazine
Editors Larry & Mary Sue Eck
P.O. Box 373 Westmont, IL 60559-0373
For subscriptions call (630) 968-4684

Websites:
www.medjugorje.org To receive monthly messages contact sshawl@medjweb.com www.medjugorje.hr Click on British flag to view website in English

The New Age Movement

Recommended reading:

Website providing information about corruption and abuse in Siddha Yoga: www.LeavingSiddhaYoga.net

Webpage providing an extensive list of articles:
www.LeavingSiddhaYoga.net/frames2.htm
See O Guru, Guru, Guru, by Lis Harris, *The New Yorker*, November 14, 1994, an important published piece that explains the problems of Siddha Yoga.

Groothuis, Douglas. *Unmasking the New Age.* (Downers Grove: Intervarsity Press, 1986). *Confronting the New Age.* (Intervarsity Press, 1988)

Michaelsen, Johanna. *The Beautiful Side of Evil.* (Eugene: Harvest House Publishers, 1982)

Pacwa, Mitch, S.J. *Catholics and the New Age.* (Ann Arbor: Servant Publications, 1992)

Post Abortion Healing

Rachel's Vineyard: weekend retreats for healing after abortion. For information, log onto www.rachelsvineyard.org, or call their toll free confidential number:
(877) HOPE 4 ME [(877) 467 3463]

Homosexuality

Courage: An apostolate of the Roman Catholic Church which ministers to those with same-sex attractions and their loved ones. For information contact:
210 W. 31st Street
New York, NY 10001
(212) 268-1010
NYCourage@aol.com
www.couragerc.net

Catholic Medical Association: an association of Catholic physicians in the United States dedicated to upholding the principles of the Catholic faith in the practice of medicine. For information contact:
National Headquarters
2020 Pennsylvania Ave. NW, #864
Washington, DC 20006
(703) 988-0588
info@cathmed.org
www.cathmed.org/publications/homosexuality.htm

Healing Ministry and Men's Community

The Servants of Divine Mercy is a contemplative, charismatic, eucharistic, and Marian community-in-formation for single, Catholic men.

The Holy Spirit Healing Ministry Internship, an outreach of *The Servants of Divine Mercy,* is a 100-hour course that trains lay people in the basics of healing prayer.

If interested in the community or the healing ministry internship contact:
Dr. Allan Weilert: (316) 733-7383 or (316) 259-1301

drweilert@theservantsofdivinemercy.com
www.theservantsofdivinemercy.com

Spiritual Pilgrimages

Pilgrimages and retreats with Patsy Soto, including the *Novena for World Peace* retreats that Jesus asked her to begin in 2003. For information contact:
His Teachings Ministry: Evangelizing as Fishers of Men
5218 Puma Ct.
North Las Vegas, NV 89031
(702) 642-8712
for-holy-souls@erols.com
www.post1.com/home/avemaria

Pilgrimages to Medjugorje combined with Father Zlatko Sudac retreat
For information contact:
Cindy Wendt (Pilgrimage Guide)
(847) 675-6024
Pilgrimages101@aol.com

Pilgrimages to Medjugorje. Accommodations with Mirjana Dragicevic-Soldo
For information contact:
Fiat Voluntas Tua
(877)-333-FIAT or (209) 835-5480
jim3fiattravel@sbcglobal.net
fiattravel.com

Sex Addiction

Sexaholics Anonymous (SA)
A recovery program based on the principles of Alcoholics Anonymous
P.O. Box 111910
Nashville, TN 37222
(615) 331-6230
www.sa.org. For meetings near you click on "meeting search"
saico@sa.org

Footnotes

[1] See Appendix
[2] Mary's message of 2-2-90. *Visions of the Children.* Janice T. Connell. (New York: St. Martin's Press. New York. 1997), p. 44.
[3] changed to lay status
[4] See website: theservantsofdivinemercy.com
[5] See above website
[6] This is the same time that Mary usually appears to the visionaries from Medjugorje. During daylight saving time, when clocks are turned forward an hour, she appears at 6:40 p.m. The rest of the year, she appears at 5:40 p.m. Thus, she appears at the same moment of the day despite how our clocks are set.
[7] Mary's message from 1986. *Richard J. Beyer, Medjugorje Day by Day.* (Notre Dame: Ave Maria Press, 1993). October 13 meditation
[8] Small hotel
[9] The real presence of Jesus in the form of a round bread wafer.
[10] For more information on Rachel's Vineyard weekend retreats see www.rachelsvineyard.org or call 877 HOPE 4 ME (877 467 3463).
[11] See "Pilgrimages" in Appendix
[12] Mary's message of 2-9-84. *Medjugorje Day by Day.* November 14 meditation.
[13] www.medjugorje.org and www.medjugorje.hr
[14] Mary's message of 8-15-85. *Medjugorje Day by Day.* June 18 reflection.
[15] Confraternity of Christian Doctrine
[16] Prayer styles of Saint Ignatius, founder of the Jesuit order of priests.
[17] See "Pilgrimages" in Appendix
[18] For more information on Rachel's Vineyard weekend retreats see www.rachelsvineyard.org or call 877 HOPE 4 ME (877 467 3463).
[19] Mary's message of 5-12-86. *Medjugorje Day by Day.* November 8 meditation.
[20] To find out about Patsy Soto's upcoming events, including the **Novena for World Peace** that Jesus asked her to begin in January of 2003, go to the website: www.post1.com/home/avemaria, write 5218 Puma Ct., North Las Vegas, NV, 89031, call (702) 642-8712, or send an email to: for-holy-souls@erols.com
[21] Mary's message of 10-20-84. *Medjugorje Day by Day.* August 4 meditation.
[22] The normal pill women use lets ovulation occur five to ten percent

of the time, and the progestin-only pill allows it to happen fifty percent of the time. Information from the National Women's Health Resource Center (NWHRC). Chart on page 2 of website under "How it works." http://www.healthywomen.org/content.cfm?L1=3&L2=112.0&L3=0.0&L4=0

[23] Mary's message of December 25th, 1991. www.medjugorje.org To receive monthly messages contact sshawl@medjweb.com

[24] "Prayer Windows" is the title of a book by Jean Gill on different ways of praying.

[25] Confraternity of Christian Doctrine

[26] Mary's message on August 25, 2003. www.medjugorje.org.

[27] In the magazine, "Call to Peace" - Bella Vista, AR USA, August-Sept 1992, a 20-page article called "A Case of Poetic Justice" asks, "The Poem of the Man-God: Divinely Inspired Prose of Doctrine of Demons?" and comes out in favor of the former. Page 15 features the quote from Maria Pavlovic, Medjugorje visionary, who maintains Our Lady has said the Poem is from her Divine Son and we may read it. Page 16 has a second quote from the visionary Vicka Ivankovich: "... The Poem of the Man-God by Maria Valtorta, ten volumes - Our Lady says The Poem of the Man-God is the truth."

[28] Maria Valtorta, *The Poem of the Man-God: Vol. 1.* (Italy: Centro Editoriale Valtortiano, 1986), Chap. 128, pp. 693-696.

[29] For information on *Courage*, visit their website at www.couragerc.net, call (212) 268-1010, or email NYCourage@aol.com.

[30] Sister Josefa Menendez, *The Way of Divine Love.* (Rockford: Tan Books and Publishers), p. 244.

[31] Mary's message of 7-4-88. *Medjugorje Day by Day.* February 12 meditation.

[32] Mary's message in 1986. *Medjugorje Day by Day.* April 3 meditation.

[33] See Appendix

[34] Mary's message of 5-24-84. *Medjugorje Day by Day*. October 12 meditation.

[35] Mary's message of 7-30-87. *Medjugorje Day by Day.* August 19 meditation.

[36] Story compiled from Janice Connell's *Visions of the Children.* (New York: St. Martin's Press, 1997), p. 10; *Medjugorje Magazine* May 2002 Special issue, p. 14; and a videotape of Mirjana telling her story to pilgrims in December, 2001, provided by Fiat Voluntas Tua.

[37] Mary's message of August 25, 1991. Sister Emmanuel, *Medjugorje: the 90's*. (Goleta: Queenship Publishing Co., 1997), p. 69.

[38] Richard Beyer, *Medjugorje Day by Day.* (Notre Dame: Ave Maria

Press, 1993), p.6.

[39] Mary's message of December, 1983. *Medjugorje Day by Day*. July 24 meditation.

[40] Wayne Weible, *Medjugorje the Message.* (Brewster: Paraclete Press, 1989), p.44.

[41] *Medjugorje Day by Day,* p. 5.

[42] Mirjana's story as told by her on Fiat Voluntas Tua pilgrimage video.

[43] www.medjugorje.org/pope.htm